Stella M. Da

BEHIN
CHALET SCHOOL

BY

HELEN McCLELLAND

Bettany Press

1996

2nd edition published in Great Britain
by Bettany Press 1996
52 Warham Road, London N4 1AT

First published in Great Britain
by New Horizon 1981
& reprinted with revisions by Anchor Press 1986

British Library Cataloguing in Publication Data
A catalogue record for this book is available
from the British Library

ISBN 0 9524680 2 6

Designed & DTPed by Green Gosling, London
Printed and bound in Great Britain
by Lithosphere, London

CONTENTS

LIST OF ILLUSTRATIONS

ACKNOWLEDGEMENTS

Accounts of my problems in finding even the basic facts of Elinor Brent-Dyer's life story have been given elsewhere (notably in *The Chalet School Revisited*, Bettany Press, 1994); and it remains as true today as it was twenty years ago that, without the wonderful help I was given during my researches, *Behind the Chalet School* could never have been written.

This revised edition has added new names to the long list of people to whom I owe a debt of gratitude. First, though, I should like to repeat my special thanks to all who gave me so much assistance with the original book. They include, as well as those in libraries, public records and newspaper offices whose names are not known to me:

> Hazel Bainbridge (Mrs J. F. Carroll), Tony Chambers, Helen Colam, Thomas Collocott, Susan Dodsworth, Judith and Peter Humphrey, Marjorie Jewell, Doris Johnson, Phyllis Kerr, the Kostenzer family, Marion Lloyd, Margaret Mann, Stanley Oliver, Donald and Elizabeth Roberts, Margaret Schofield-Palmer, Sybil Smith, Joyce Thorpe, Edward West and Judy Whale; and the late Mrs Blake, Hilary Bray, Ernest Bullock, Rose Farr Smith, Olive Farrar, Mrs Griffiths, Herbert Howells, Phyllis Matthewman, Isobel Miller, Hope and Noel Moncrieff, Eva Oliver, Vivien Pass and Mary Starling.

In connection with this new edition — which could well have been retitled *Further Behind the Chalet School* — thanks are due first to Pamela Howe, whose BBC programmes not only unlocked a store of new information but also provided my introduction to Elinor's half-nephew, Mr Charles Dyer, son of her vanished half-brother, Charles Arnold Lloyd Dyer. Mr Dyer has been most helpful in filling in some of the gaps in Elinor's early life, and it is due to him that I have now been able to give a fuller account of this period and of Elinor's father.

I want also to thank my dear friend, Chloe Rutherford, for all her encouragement and especially for sharing her personal memories of Elinor, as well as for generously allowing the use in this book of copyright material.

Others, too numerous to mention individually, have contributed valuable new information during the years since *Behind the Chalet School* first appeared, including many members of the New Chalet Club and of Friends of the Chalet School and other Chalet fans around the world. I am deeply grateful to all of them; and I would like to thank particularly:

> Fen Crosbie and Polly Goerres — for their tireless enthusiasm in pursuing clues; Rosemary Auchmuty and Juliet Gosling of Bettany Press and their editor Joy Wotton, with whom it is always a pleasure to work; Beth and David Varcoe for their dedicated researches in Herefordshire; Luella Hamilton and Olga Hargreaves for detailed and enlightening comments; and David Russell Halliwell for solving one of the mysteries.

Finally, I want to thank my husband and daughters, AK, CHK and AMK, who, despite being at times less than enthusiastic about the Chalet School, have always given me invaluable support.

Helen McClelland, February 1996

COPYRIGHT ACKNOWLEDGEMENTS

All extracts from the Chalet School series, the La Rochelle series, *The Lost Staircase* and the Chalet *Club News Letters* are quoted by kind permission of the publishers, W. & R. Chambers and Harper-Collins; and of Mrs C. P. Rutherford, Miss Brent-Dyer's executor, who has also kindly allowed quotations to be used from letters, an unpublished poem, and from *Elizabeth the Gallant* (published by Thornton Butterworth).

The short extract from Elinor M. Brent-Dyer's *The School by the River* is quoted by kind permission of the publishers, Burns & Oates Ltd, and of Mrs Rutherford.

Quotations from Miss Angela Brazil's autobiography, *My Own Schooldays*, and from school stories by Miss Brazil — *The School in the South*, *A Fourth Form Friendship*, *The Fortunes of Philippa*, *Bosum Friends* and *The Third Class at Miss Kayes* — are included by kind permission of the publishers, Blackie & Son Ltd.

Four short quotations from *You're a Brick, Angela!* by Mary Cadogan and Patricia Craig are included by kind permission of the publishers, Victor Gollancz Ltd.

An extract from the 1973 edition of the *Benenden School Magazine* is quoted by kind permission of the Editor.

For the use of photographs and other illustrations, warmest thanks are due to:

Charles Dyer: Photograph of Elinor M. Brent-Dyer as a child.

South Tyneside Central Library: Photographs of Westoe Village and Winchester Street.

Mrs Eva Oliver: Photograph of St Nicholas's School *c.* 1908.

Executors of the late Mrs Olive Farrar: Photograph of Ernest Farrar.

Mrs J. F. Carroll (Hazel Bainbridge): Photograph of Hazel, Julian and Edith Bainbridge.

W & R Chambers Ltd: Photograph of Elinor M. Brent-Dyer (1963); various illustrations by Nina K. Brisley.

Foto Angerer: Photograph of Pertisau and the Achensee

Vivian's Studio, Hereford: Photograph of the Margaret Roper School (1941); portrait of Elinor M. Brent-Dyer (1954).

Mrs C. P. Rutherford: Snapshot of Elinor M. Brent-Dyer and Mrs Phyllis Matthewman.

Mrs Christine Keyes: Photograph of the commemorative plaque at Pertisau.

Behind The Chalet School
is affectionately dedicated to
the memory of
Georgina Grace Moncrieff
who introduced me to Elinor's books
and to so many others

PROLOGUE

THE LONG ROAD

> Higher and higher they climbed . . . till at last they reached the great Alp . . . and there before them, dark, beautiful, and clear as a mirror, spread the . . . [Achen] See, with its three tiny hamlets and two little villages round its shores, and towering round on all sides the mighty limestone crags and peaks of the mountains . . .
>
> From the landing stage to the Chalet was a good ten minutes' walk, and then they saw the welcoming lights . . .
>
> They were at the Chalet School at last.
>
> (*The School at the Chalet*, 1925)

In fiction, it had taken Madge and Joey Bettany, whose arrival at the lovely village of Pertisau-am-Achensee is described above, only about a day-and-a-half's journey by boat and train to reach the Tyrol. In real life it had taken Elinor Brent-Dyer more than thirty years.

At the time of her visit, in 1924, she was just an unknown schoolteacher who happened to choose Austria for her long summer holiday. Yet, when she died some forty-five years later, she was considered important enough to be given obituary notices in many of the national papers, among them an appreciative half-column in *The Times*.

It had all come about because of that holiday in Austria. For on her return Elinor had written a school story with a Tyrolean background: *The School at the Chalet* (published a year later, in

October 1925); and this story, along with the mammoth series that followed — in all fifty-nine books — had proved fantastically popular. The books were reprinted over and over again, while fan mail arrived in increasing quantities from all around the English-speaking world. Perhaps Elinor's name did not become as familiar to the general public as that of Angela Brazil, the best known of all school-story writers, but even Miss Brazil never had a fan club with rising 4,000 members, as Elinor Brent-Dyer had during the 1960s.

And it is worth stressing that it was not during the heyday of the school story that this Chalet Club existed: had there been such a club in the twenties or thirties it would not have been so astonishing. That the Chalet Club was a going concern as recently as 1969 underlines what must be the most remarkable feature of the Chalet books: the way in which their popularity still endures, right up to the present day. For despite the school story being generally out of favour now, more than 100,000 Chalet School paperbacks are regularly sold each year; and hardback copies are eagerly sought in the secondhand market, where the prices of first editions and certain scarce titles can often reach three figures.

Yet more unexpected: today in the 1990s the original Chalet Club has two flourishing successors, numbering between them well over a thousand fans; and, although seventy years have passed since the Chalet School's first appearance, the publishers continue to this day to get letters from Chalet enthusiasts in many parts of the world. A number of these letters will be cited in Chapter XXI, which deals with the whole matter of the Chalet legend. But one may be mentioned here: it arrived in July

1979 — the writer being obviously unaware that Elinor had died ten years earlier:

> Please forgive my writing to you, but I have always wanted you to know how much I loved your books and what they meant to me . . . I was a complete Chalet girl, and could have recited your books by heart when I was young. I just lived for the next one to be published.
>
> They [the books] were my reality — not my own surroundings.

That last sentence could fittingly be applied to Elinor herself. She, too, had always tended to prefer her own fantasy lands to the real world. And from the moment that the Chalet School was born, soon after her arrival at the Achensee, this tendency was to grow ever stronger.

It had taken her more than thirty years to reach the Tyrol, and to find her life's work. But then she had had to come a long way.

Elinor M. Brent-Dyer as a child. Photograph possibly taken by her father, Charles Dyer, and found in his possession. Given to Helen McClelland by Charles Dyer, son of Elinor's half-brother Charles Arnold Dyer.

CHAPTER I

A FAR CRY FROM THE TYROL

> They had five bedrooms, counting the two attics, but no bathroom. The family still took their tubs in the scullery in a long zinc bath, that hung from a couple of hooks during the day, and had to be filled with a bucket.

When Elinor wrote that description of Rosamund Lilley's home — in *A Problem for the Chalet School* (1956) — she could have been drawing on her own early memories. For at 52 Winchester Street, the house in South Shields where she had grown up, there was no bathroom. There was no inside lavatory, either, and no running hot water. Cold baths were probably the order of the day in Elinor's childhood home. And this may explain why her Chalet School girls are so often pictured cavorting merrily into cold baths, to emerge 'glowing from the icy sting of the mountain water'. But this is running ahead too fast. To give Elinor's story a proper beginning it is necessary to go back many years, to 26 April 1893, the day of her parents' wedding.

Charles Dyer and Eleanor Watson Rutherford were married in South Shields at the parish church of St Hilda: a dark squarely built edifice, with an oddly small, rather undernourished-looking, tower, which must be the town's best-known building.

The bride came from a family with deep roots in the north of England. One of her grandfathers had been a local miller, the other a parish schoolmaster, and her forebears on both sides had belonged to this corner of the north-east for generations back. She herself had lived all her twenty-four years in South Shields — for the past eighteen of them at the house in Winchester Street that would remain her home after the marriage, and she had grown up surrounded by family. For although her father, Isaac Henzell Major Rutherford (of whom more in due course), had died seven years previously, her mother was still living; and she had numerous relatives in and around South Shields, including two married brothers in the town itself.

On the other hand her bridegroom, a thirty-six-year-old widower whose full name was Charles Morris Brent Dyer, was a newcomer, having arrived only recently in the north-east. He, like his father and grandfather, was a native of Portsmouth — a place that is frequently mentioned in the early Chalet books — and his widowed mother had continued to live there until her death in 1891. His father, William Dyer, had been a ship's carpenter in the Royal Navy, but he was drowned at sea when Charles was still a schoolboy; and it was due entirely to the generosity of his godfather that Charles was able to complete his education and, in due course, to enter the Navy. Here he had achieved the rank of commissioned officer — something of which Elinor was always to speak with pride; but a bout of ill-health had obliged him to take early retirement. He had then trained and qualified as a surveyor at Lloyds; and it was to work in this latter capacity that he had come to South Shields with its busy docks and shipyards.

At the time *Behind the Chalet School* was first published, Charles Dyer remained a shadowy figure; but even then it was clear that he was not fated to enjoy good fortune in marriage. His first wife, a Portsmouth girl named Helen Arnold, had died only five years after their wedding. And his second marriage was not to last, in any real sense, for even that short time.

Charles and his new wife (she was always known as Nelly, and from now onwards this name will be used here) set up their home at 52 Winchester Street, which they were to share with Nelly's mother, Hannah Rutherford. And this arrangement certainly offered practical advantages: the red-brick Victorian terraced house would have been too large, with its three storeys and attic floor, for Hannah to occupy alone; yet she could not have sold it, because legally it belonged to her only on trust for her lifetime. After that the terms of her late husband's will were automatically going to bring the house into her daughter Nelly's possession. Hence it would have been pointless for the newly married couple to buy another house, even if they were financially in a position to do so.

That the house-sharing plan had drawbacks must be obvious. They included for Charles Dyer the classic snag of a resident mother-in-law. One, moreover, of sturdily independent character, who would not only retain ownership of the house but had for many years been accustomed to acting as its head.

From Nelly's point of view things looked different. She, as her parents' youngest child and only surviving daughter, had always been cosseted, and the house had been her home since she was six years old. It might well have seemed to her convenient that her mother was living upstairs, ready with advice and help. Most of all Nelly would have appreciated this when the time came for her first baby to be born, since there was probably no question in those days of the birth taking place in hospital. At all events, the child who later became well-known as Elinor M. Brent-Dyer was born at 52 Winchester Street, the house where she was to live until she was nineteen. The year was 1894, the date Friday 6 April; and the birth certificate gives the baby's names as GLADYS ELEANOR MAY DYER.

It is safe to guess that both Nelly and Hannah thought that the baby was beautiful. However there is no possibility of learning how Charles Dyer reacted to his daughter's arrival. He did go and register her birth, and he was not at this period working away from home. But of course babies were nothing new so far as Charles was concerned: he, by his previous marriage, already had a son, Charles Arnold Lloyd Dyer — born in 1888, two years before the death of the first Mrs Dyer. And this little boy is surrounded by one of the strangest mysteries in Elinor's background.

Charles Arnold was barely five at the time of his father's second marriage; and it would surely have been natural for him to have come and lived for at least part of the time with Charles and Nelly, once they had settled down at Winchester Street after their wedding. By this juncture his grandparents had all died, he had no other close relatives, and there was ample room at 52 Winchester Street. Instead, it appears that he was condemned to continue a pathetic kind of wandering passage between lodgings, being left for the most part in the care of various landladies. And at no point does he seem even to have visited the Winchester Street household.

Altogether, this half-brother of Elinor's represents a curious enigma. There is documentary evidence for his birth, as well as for the fact that he was still living in 1911, at the age of twenty-three. And it has now come to light that he later married and had a son — yet another Charles Dyer. But what became of him in the mean time is unknown. Oddest of all — among those who supplied information about Elinor's early life, including some who appeared to have known her and the family reasonably well, not one person could recall ever hearing a word of Charles Arnold's existence.

Elinor herself may not have know of it in her youth, for much was concealed from children in those days. But later she did learn about this vanished half-brother, and it is tempting to speculate about a passage in one of her books, *The School at the Chalet* (1925), which describes the extraordinary behaviour of Grizel Cochrane's widowed father. Grizel's mother had died when she was five. 'After her death, Mr Cochrane had sent the child to his mother's, and led a bachelor life for the next five years.' Then 'he had married again, most unaccountably, without informing his second wife of the fact that he had a [child].'

Could it be that this unlikely sounding episode was actually based on real life? And, if so, might not the second Mrs Dyer have reacted like the second 'Mrs Cochrane' who, we hear later, 'had never forgiven her husband for not telling her of Grizel's existence'? Of course this is only speculation. On the other hand, it has now been established that the rift which gradually widened between Charles Dyer and his second wife did partly originate in disagreements over the small Charles Arnold.

Whether or not other things contributed to the trouble is unclear. But certainly the couple were very different in both temperament and outlook. Charles was apparently an extrovert, outspoken in manner and bohemian in tastes. He played the organ, was an accomplished amateur photographer, and tended — it seems — to be a little too fond of drink and pretty woman. Whereas Nelly, who by all accounts was herself a pretty woman, was far more conventional in attitudes and tastes. The two did share musical leanings, for Nelly, in her daughter's words, anyway, was 'a brilliant amateur pianist'; perhaps a characteristic exaggeration on Elinor's part? Be that as it may, later reports about Nelly clearly indicate that she was throughout life a person who attached great importance to received middle-class opinions.

Whatever caused the problems originally, let alone the rights and wrongs of the matter, trouble appears to have begun quite early in the marriage and to have been well established by the time Nelly Dyer's second child was born. Nelly had become pregnant again only five months after Elinor's birth, and the baby, a boy, arrived on 28 June 1895.

This time it was not the father, but the mother who went to register the birth, something that was a little unusual in 1895: and the choice of the baby's two names — he was called HENZELL WATSON — was significant, as both were closely and exclusively associated with his mother's family: Watson was the second of Nelly's own names, having been her mother Hannah's maiden surname; Henzell was the favourite and the most frequently used name in the Rutherford family. (Clearly the Rutherfords were proud of their connection with the Henzells: a family of Huguenot origin, who had fled from France and come to carry on their craft of glass-manufacture in and around Newcastle-upon-Tyne; and Elinor herself was always pleased to claim her French ancestry.)

Altogether it is hard to escape the impression that when Nelly chose those two particular names, Henzell and Watson, she was deliberately establishing her own family's claim on the child to the exclusion of his father. Especially bearing in mind that it was against the normal custom of the day for a first son — as Henzell in effect was — to receive no name from the paternal side of his family.

At any rate two things are certain: in the 1898 street directory for South Shields, based on facts supplied in 1897, the name of Charles Dyer no longer appears at 52 Winchester Street, although it had done so in the two previous years; and, after the closely spaced births of Elinor and her brother, there were to be no more children.

Elinor, then, was probably no more than three years old when her father finally walked out. Or, to be fair, perhaps he was pushed. But either way, and typically of that small-town world in which Elinor grew up, the loss of social face involved was considered almost as grave as the loss of a husband and father.

The residents in Winchester Street placed a high value on respectability. Perhaps some of them might only recently have drifted across the barrier from upper-working to lower middle class; but among their number were lawyers, officials of the gas company and the proprietors of an exclusive Young Ladies' Academy. Besides, the street was situated in the 'right part' of South Shields — in other words, in the area bordering the sea-front and the select Westoe Village, and on the far side of the town from the docks and shipyards, where at this date mean little houses thronged higgledy-piggledy, in a maze of narrow streets beside the Tyne. Winchester Street was also at a safe distance from the Harton Workhouse, a survival from the bad old days, which was still casting a grim shadow over working people's lives. On the other hand it was within a stone's throw of the beach, and of Bents House, a handsome private estate on the sea-front (now a public park).

Undoubtedly, then, Winchester Street was respectable. And to Nelly Dyer's family, clinging as they were to the skirts of this middle-class respectability, Charles's disappearance represented not only emotional upheaval but social disaster. In those days, almost a century ago now, the whole question of 'What — will — people — say?' was charged with an importance that is difficult to appreciate today; but plainly this side of things did matter a great deal to Elinor's mother and grandmother, as demonstrated by the enormous pains they took over hushing things up.

How they managed to succeed in doing this is mysterious. Nelly and Hannah can hardly have gone so far as actually to announce Charles's death; but Nelly could possibly have assumed widow's garb, as was traditional in those days. And, one way and another, the impression was gradually spread around that Mrs Dyer was now a widow, having lost her husband. Of course, in a way, she had 'lost him' — a euphemistic expression that Elinor herself was to use, many years later, in a letter to her publishers where she explains: 'I never knew my father, because we lost him when I was three years old.'

Relatives and friends must have known the facts. Neighbours may have guessed. But apparently there were blind eyes turned and deaf ears, and only the most hushed comments were whispered behind the lace curtains. With the result that, after a few years had passed, the myth of Nelly Dyer's widowhood was being generally accepted.

But what version of the story did Nelly give to her children? Of course at only three and two respectively they could not have understood the true state of affairs, but they were quite old enough to have noticed their father's continued absence and to have been acutely aware, as small children are, of the tensions in the atmosphere around them. And Elinor, at least, was of an age to have asked questions repeatedly.

Today, we can never learn what answers she received, for at no time in her life does she appear to have spoken, even to close friends, about this unhappy passage in her childhood, or its aftermath. Nor in this case do her books offer enlightenment, since none of them deals with the plight of a family deserted by their father. On the contrary, her fictonal fathers, with a few notable exceptions (those in the Chalet series include Captain Carrick, the callous and unscrupulous father of Juliet, and Margot Venables's ne'er-do-weel husband, Stephen) are usually portrayed as figures of almost preternatural reliability. Something that may in itself be significant, for when Elinor endowed these story-book fathers with so many admirable qualities she could have been compensating for her own childhood loss.

It seems hardly conceivable that Elinor and her little brother were among those who were encouraged to believe in Charles's death. Yet this was an era when the precept 'Not in front of the children' was almost religiously followed, so there remains a faint, dreadful possibility that, for at least a time, she and Henzell were deceived. Undoubtedly their childhood contemporaries were; as was borne out in a striking way — and quite unconsciously — by one friend who had known Elinor and the Dyer family well during those early years, the late Mrs Phyllis Matthewman. In a letter, dated 24 May 1974, Mrs Matthewman began a description of her first meeting with the eleven-year-old Elinor: '[She] was about a year older than I am, and she lived in South Shields with her widowed mother and her brother.' Nor was this a case of someone exercising discretion. Mrs Matthewman was visibly astonished to learn, all those years later, that in 1905 — the time she was describing — Elinor's mother was very far from being a widow; was not, in fact, to be widowed for a further six years.

And not only was Charles Dyer still alive. He was actually living on the other side of South Shields: it was the other side in every sense, for although barely a mile from Winchester Street for the seagulls, which are rarely silent in South Shields, it was a world away in social terms. This bizarre situation was first revealed by the street directories: here, after a gap of eight years, the name Charles Dyer suddenly reappears in the 1905 directory, and it is then regularly included until the 1911 edition.

Charles, at some point in the interval, had joined the Merchant Navy and he was now a master mariner. Quite possibly he spent long periods at sea, and was relatively seldom at his address in the Laygate. Nevertheless, the fact that he was actually resident in South Shields, however seldom, inevitably raises speculation as to whether Elinor and Henzell could possibly have remained ignorant of their father's continuing existence. In 1905 they were eleven and ten years old respectively; and the South Shields of those days was a very small community. However hard Nelly worked at keeping things dark, there must have been an ever-present danger that someone would give the secret away.

Whether the children were ever allowed to see their father is another matter. If they were, the meetings must unquestionably have taken place in the darkest of secrecy. And one small piece of evidence does exist to indicate that Elinor may indeed have seen her father some years after she was three. It is provided by a photograph that was among Charles Dyer's possessions (and passed to the author of this biography by Charles Dyer, his grandson and Elinor's half-nephew). This picture, (page 4) the earliest known of Elinor, shows a rather wary, inward-looking little girl, with long straight fair hair, and a somewhat mournful expression. Not that the photograph in itself proves anything. But it is significant that the child portrayed is unquestionably more than three years old. No date appears anywhere; but a reasonably informed guess would put Elinor's age as near enough six or seven at the time. So, how did this photo come to be in Charles's possession, if he really had not seen Elinor since 1897? Nothing suggests that Nelly Dyer would ever have sent it to him. Yet, on the other hand, if — and this must remain a large 'IF' — Charles was occasionally allowed a visit from his children, he could have taken this photo himself, bearing in mind his acknowledged skill as a photographer.

Whatever the facts of the situation, either way it was extraordinary. On the one hand, the children would have been innocent victims of the myth that Charles was dead. On the other, they were perforce accomplices in concealing not only his existence but, perhaps, also the fact that from time to time they paid him visits in secret. And there can be no question that the atmosphere of secrecy and evasion surrounding Elinor's childhood did radically affect the development of her character.

Besides, there was another complication in the tangled skein of events — one it is virtually certain Nelly Dyer would never have mentioned to her children. Charles had at some point set up house with another woman; and when he eventually departed for the last time from South Shields, it was to her house in Forest Gate, East London, that he went to live. And Emily Sarah Drowley not only presented Charles with yet another son — and

Elinor and Henzell with a second unknown half-brother — she also gave him something that Nelly had not, apparently, ever provided: a home for the elusive Charles Arnold Lloyd Dyer, who also lived at the house in Forest Gate. It was here that Charles made his will, in the summer of 1910; and here that he died of cancer on 30 July 1911 — barely a fortnight after his 55th birthday.

The death was notified by his eldest son, who is also named in the will, a brief but revealing document which begins, after the usual preliminaries: 'I leave the sum of £150 to my son, Charles Arnold Lloyd Dyer'. (That was worth something more like several thousand in 1990s terms.) And everything else of which Charles died possessed, he left to Emily Sarah Drowley. Not content with that, he then added: 'And I make no provision for my wife, Eleanor Watson Dyer, from whom I am living separate and apart by deed of separation. Nor for her two children.'

There appears a frightening bitterness about the addition of 'that 'I make no provision'; and in the contrast between 'her' two 'children' and 'my son'. The latter also makes clear that Charles and Nelly did become estranged, at least in part, over Charles Arnold. And, more recently, this has been confirmed by Elinor's half-nephew.

For Nelly Dyer the will must have been both painful and humiliating. And it would be hard to believe that she allowed Elinor and Henzell, even at seventeen and sixteen years of age, to read it. Indeed, if Nelly continued the pattern of concealment she had begun fourteen years earlier, it is likely she destroyed any copy of the will that came her way.

But she cannot so easily have destroyed her memories.

CHAPTER II

TURN-OF-THE-CENTURY CHILDHOOD

In one important respect Elinor's mother had been luckier than many other deserted wives; for although her husband was the family's official breadwinner she did not have to face acute financial anxieties after his departure. And for this fortunate state of affairs she had to thank her father, the late Isaac Henzell Major Rutherford.

Isaac, like a number of Elinor's forebears, had spent his working life in the Merchant Service. Here he had quickly risen to become a master mariner, and by hard work and thrift had managed to amass a considerable fortune. In addition he had bought 52 Winchester Street — a good-sized freehold house in a residential district — which, together with almost all his money, had been left in his will, first to his 'dear wife Hannah' on trust for her lifetime and after that outright to his daughter, Nelly. Moreover, Isaac and his lawyer had carefully tied things up to ensure that Nelly would enjoy her inheritance 'free from the debts, control, or engagements of any husband with whom she . . . [might] intermarry'.

Without that clause in her grandfather's will, Elinor's childhood might have passed in far less comfortable surroundings. As things were, Isaac Rutherford's capital, sensibly invested, produced an income that was amply sufficient at that time for a small family living in their own house. Besides, it is virtually certain that some payment by Charles Dyer towards the maintenance of his wife and children was arranged in the deed of separation.

One way and another life was probably comfortable enough at 52 Winchester Street. Living was cheap, too, in those pre-1914 days, with milk costing a mere penny (not quite a $\frac{1}{2}$p) a pint, butter about 2$\frac{1}{2}$p a pound, eggs 2p or 3p a dozen and the best meat perhaps 7p a pound. And although a direct comparison of prices can be misleading, since the value of money has plummeted during this century, there is no question that Elinor's mother was spending far less, not just in money but in real terms, than a housewife must now in the 1990s. Nelly could, for instance, have bought a hundredweight sack of best coal for a shilling (5p) or less — which means that, even making allowance for the changed value of the pound sterling, coal was then in effect many, many times cheaper than it is today. Not surprisingly then, coal fires were a feature of most living-rooms at that period; and Elinor was always to retain from her childhood days a preference for the cheerfully burning open fire (a preference to be shown also, in the later Chalet books, by Jo Maynard who insists on having an English-style fireplace installed in her Swiss home).

It is not surprising either, with money going so much further, that most of the households in Winchester Street were able to afford a living-in maid — that coveted status symbol of the times; especially when her wages were only about 20p a week. Elinor's mother, for one, seems always to have employed a maid-of-all-work, and most probably had other help in the form of a visiting washerwoman at least once a week; perhaps a sewing-woman from time to time, as well.

No wonder that the idea of household help being always readily available, somewhere in the background, underlies all Elinor's pre-war stories. It is more unexpected, though, that this impression should linger in the books she wrote during the war and post-war periods; for by this time she and her mother were struggling along in a huge house with little domestic assistance. But then it often happened with Elinor that the ideas acquired during her early life remained with her to the end.

Indeed it becomes clear that Elinor was in so many ways the product of her early environment that, in order to understand her character or even certain aspects of her books, it is essential to have some picture of daily life in her childhood home. And here she herself has given no direct help. On the contrary, throughout her life she was always uncommunicative about anything that concerned her background. More than that, she was sometimes positively misleading. Nor did the most urgent pleas from her fans and her Chalet Club members ever succeed in drawing more from Elinor than three short and carefully edited paragraphs. This meagre account of her life story, which appeared under the heading 'Something about Me' in the Chalet Club's newsletter for June 1963, begins: 'I was born near Newcastle-on-Tyne and can boast of having lived under five monarchs' — a sentence that is less straightforward than it appears; for, by 1963, Elinor had in fact lived under *six* monarchs, counting from Victoria to the present Queen inclusive. Perhaps she genuinely forgot one. Or perhaps she miscounted, arithmetic being always one of her weak points, as she herself was ready to confess and the books frequently confirm. ('There were twelve [in the] Fourth . . . twenty-two [in the] Third . . . twenty-one juniors . . . six in the Sixth Form and eight in the Fifth, making up the school to the number of seventy' — *The Rivals of the Chalet School*, 1929 — a sum that, after many attempts, would still seem to total sixty-nine.)

But quite possibly that slip over the number of monarchs was not accidental, since Elinor did often tend to try and lop a few years off her age, in particular when her writing career was concerned. And nothing so unusual about that. It is much more striking that she should have taken such pains to avoid naming the actual place of her birth and upbringing. This might, of course, have been due to snobbishness: in part her own, for reputedly Elinor in real life was less free from snobbish ideas than are some of her fictional characters; but mainly to her long experience of other people's. There can be little doubt that once she had encountered that exclusive world of the girls' boarding-school (as a young teacher during the 1920s) Elinor would have found it best to forget her own comparatively humble North Country origins. Today many social ideas have been turned inside out; but at that pre-war period the boarding-school girl, in fact as in fiction, was not expected to come from a place like South Shields with its working-class image of shipyards, collieries and seaside boarding-houses.

In any case Elinor had a far more compelling reason to fear being traced home: for, brought up as she had been, she understandably shrank from the possibility that outsiders might learn of her parents' broken marriage and that her own home background had been so different from that of the happily united families she portrayed in her books.

Maybe it appears extraordinary that anyone writing in the permissive sixties would bother to hide things so unsensational. But Elinor's habit of concealment had by this time been established for too long to be broken; after all, evasion had formed an integral part of her life for sixty-six years — ever since those smoke-screen tactics adopted by Nelly Dyer at the time of Charles's departure. And this may also explain why, in the course of a hundred published books, Elinor makes no use of her own Tyneside background, or of anything too closely connected with it. The one exception to this is the recently discovered *Jean of Storms* (a full-length novel which was serialised in the *Shields Gazette* during the spring and summer of 1930). And there were to be no autobiographies. Not even one as deliberately unrevealing as Angela Brazil's *My Own Schooldays* (Blackie & Son, 1925).

However, despite Elinor's heavy silence on the subject, it is still possible to obtain the required picture of her upbringing, and to learn much about her turn-of-the-century childhood, because so many of her contemporaries in South Shields were eager to fill in the background. And, despite the passage of many years, Elinor's memory had remained amazingly vivid in South Shields. But then, in the phrase often used by her friends and acquaintances: 'Elinor was not the kind to be easily forgotten'.

One thing emerges clearly from the various accounts: the children of Elinor's generation led far simpler lives than do most children today. Thus it can be taken for granted that Elinor and Henzell went early to bed, and, like the girls of the Chalet School, at an absolutely fixed time, that was seldom later than 8 p.m. until they were into their teens. Long afterwards Elinor, whose childhood home was without electric light, would record a memory of bedtime journeys through the shadowy unlit house:

> How dark it was in the passage! She had to go past the stairs, and who knew what awful thing might not be lying in wait for her, concealed half-way up? Supposing a long, skinny hand came through the railings and clutched her hair!
> (*Gerry Goes to School*, 1922)

Regular hours would also have characterised the day's timetable, with simple home-cooked meals appearing at fixed times. No convenience foods, either; no cornflakes, potato crisps or Coca-Cola. All most wholesome, no doubt; but the gusto and frequency with which Elinor writes of continental menus might imply disenchantment with the more everyday type of English fare; and certainly remarks to the effect that, 'English food's all very well . . . but I *love* what we have here in the Tyrol' (*The Head Girl of the Chalet School*, 1928) can be found in many of her books.

Children's amusements were also simpler in those days. And with television still a number of decades away in the future the favourite indoor pastimes included Ludo, Halma, Beggar-my-Neighbour, and the other old-fashioned games often played by the families in Elinor's early books; as well as jigsaw puzzles and the various paper-games and quizzes for which Elinor retained a lifelong passion.

Out of doors, in the quiet streets around her childhood home, the local children played singing games, or 'Hitchy-Dobber' (the Tyneside version of hopscotch); and since the Winchester Street houses had no gardens, only quite small back yards, Elinor and her small brother must often have longed to join in, although in view of Nelly Dyer's tendency to adopt middle-class prejudices it is most unlikely they were allowed to do so.

More probably the two children had to content themselves with watching from the window of the front parlour. And at least there was plenty for them to see and hear. Every morning the housewives of the day, or in some cases the maid, would sweep the pavement before the house and carefully whiten the doorstep. Sometimes the women who sold the whitening material came round, carrying their wares on their heads in baskets and shouting out 'Chalk, or Rubbing Stone!' as they trudged along. Then there were the tradesmen who drove their carts slowly up and down the road, looking for customers to buy milk or vegetables or coal. From time to time a carriage, bearing perhaps the doctor or one of the grand folk from Westoe Village, made its stately way past, the horses' hooves clip-clopping smartly on the cobbles. On certain days the organ-grinder's music could be heard. And just once in a while came the sound of galloping horses, which would instantly have drawn everyone, children and adults alike, to the windows, for that meant a fire, an event that was always exciting — provided, of course, that it was happening somewhere else.

The ordinary day's routine for Elinor and Henzell would also have included the regular morning and afternoon walks that were later to be a feature of life at the Chalet School; and occasionally the two might have been taken for a trip in the ferry that chugged its way across the Tyne estuary between North and South Shields; or else to ride in one of the quaint-looking horse-drawn trams, which passed along the top of Winchester Street; though, oddly enough, this particular form of transport does not seem to have appealed greatly to the young of Elinor's day: 'We children despised the trams', according to one of her contemporaries. 'We thought they were only for old, old ladies, in black feather boas.' But of course most people at that time were excellent walkers, as emerges in all Elinor's early books where walking, even for long distances, is obviously taken for granted as the everyday thing.

In many ways it sounds a peaceful time; and, despite its troubled beginning, daily life was generally ordered and peaceful for the Dyer children. Not that they can have failed to learn that life had other and far less pleasant sides: South Shields had a large share of poverty and unemployment, and during Elinor's childhood there were often long queues to be seen at the soup kitchens that, from time to time, were set up in the town. Nor was it unusual to see people begging in the streets.

Elinor did clearly grow up with some awareness of poverty; and she was to convey in her stories a strong feeling of the better-off person's obligation to help those less fortunate. Perhaps her attitude does often sound a note of Lady Bountiful that is out of tune today, but this, to be fair, is something that must be judged in its period context. As must also her ideas on the subject of illness — a recurrent theme in all her books. Here it is essential to remember how many diseases which have all but vanished today were common throughout Elinor's early life. Tuberculosis, for example, used then to cause literally hundreds of deaths each year in South Shields; diphtheria and scarlet fever were prevalent, and could often be fatal; even smallpox was not unknown. And, among the middle classes at least, illness was taken far more seriously than it usually is today. The most ordinary cold might have confined a child to its room for a week or more — as happens frequently in the Chalet School books; and measles, which many children now get through in a few days, would have meant for Elinor and Henzell about three weeks in bed, the first part of the time in a darkened room. Besides, in those days being 'in bed' meant exactly what it said; there was no larking around the house in pyjamas.

Altogether illness played an important if unpleasant part in most people's lives, and this may explain why Elinor developed a considerable preoccupation with the subject, and why there are so few of her books in which someone is not ill, less or more seriously, in the course of the story.

Her characters also suffer a good deal either during or in anticipation of visits to the dentist. Whether Elinor herself shared that dread of the dentist shown by Joey Bettany in the Chalet School stories is not known, but it appears that her early dental experiences were painful; and certainly she did not manage to keep her own teeth much past the age of forty. It would be hard to blame Elinor, or anyone else, for dreading the old-fashioned type of dentistry: without pain-killing injections and all today's numerous other improvements, it must have been a grisly business. And people were just expected to grin and bear it. Children as well.

That they mostly did so was due no doubt to their tougher upbringing; for there can be no question that children then were expected to be more stoical, as well as being more submissive and obedient to their elders. A strict upbringing was the fashion of the day and, as put by an old acquaintance of Elinor's, Miss Mary Starling, who grew up in South Shields at exactly the same time and in a very similar environment: 'Parents were parents then and did not try to be just "pals".' Her own father and mother, to whom she was devoted, 'were strict and demanded deference'; and she and her brother and sister 'were usually obedient as most children were'.

This lady recalls, too, the regular church-going that unquestionably formed as important a part of Sunday in Elinor and Henzell's childhood as it did in hers:

> The Sabbath was strictly kept . . . We went to morning and evening service, and to Sunday School at 2.30 p.m. After morning service my sister, who was two years my junior, and I went to Grandmother's. We had to tell her the text of the

> sermon and the headings of the preacher's theme. We had a consultation at the gate before we went in!

It is easy to picture Elinor and the little brother who was only one year *her* junior being catechised in this time-honoured fashion. That the family did go regularly to church, and that it was the Church of England to which they belonged is clear from the information supplied by various friends. However there are hints in Elinor's one and only North Country story (*Jean of Storms*) of a more fundamentalist influence at work somewhere in her background. The eponymous heroine of this story is much concerned that her little niece shall learn to think of a loving God, and not grow up to fear hell and the devil lurking round every corner, in the frightening way that — we gather — she had herself been taught as a child. And there is a personal note beneath some of the descriptions in this story. Nevertheless there can be no question about the great importance of religion to Elinor personally; it is demonstrated throughout her writings. And the important role it plays in her books will form the subject of a later chapter.

A final word on Elinor's upbringing. All in all, the indications are that it was entirely typical of its period. Moreover, it can be seen that all Elinor's most deeply rooted convictions were planted during the first two decades of her life, and that many of the themes which recur over and over again in her books had their origins during those early years.

Which is why it has seemed so essential, in this chapter, to try and give some general impression of the period.

CHAPTER III

SCHOOL WAS A LIFE SENTENCE

THE SENTENCE BEGINS

It was around the year 1900 that Elinor began what eventually proved to be half a century's personal experience of school. For that, give or take a few years here and there, is the impressive total when her own school-days are added to the time she spent as student, pupil-teacher, teacher and finally as headmistress of her own school. Moreover, this takes account only of real-life schools. In fiction, once her Chalet School was firmly established, Elinor was never really to leave school until the day she died.

By the time that Elinor was old enough to be thought ready for school, two or three years had gone by since Charles Dyer's departure. The household at 52 Winchester Street had settled into its new pattern. Nelly Dyer was in sole charge — although she did have the backing of her mother, Hannah Rutherford, until the latter's death in January 1901. (The deep impressions made by this event on the six-year-old Elinor will be considered in Chapter VI.)

Undoubtedly the question of finding a suitable school for Elinor was one that gave rise to much discussion between Nelly and Hannah. There was no lack of choice: quite close at hand they had Westoe Infant School and Ocean Road and Baring Street Board Schools. Many of the neighbourhood children attended these schools. But it seems unlikely that Nelly and Hannah would even have glanced at them; for, although not rich, they were sufficiently well-off thanks to Isaac Rutherford's provisions to afford at least modest school fees. In any case, Mrs Dyer, as later reports make plain, was always anxious to maintain her family's middle-class status. Hence her thoughts, and her mother's, are likely to have gone straight towards the fair number of private schools in their district. One was only a few doors away from them in Winchester Street. However this one, along with many others, was passed over in favour of a small select establishment, run by the redoubtable Misses Alice and Henrietta Stewart.

By 1900, the Misses Stewart had been directing their school for almost twenty years. Both were in their forties; and they were, in the words of an ex-pupil, 'two very fine ladies'. Indeed who, looking at them in the school photograph could doubt it? One glance puts beyond belief any idea that either lady could ever have been 'guilty of the slightest deviation from the strictest propriety' (unlike poor little Miss Phoebe in J. M. Barrie's *Quality Street*). Perhaps their school was smaller and, judging from advertisements in the local paper, offered fewer facilities than did some of the other private schools in Westoe. But it enjoyed a reputation for unimpeachable respectability, and was attended by many of the local girls whose parents had middle-class aspirations.

Whether the school also offered a high standard of teaching is more difficult to establish. Elinor never referred directly to her own early education. But it is possible to read between the lines of her books that something, sometime, had caused her to have and retain throughout her life an outsize grudge against old-fashioned teaching methods. Time and again she brings her stories round to this subject, getting launched into it right away with her first published book, *Gerry Goes to School* (1922). This story tells how Geraldine Challoner, who has been brought up by two elderly great-aunts, comes at the age of twelve to live with friends, and is then sent to a modern high school. Here, on her first day, she is questioned about her work to date:

> 'Now, Geraldine,' began the young mistress . . . 'what arithmetic have you done? . . . fractions, vulgar and decimal? Can you do proportion, or simple interest? What about percentages and square measure?'
>
> 'I — I don't know,' faltered Gerry alarmedly. [As well she might in the face of that Red-Queen-like questionnaire] . . . '
>
> 'What history did you use, child?'
>
> 'Mrs Markham and Little Arthur,' replied Gerry, with a horrible feeling that Miss Hamilton would be surprised. In point of fact that young lady had much ado to keep her countenance.

Things then go from bad to worse when French and geography are touched on. But the climax came when:

> [Miss Hamilton] inquired, more in fun than anything else . . . 'And did you use *Magnall's Questions*, too?'
>
> 'Ye-yes,' faltered Gerry.
>
> 'You did! Good gracious!'
>
> Miss Hamilton was silent for a moment with sheer wonder. The tears came into the child's eyes. Oh, how terribly old-fashioned she must seem, she who had never done any algebra, or geometry, or physical geography, and who had

> been taught out of such a book as *Magnall's Questions*!

This latter book, the *Historical and Miscellaneous Questions, for the Use of Young People*, by Miss Richmal Mangnall — to give the author her correct spelling — was originally published in 1800 and frequently revised and reissued. (And Elinor is not alone in misspelling the name: James Joyce also refers to *Magnall's Questions*.) Much beloved of Victorian governesses, the little catechism ranged undaunted over world history, beginning very properly with 'the creation of the world by the Almighty . . . 4,004 years before the birth of Christ'. It touched also on Science, Astronomy and Heathen Mythology, as well as providing 'Questions on Familiar Subjects'. There is no possible doubt that the Misses Stewart would have known this book; and could still have been using it during Elinor's time in their school.

In the above extract from *Gerry Goes to School*, the situation is shown mainly from the pupil's (Gerry's) angle. In *Jo Returns to the Chalet School* (1936) a similar situation is presented from the viewpoint of the staff:

> 'Polly Heriot is a nice bright child,' declared Miss Wilson . . . 'But oh, my goodness! her prior methods of education leave a good deal to be desired.' And she surveyed the young lady's botany exercise with a rueful smile.
>
> 'What's wrong with it, Nell?' asked Miss Annersley . . . 'It looks neat enough.'
>
> 'That's as may be. The trouble is that it's at least fifty years behind the times!' retorted Miss Wilson. 'Just look at those *niggling* little sketches!'

'Oh, she's out of date,' agreed the English mistress [Miss Annersley]. 'Her essays aren't essays at all — they're good little "compositions", all nicely spelled, written, punctuated, and paragraphed, and without an original idea in them. Polly Heriot is an original young person when she isn't trying to express herself on paper.'

'Her arithmetic is enough to turn anyone's hair white!' groaned Miss Leslie from the other side of the room. 'Oh, beautifully neat, and set down with ruled lines and carefully formed figures. But I'd give a bookful of all this meticulous working for one untidy page of to-day's methods!'

'She's a problem,' commented Miss Wilson . . . 'She doesn't even know how to do arithmetic. Her science is conspicuous by its absence; botany, mid-Victorian; geography, the limit — have I shown you the centipedes she draws for mountain-ranges? What's her history like, Con?'

'Oh, matches with the rest. Just what you'd expect — fearfully biased stuff, and no idea of standing back and taking a good, general view of things,' said Miss Stewart. [No connection with the ladies of Elinor's first school.] 'She knows all the dear old stories . . . As for anything outside of *English* history, Europe and the rest of the world might never have existed, so far as she's concerned!'

'Well, she's a problem,' repeated Miss Wilson.

And ten years later, in *The Lost Staircase* (1946), Elinor was still thumping the same tub. Only here the sides are reversed, for now it is not the pupil but Miss Mercier, the teacher who suffers from outdated ideas:

> 'We had better begin by going through the books you have been using,' she said. 'Please bring them here.'
>
> Jesanne . . . laid them before her governess. Inwardly she wondered what that lady would make of them, for already she knew that Miss Mercier's ideas of education were based on her own schooldays, while these books were modern of the modern.
>
> Miss Mercier picked up the first and looked at it. 'H'm! Empire history. Have you gone far in this?'
>
> 'Just up to the conquest of Canada,' said Jesanne.
>
> 'I see. What else have you done in history?'
>
> 'A general survey of the history of England — more detail when it deals with New Zealand, of course; and history of New Zealand up to the present day.'
>
> 'I see. Well, for the present I think you had better do detailed work in English history. It is shameful for an English girl not to know the history of her own country.'
>
> 'But I am not English,' said Jesanne demurely, 'I'm a New Zealander.'
>
> 'You will be English now,' said Miss Mercier, shortly — the demureness was not lost on her.

So far the honours are fairly even. But, alas for Miss Mercier, methods of teaching even English history have undergone transformations:

> To begin with . . . [this book] was not divided up into reigns, but into great movements. For example, the whole of one chapter dealt with the Reformation, and covered the reigns of Henry VIII, Edward VI, Mary I, and Elizabeth. The

position of England with regard to the Continent formed the subject of another chapter, and covered the same period. It was very distracting.

And then Jesanne had been taught to think for herself; to reason from cause to effect, and to find out effect from cause. She asked questions, as she had been trained to do . . . and they were questions that Miss Mercier, who had never bothered with logical reasoning, found difficult to answer.

Nor were things any better when it came to mathematics; while geography was to prove equally bothersome, 'what with land-tilts, continental shelves, and influence of climate and so on.'

For, as Elinor sums up the matter, 'Miss Mercier's schooldays belonged to the beginning of the century, before methods were revolutionised.'

And that last goes for Elinor too. That *her* schooldays, like Miss Mercier's, had 'belonged to the beginning of the century' is beyond dispute. But whether the teaching methods in the Misses Stewart's school could justly be condemned as inadequate — that can only remain a matter for speculation. However, one thing stands out if a comparison is made between the first and third of the above extracts: Elinor has far more sympathy with Gerry's predicament than she has with Miss Mercier's. Clearly she identified more with Gerry. And it might also be that she looked down, just the tiniest bit, on Miss Mercier. After all she, unlike the governess, did manage eventually to rise above probable deficiencies in her early schooling.

Perhaps that in part was just her good fortune: Elinor was eventually to continue her education at an establishment very different from the Misses Stewart's. But no doubt the achievement had demanded also a great deal of effort on her part, as well as much sheer hard work in the way of self-education.

OGLE TERRACE TO WESTOE VILLAGE

From the very beginning she had been ready, even anxious to learn. 'At three I taught myself to read [she relates in 'Something about Me'], and by four I was reading fluently . . . That year my mother also taught me to print.' Of course Elinor is sometimes unreliable about dates and ages, and there is no hard evidence to back up these statements. On the other hand, a very old friend does have it well established in her memory that 'Elinor, like my sister and myself, was a fluent reader from the age of four'. So, on balance, it is probable that she really was well advanced for her age when she first arrived at the Misses Stewart's school.

During her early years there the school was housed in Ogle Terrace, a solidly built Victorian street that was not far from, and not altogether unlike, Winchester Street. Ogle Terrace was, however, considered to be a trifle superior. The houses were in fact larger; the curtains over the windows were possibly of better quality Nottingham lace; there may, in the sombre living-rooms have been fewer ships-in-bottles and more busts of Shakespeare; larger aspidistras, taller whatnots, yet more massive marble clocks on the ornamental mantlepieces. But in both roads the style of house decoration was undoubtedly similar, with browns and greens the favourite colours; and the pictures would almost certainly have included *The Soul's Awakening* or *The Stag at Bay*.

In adult life Elinor was to acquire very different ideas about houses, rooms and decorations, as her

Westoe Village, 1906, where Elinor attended St Nicholas's School.

Winchester Street (now demolished), where Elinor was born and grew up, seen here in the 1950s.

books make clear with their many detailed and affectionate descriptions: living-rooms that are light, spacious and simply furnished, bedrooms that are white-painted and flowery-chintz-curtained are to be found in the homes of all her favourite characters. Nevertheless that dark heavy Victorian setting at Ogle Terrace was one where the small Elinor could have felt quite at home.

Until Elinor was about twelve, the Misses Stewart's school — it was almost always called just that, although its proper name was St Nicholas's — remained in Ogle Terrace. But then, sometime during the year 1906, a great day arrived when the two ladies moved out, taking their school with them, to a large house in Westoe Village. And that, as everyone knew, was quite the most desirable residential district in all South Shields.

In 1906, Westoe Village really was a village; the central part, which is all that now remains, was surrounded by farmlands; and stately homes were not lacking: Westoe Manor House, then the residence of a wealthy iron founder, and Westoe Hall, home of Sir James Readhead and his family, were close at hand. Even as lately as 1951 the district retained a rural character. Then in that year the last farm vanished beneath the new Marine and Technical College buildings. However the street where the Misses Stewart had their school (incredibly, until the 1930s) is now part of a conservation area, and from outside their house has changed little in appearance since Elinor's school-days. The street itself, too, with its cobbled road and line of handsome trees in the centre, still looks much as it did. And although that narrow lane at the far end no longer leads into real countryside both Manor House and Hall have managed to survive the years.

Westoe Village in 1906 must have been a revelation to the twelve-year-old from Winchester Street. These houses were of impressive size, many of them villas with large gardens, some even had stables and coach-houses. The families who lived in the village were the best families: they had staffs of servants; they drove round in carriages; their gardens were tended by gardeners and under-gardeners, their children by nannies and under-nurses. It was a new world. And it was also Elinor's first introduction, even at second-hand, to gracious living. She was never to forget it.

And to think that some of the girls in her school actually had their homes in Westoe Village, and lived there all the time . . .

One of these lucky beings was called Olive Mason (later she was to marry a gifted young composer whom Elinor greatly admired); and for a time Olive, six years the older, became Elinor's idol. 'Your name may be Olive but *you're* as fair as fair' was a typically phrased compliment that the small Elinor often repeated. And she would follow Olive round devotedly, carrying her books and occasionally offering a posy of wild flowers.

However it is plain that her beloved's name, Olive, displeased Elinor; perhaps it recalled those gloomy Victorian drawing-room walls. And doubtless she would have liked to see it changed. She herself was to change her name at several points during the first thirty years of her life. Christened Gladys Eleanor May, she does not appear ever to have been known by the first of these names, although as late as 1913 she was still using it in her signature. At school, and at home in the early days, she was always called May — the name by which her mother addressed her to the end. Later she took to Eleanor, with that spelling; at college she proclaimed herself to be Patricia

Maraquita, and wrote this name in all her books; after college she reverted to Eleanor, but usually shortened it to 'Len'. And it was really only in the mid-1920s that she finally settled into Elinor. Thereafter (apart from her time as headmistress, when the nickname B.D. was much used by her schoolgirls) it was as Elinor that she remained.

But, to return to the days of the Misses Stewart's school — what kind of child was Elinor (or May) at this stage in her life?

ELINOR AND/OR MAY

First of all, what did she look like? The earliest photograph available (apart from that discussed in Chapter I) was taken about 1908, and shows her in the St Nicholas's School group. The only other evidence is hearsay, and it is not easy to get an exact description of her colouring. Some friends have called her hair brown, others light brown; and one actually used the word 'corn-coloured', which would have delighted Elinor, who frequently used it herself in her books. All agree that the hair was straight by nature, and later pictures confirm this; so obviously a curling agency of some kind, tongs or papers, must have been at work before that school photo was taken.

From the photo (see page 57) it can be seen that Elinor's hair was thick to the point of being bushy, and was at least shoulder-length. But of course at that time no girls ever had their hair cut short. Or rather — no girls who went to schools like the Misses Stewart's. 'The girls from the workhouse were the only ones with short hair' wrote an ex-pupil of another South Shields school, then in her seventies: 'We always felt sorry for *them*.'

As to build, Elinor looks quite well-grown for her

age (thirteen or fourteen in the photo) and she is described as being 'on the solid side'. This she undeniably was in later life. However she did share the knack some plump people have of being able to move very lightly on her feet; and later this was to be a great asset when she became interested in folk dancing.

Her best point, according to several people, was her complexion — described by one acquaintance as 'a really lovely pink-and-white'. But this apart it seems that Elinor was considered to be plain. For one thing, her features were very large — something not revealed by this early photograph, but clear in later ones. Elinor seems to have taken after her father in appearance, and it could be that she inherited her heavy physiognomy and sturdy build from Charles's mother, Christianna Dyer, who came from a South African Dutch family. Besides, Elinor did have — not exactly a squint, but one eye that was 'slightly turned', or 'wandering' or 'swivelled round' (there are various descriptions). Later she was to undergo an operation which partially corrected this. But she never lost a habit which may originally have been connected with the eye trouble, of holding her head a little to one side. This tendency can be seen both in the St Nicholas' school photograph and in one taken about 33 years later with her own school group (see page 227).

And that Elinor was not indifferent to her lack of beauty can be deduced from her stories. In all of them, outstandingly good looks are lavished on a majority of the characters, but with two significant exceptions. Neither Joey Bettany in the Chalet books, nor Janie in the so-called La Rochelle Series, is in the least pretty. Yet these two are among Elinor's preferred heroines, Joey being unquestionably her prime favourite; and there is surely self-revelation beneath such passages as the following (from *Jo of the Chalet School*, 1926), where Joey, aged thirteen, has just given a Christmas parcel to her (much) older sister, Madge:

> She opened it, and there lay a little miniature of Joey, set in a narrow silver frame. 'Joey!' she cried. 'Where did you get this?'
>
> 'Miss Durrant did it,' explained Jo through a mouthful of chocolate.' . . . 'Do you like it?'
>
> '*Like* it!' Madge . . . looked from Joey of the picture to the pyjamaed figure curled up beside her . . . 'It is just what I most wanted, and exactly like you!'
>
> Joey considered it with her head on one side. 'No one on earth could call me beautiful, could they?' she said with unexpected wistfulness in her voice.

Joey, of course, was to grow up 'striking-looking', even 'distinguished'. And according to Mrs Phyllis Matthewman, who saw things with the unclouded eyes of a childhood friend, Elinor too, in later life, could sometimes look distinguished — 'when she took the trouble to get herself up properly'.

However, there is no denying that, back in her school-days, Elinor was not pretty; and it is possible that a feeling of inferiority about her looks may have contributed to making her self-conscious. Opinions about her do differ, but the general impression seems to be that she was not very popular among her contemporaries at the Misses Stewart's school. Perhaps an account Phyllis Matthewman gives of their early acquaintance may help to explain this: 'Elinor was introduced to me as someone I could play with — my aunts were friends of her mother. I'm afraid I wasn't very pleased. She was, at that time, very loud in her manner and apt to attract a good deal of amused attention from people who overheard her. It rather made me curl up.'

Now it would certainly come as a shock to anyone who knew Elinor only through her Chalet books to hear that she could, even at eleven years old, have been so noticeably 'loud'. At the Chalet School such emphasis is always laid on the importance of quiet good manners and gentle voices. Particularly in public:

'Miss Bettany was always careful to impress on the girls the necessity for good behaviour out of doors.' And when, on a rare occasion, this 'necessity' is temporarily forgotten, Mademoiselle has only to remind the school: ' "You must not shout thus, but speak with gentle tones and softly. It is not well for you to make visitors think that we of the Chalet School are rude — rough — noisy.' They stopped at once' (*The Princess of the Chalet School*, 1927).

Elinor as a child may not have been either rough or rude, but she was almost certainly noisy. Even her closest friends have remarked that her manner, although it did lose that actual loudness that so disconcerted the youthful Phyllis, remained throughout her life pronounced, not to say exuberant. And it cannot be imagined that the young ladies at the Misses Stewart's school were encouraged to behave with exuberance: Elinor's boisterous behaviour must often have brought her into conflict with the authorities. Still more important, she probably caused frequent embarrassment to her schoolfellows, since most children do abhor being made to feel conspicuous.

Besides, there could have been another reason for her possible unpopularity. Elinor was undoubtedly a clever child who could have benefitted from a more high-powered academic education; she was perhaps better at her lessons than others who were considered by their fellow pupils and their teachers to be more socially acceptable. If so, being Elinor, she would not have hesitated to point this out: all her life she was to be 'a very forthright person' — and even, in the words of one acquaintance, 'a very assertive person'.

However it was mainly those in her own age group who were out of sympathy with her. A number of the younger children apparently liked her very well. One, Miss Kathleen Page, who was a junior when Elinor was a 'big girl', remembered her with much warmth; and particularly in connection with outings to the beach. In a letter Miss Page described how, during the summer, the school would often walk across the fields from the village, and go down the rough grassy path to a beach called Mans Haven — incidentally a distance of around two miles each way, and they, like the girls in the Chalet books, thought nothing of it. On these excursions Elinor was always ready to entertain the little ones: 'I can see her now, sitting on a rock telling us stories which I loved'.

Here too a pattern was gradually being established that would continue into adult life. Elinor often tended to get on better with people younger than herself. Perhaps they found it easier to accept her rather larger-than-life manner. Perhaps she just felt more at ease with them.

CHAPTER IV

READING, WRITING, MUSIC

The description of Elinor holding the younger children enthralled with her stories will undoubtedly remind Chalet School readers of Jo Bettany, who is often pictured doing exactly the same thing.

Elinor and Jo both had the real story-teller's compulsion, which in Elinor's case seems to have existed from the time when she was first able to speak coherently. Thus when Nelly Dyer taught her four-year-old daughter to write she may not have been acting from purely disinterested motives. According to Elinor, anyway, her mother was 'sick of being perpetually asked, "Will you write down a story I've 'magined [sic], please?" '; and Elinor continues: 'Before that [i.e. learning to write], I had told the stories — to my little brother and the cat'. Most likely also to anyone else who could be persuaded to listen. To the end of her life Elinor was to remain a great raconteuse: 'She could make a most amusing speech — just like that, anytime,' a friend, Miss Rose Farr Smith, wrote of her in the 1960s.

It is a pity that phrase about her little brother and the cat sounds rather twee, for the picture it paints is probably quite faithful to reality. Elinor and Henzell were very close in age, and they must have been thrown very much together by the circumstances of their early home-life. 'Rex and I never say much, but we've been pals all our lives. I'm only eleven months older than he is', Madeleine in *Seven Scamps* (1927) says of *her* brother (at this point he is in danger at sea during a violent storm): adding significantly, 'I don't remember a time when he wasn't there'. And, although Elinor was fourteen months older than Henzell, that last must have been exactly true for her as well.

As to the cat — the only surprising thing is that the noun should be in the singular, because it appears that Elinor's family had a quite remarkable fondness for cats, and that there were always several of them around at 52 Winchester Street. Not one person describing the house (or, for that matter, Elinor's later homes) has failed to mention those cats; and one friend, blunter than the rest, states that the animals did not always make their presence known by sight and sound alone: 'Sometimes that house really did reek of cats,' she recalls. And, years later, a lodger in Elinor's Hereford house made a similar complaint.

However there can be no question that, with or without a cat in attendance, Elinor continued to pour forth stories, since comments to the effect that 'she was always scribbling away, all her life' are among those most frequently made by her friends. Nor, seemingly, did her earliest efforts all go unrewarded, her first public success as a writer coming, at least allegedly, at the age of five, when she won a magazine competition with a moral little story entitled *Lotty's Fright*: it was 'all about a naughty little girl who borrowed her cousin's new bicycle without permission and ended up with a broken arm as a result'.

Here the particular choice of plot is interesting; for it suggests that at five years old Elinor was already fascinated by the idea that misdeeds could often bring their own, as it were, built-in punishment. This was to become a regular theme in her books: examples leap to mind. In *Jo of the Chalet School* Jo Bettany disobeys a strict order forbidding attendance at an ice carnival, slips during the festivities and sprains her ankle badly. Characters in various books, notably *The Rivals of the Chalet School*, disregard bans on skating before the ice is officially pronounced safe, and are involved in near-fatal accidents. Eustacia Benson, who (in *Eustacia Goes to the Chalet School*) is running away from school mainly as a gesture of defiance, also meets with an accident: this causes severe injuries to her back, condemning her (like What-Katy-did-Carr before her) to many months in bed. Joyce Linton (*The Chalet School and the Lintons*) is punished for her participation at a midnight feast, not with the conventional lines or French repetition but by a violent and frightening bout of sickness. In *A Chalet Girl from Kenya*, Emerence Hope disobediently leaves the path during a walk and . . . But the examples of people bringing punishment on themselves are literally too numerous to cite.

Not that children in Elinor's books are immune from penalties imposed by parents or teachers. Far from it. Scoldings, fines, docked half-holidays, confiscated pocket money, lines, repetition — some or all of these occur in most of the school stories. And in all the books people are frequently 'sent to bed'.

There is naturally no corporal punishment in any of Elinor's school stories. The schools portrayed were just not that kind. However, in the various fictional families spankings do occur from time to time, and are described; and even in the Chalet series odd remarks, passed to the effect that such and such an insubordinate girl 'could do with a good whipping', tend to reinforce the impression that personal chastisement was familiar in Elinor's childhood. Certainly the belief in formal punishments as an essential part of children's upbringing was generally accepted at that time — enduring indeed until much nearer the present. And Elinor absorbed this notion along with many others now totally out of fashion.

The idea of retribution features again in her second published story, to judge by its title anyway. 'At twelve I sent a short story called 'Jack's Revenge' to *Sunday*, a children's magazine which we took in. It was accepted and paid for — 10s. [50p].'

Now this is a little puzzling: not the event, which could well have happened, but the details, which do not match the facts. Yes, a story by Elinor entitled 'Jack's Revenge' — Jack, by the way, being not a boy but a dog — did appear in *Sunday* (as the magazine *Sunday Reading for the Young* was familiarly known). But the year of its publication was 1914. And in 1914 Elinor was not twelve but twenty years of age.

However, the possibility that Elinor did contribute to another Sunday periodical at a relatively early stage has some independent backing from a contemporary of hers, Miss Mary Starling, who remembers being introduced to Elinor when both were in their teens, and 'looking upon her with something akin to awe when I heard that she had had stories accepted and published in the *Sunday Companion*, a magazine which we at home took in regularly'.

And one scrap of evidence can be found — in *Gay from China at the Chalet School* (1944) — to show that Elinor was certainly familiar with the periodical in question: 'Gay meekly handed over the magazine . . . Grandma . . . looked it through from cover to cover . . . "Lot of trash!" she snorted. "When *I* was a young girl I only read the *Sunday Companion* . . . And *then* my father tore out the serial first." '

'Grandma' in the above extract makes very clear her opinion of that 1944 girls' magazine. But the sixteen-year-old Gay Lambert, or her real-life equivalent, might well have reacted in a similar way to the *Sunday Companion* — especially to those serials that were ripped out by the stern Papa. Good strong melodramatic staff they were; and if the *Sunday Companion* arrived regularly in Elinor's childhood home she must have had a splendid time reading the weekly instalments — as read them she certainly did, given the opportunity, being apparently the kind of child to read anything she could put her hands on.

Of course the children of her time had nothing approaching the sheer quantity of books being specially written for them that children have today. But they did not lack varied reading material. Even leaving aside all that might be labelled 'adult literature' and the acknowledged children's classics — *Treasure Island* and so on — there was a wide choice among the works of 19th-century and earlier writers. Elinor often mentions affectionately Louisa Alcott, Mrs Molesworth and Mrs Ewing; and she makes clear her admiration for Charlotte M. Yonge, an author who is unfashionable nowadays but whose novels, both family and historical, did have a perceptible influence on Elinor's own ideas and writings.

In quite another vein there were such writers as Marryat, Ballantyne, Rider Haggard, Fennimore Cooper, Henty and Weyman: Elinor and her brother possessed many of their books; and the adventure stories for boys that Elinor wrote during the 1950s may owe something to her early reading among these authors.

It is worth noting, too, that a number of children's

books which are now rated as classics were published during Elinor's early years, and probably were included in her reading. Among them were Rudyard Kipling's two Jungle Books and *Stalky and Co.* (a favourite book of Elinor's); all the best known stories by Edith Nesbit; *The Wind in the Willows*; and both *The Little Princess* and *The Secret Garden* of Frances Hodgson Burnett (the latter another favourite).

Perhaps Elinor, at eight years old in 1902, was temporarily beyond the age for *Peter Rabbit*, which was first published that year. In any case it was around this time that she was having her first introduction to the girls' school story: here she would not at first have met books by Angela Brazil, that symbol of the genre, for Miss Brazil did not begin producing 'The Works' (as she herself often called them) until 1907; but L. T. Meade, who is usually given the credit for having orginated the whole thing, had been busy ever since her *A World of Girls* in 1886, and Elinor can hardly have escaped reading a number of these rather cloying books.

Another writer whose school stories she encountered at this stage was May Baldwin. And possibly the idea which, twenty-odd years later, was to set going the whole vast Chalet School series could have grown from Miss Baldwin's early books; for among them are several about schools on the Continent: *A Popular Girl* (1901), for instance, is a 'tale of school life in Germany'; and *The Girls of St Gabriel* (1905) an account of 'Life at a French School' — one that seems nowadays of paralysing boredom, but perhaps Elinor at eleven found it entrancing.

However that may be, the stories of May Baldwin are not included on any of the lists of recommended books which the adult Elinor compiled at various times for her Chalet Club members. These, selected mainly from established writers, contain no surprises; although it does rather date Elinor that G. A. Henty and O. Douglas (pseudonym of John Buchan's sister, Anna) should be among the chosen.

Apart from continually urging the club's members to read as much as possible, Elinor was also anxious that they should get into the habit of buying books. Of course she, as a writer, might have been thought to have an interest in this; but in fact she was herself a lifelong collector of books. 'I began collecting them when I was only seven', she wrote in 1965; adding ruefully that, when faced with a house removal, she 'had over 3,000 to sort out'. And in the 1970s enough of that collection survived to make Elinor's estimate quite realistic, as well as to furnish evidence of her varied tastes.

Her books also give every sign of having been well read. Altogether, what with all the reading and writing she did, it is remarkable that she ever managed to fit in any other interests. In fact she had many, and one in particular which, like books and writing, dated from her very early years: 'On my fourth birthday I had my first music lesson and thereafter music was as important a part of my education as any other subject', we learn from 'Something about Me'. (Surprising, really, how much information those few lines do contain.)

Here there are unmistakable echoes of the Chalet School, for the latter part of that statement cannot fail to summon up Mr Denny, the school's eccentric singing-master. 'He was a dreamy, irresponsible being who declared . . . that music should have the first place in every school' — so runs the description in *The Princess of the Chalet School*. And in book after book all through the series it is confirmed that 'if . . . Mr Denny had had his way, all lessons would have been based on music. He quoted what Plato had to say on the subject in season and out' (*Eustacia Goes to the Chalet School*).

Whatever Plato may or may not have said, it would seem hard to put Mr Denny's ideas into practice in ordinary schools. Although Elinor for one might have enjoyed her maths lessons more if geometry theorems had been expressed in plain chant, and quadratic equations sung to fugues by Bach or Handel, two of her preferred composers. Bach was in fact always her supreme favourite; others whose music she mentions enjoying particularly include Beethoven and Haydn. At one point she described her musical tastes as 'severely classical'; but since on another occasion she avowed a 'love [of] the music of Ravel, and of Franck and all that school', her definition of the term must have been fairly elastic.

Anyway her books establish beyond doubt that music really did mean a lot to Elinor: her appreciation and enjoyment shine through in her writing. And her musical studies (of which more in a later chapter) also gave her something that is unusual among writers of schoolgirl fiction: a knowledge of just how much toil and sweat and grinding effort, never to mention talent, is required to make a concert performer. 'At my age, and if I'm to make music my career as I intend, I simply haven't time to waste', fifteen-year-old Nina Rutherford (in the rather unfortunately titled *A Genius at the Chalet School*, 1956) explains to her guardian, 'I ought to be doing six hours' practice a day. And there's all the theoretical side . . . '

Which is fine as far as it goes. But talented teenagers who aspire to six hours of daily practice can be found in other school stories. So it is more interesting to find that Nina had been warned 'from her earliest days . . . about the hardships and disappointments she must meet if she went in for concert work . . . that there would never come a time when she might rest on her oars unless she meant to give it up for good . . . that it was a hard life . . . with perpetual travelling . . . requiring great powers of self-control so that no matter how unhappy or poorly she felt she should not disappoint her audiences'.

Even this, although the points stressed were all worth making, does not prove that Elinor had any inside knowledge of musical matters. However there is, in a later chapter, a description of how Nina sets to work before a concert, and this has the authentic ring that comes from experience (albeit only at a far humbler level — Elinor herself being apparently no performer).

> She would, of course, play from memory on the Monday, but there were two or three cadenzas that were not clear enough for her liking and she set to work on them, reading the music first to fix them more securely in her memory, then playing them, at first, slowly, then faster, until they were right up to time and rippling from her fingers with perfect evenness, every note receiving its proper value.
>
> This took half an hour. Then she closed the music and proceeded to play the whole thing right through, listening to herself as she had been taught, with an ear alert for any slips. Twice more she played it. [Etc., etc.]

Now that passage hardly represents lively writing for children. But it has deliberately been quoted uncut because it is the details which are important in this context. For they establish that Nina really does know the proper way to practise (two experienced professional musicians are prepared to vouch for that). As for the writing — *A Genius at the Chalet School* is the thirty-fifth book in the series, which by 1956 had been going on for more than thirty years. No wonder if the style had by this time become rather pedestrian.

Elinor had not always lacked the ability to make a musical child come to life. When her presentation of Nina Rutherford in 1956 is compared with that of Margia Stevens, chief musical talent in the early Chalet School books, the contrast is striking. For one thing, that injudicious term 'genius' is not applied to Margia. unless occasionally by her contemporaries. Elinor is content with calling her 'intensely musical', and making it clear that she was 'expected to do great things in later years, for she was gifted beyond the ordinary'. But the main difference is that, where Nina obstinately refuses to leave the printed page, Margia is quite a human schoolgirl, however talented. She can actually grumble when some enthralling ploy with her chums is interrupted because of her musical training:

> 'Herr Anserl has come up to give you an extra lesson, Margia, and . . . [Miss Wilson] said I was to tell you to go *at once*!'
>
> Margia's face clouded over. 'Bother him!' she said ungratefully. 'What does he want to do that for? I had a lesson yesterday, and that's enough for one week!' (*The Chalet School and Jo*, 1931)

Not that Margia really lacks enthusiasm for work. In a later book (*The New House at the Chalet School*, 1935) Elinor makes this plain when Margia has an encounter with the new matron, an unpleasing lady whose attitude to music is strictly no-nonsense: 'If you expect me to believe that any girl isn't overjoyed at getting *out* of her practising, you've made a mistake,' she proclaims at one stage.

The said Matron Besly, being a new arrival at the Chalet School (she doesn't stay long, either), is unaware that 'Margia's love of music amounted to a mania', and in she sails with all guns firing.

> 'What are you doing over here?' she asked sharply. 'And what do you mean by grinning at me like that?' . . .
>
> 'Mademoiselle sent me over here to practise, as the piano I generally use has gone — two strings snapped with the heat,' . . . [Margia] explained . . . 'And I beg your pardon, Matron, but I wasn't grinning — at least, I didn't know that I was. You see, I'm so longing to get at my new Brahms.'
>
> 'Rubbish!' said Matron, curtly. 'Don't tell me such nonsense as that!'

But Elinor clearly understood the possibility that this idea was far from rubbish and nonsense. Although not gifted with the fictional Margia's ability to play the piano, she was genuinely able to share such feelings about music. And this capacity for getting inside a musical character, along with her more realistic view of the music profession, singles out Elinor from most other writers in her field. Elsie Oxenham, for one: Miss Oxenham, on good authority, cannot be faulted where folk dancing is concerned; but she always manages to give an impression that things are far too easy for her budding musicians: Queen's Hall (akin to the Royal Festival Hall of today) is, as it were, just at the end of the school concert platform. And with Angela Brazil there is something about her schoolgirl performers that suggests more acquaintance with the romantic party piece than with the five-finger exercise.

However, to balance things a bit, neither of those ladies ever made such an out-and-out blunder as Elinor once did in writing about a staff evening at the Chalet School (*Exploits of the Chalet Girls*, 1933): for during this entertainment: 'four of the Sixth [Form] played a movement from one of Brahms' Quartets for violin, viola, 'cello and *flute* [sic]. It went very well.'

And maybe it did go well. But unfortunately, and to the possible chagrin of many flautists, Brahms never wrote even a single flute quartet, nor indeed any chamber music work that includes the flute.

That really must have been an off-day for Elinor; and not much excuse for her, either. Because, as she herself often pointed out, her musical education, though perhaps less thorough than she claimed, had undeniably been lifelong.

CHAPTER V

SCHOOLMISTRESSES AND SCHOOLGIRLS

The music lessons that began on Elinor's fourth birthday were to be continued through and even beyond her school-days; and at first her mother used to supervise her practice, so no doubt it was as regular as that of Margia Stevens at the Chalet School, or Gerry Challoner in *Gerry Goes to School*; although it perhaps did not include such impressive quantities of scales and arpeggios, finger exercises and studies (Czerny's *Etudes de la Velocité* are frequently mentioned in the stories).

Whether her piano lessons took place at school or elsewhere is not known. The Misses Stewart's school did of course have a piano teacher; indeed such a school could hardly have done without one in those days, when to play the piano a little was considered to be a necessary accomplishment for young ladies.

Nor was piano playing the only attraction offered by St Nicholas' School. According to the Misses Stewart's advertisement there was Swedish drill, for instance — the instructress at one time being a Miss Wilson, a name with strong Chalet School echoes. Also, and no doubt a matter for some complacency, a fully qualified Froebel teacher for the Kindergarten. However it is noticeable that the school's advertisement does not until quite late in Elinor's time mention any other qualified staff, which would rather imply that there were none. The two Miss Stewarts were almost certainly unqualified as teachers themselves, although both had behind them years of experience in their school, and one sister had also worked as a private governess.

For some reason, though, it was not this sister but the younger of the pair, Miss Henrietta, who took charge of the teaching at St Nicholas's. In the photograph (opposite) she is seated in the second row, the further right of the two ladies in black. Her elder sister, the lady in the terrifying hat who is seated beside Miss Henrietta, appears to have acted mainly as housekeeper, organising the catering, doling out the morning milk and so on. But she was obviously much concerned with the general running of the school and must have had a hand in all decision- and policy-making. Also, at a guess, with discipline.

Other mistresses to be seen in the photo include: mathematics, (did she and Elinor often clash?) third row, immediately behind the elder Miss Stewart; art and dancing, on extreme right of second row from the back; the French 'mamselle' — unmistakably French — in the third row, third from the left; and the Kindergarten teacher, second row, third from the left.

It can be seen that the latter's charges in the Kindergarten included a number of small boys. Pretty minuscule they look, too, but then not one of them can have been more than eight at the most, for by the conventions of the day it was around the age of eight that masculinity was adjudged really to set in, forever debarring boys from attending the same school as their sisters. From this point onwards the pressure was heavy on a boy to become 'manly'. And this included a lot of things: the whole of the stiff-upper-lip cult, of course; and perhaps little matters such as no longer wearing button boots, which, in some circles at least, were thought 'sissy'. All rather odd in a generation that was still putting small boys up to the age of three or even four into petticoats and dresses.

St Nicholas's School (known as the Misses Stewart's school), taken in the garden of the school's premises about 1908. Elinor (May) is in the second back row, fifth from the right. Miss Stewart is in the second row, wearing a hat, with her sister on her left.

Elinor's brother, Henzell, was one of those who spent a couple of years in St Nicholas's Kindergarten. But that had been during the school's Ogle Terrace days; by the time this photograph was taken Henzell was at least twelve, and had long since moved on to the boys' high school.

The photograph does not make it clear whether the school had an official uniform or not. The younger children's clothing shows a fair amount of variation, but many of the older girls are dressed similarly in blouses and skirts. (And only to think that in those days 'a skirt for lasting wear', as advertised in the *Sunday Companion*, could be bought for a mere three shillings and eleven pence — just under 20p.)

Oddly enough, some of those 1908 garments look not unlike the clothes worn by some girls of the present day. However there is no doubt at all that the garments the camera does not tell us about were very different. Underclothes, to begin with — though they would surely never have been mentioned: the usual generous array included invariably a chemise, drawers and petticoat, of cotton or flannelette according to season; in cold weather a woollen vest or combinations would have been added; possibly stays; but no bras — in the present-day sense they were unknown; and, just to add to the joys of life, for Sundays the cotton petticoat and drawers were usually starched, which really must have made a torture of those prickly horsehair sofas that were all too popular at the time. But then comfort was hardly important. Legs, for instance, were always encased in long stockings: in winter these were woollen and usually black; even in summer they were long, although at least they were made of cotton, and mostly white.

Today's schoolgirl, going comfortably bare-legged

in hot weather, could spare a bit of sympathy for seventeen-year-old Madeleine in Elinor's *Seven Scamps* (1927): during a summer holiday in Guernsey she actually has to spend precious time mending one of her stockings, and it is clear she wears them as a matter of course.

Girls at the Chalet School also wear stockings more often than not, at least in the early books of the series, and from time to time this can make rather odd reading nowadays. As, for example, when Joey and Elisaveta, aged fourteen and twelve, are making a hair-raising (and unforeseen) mountain escape: here, although both the narrative and the illustration on the original dustwrapper make plain they are wearing only summer dresses, they must nevertheless be stocking-clad, since they are able to remove the said stockings and cut them up to make an improvised rope.

And this particular scene throws some interesting light on the attitude of Elinor's generation towards the whole subject of underclothing:

> Still . . . [the stocking rope] was not nearly long enough. They would land on a fairly steep slope, and they dared not risk a drop, [So how to lengthen that rope?]
>
> 'Our frocks?' suggested Elisaveta.
>
> Joey shook her head. 'No; I don't think we'd better do that. People might have fits if we wandered to Briesau in only knickers and camis.'
>
> This was so true that . . . [Elisaveta] said no more. (*The Princess of the Chalet School*, 1927)

Well now — was it a matter of life and death to get down that precipice or wasn't it? In fact, when the passage is read in context the urgency of the situation is clear; and, apart from this moment, the whole escape sequence is well managed. But then it is impossible today to appreciate Joey and Elisaveta's dilemma. The elder Miss Stewart though, a lady who even in summertime wore a hat when being photographed outside her own house, would undoubtedly have grasped the niceties of the problem. Elinor too could understand, for that was the way she had been brought up.

To return from that Austrian mountainside to the St Nicholas's school photograph — it is obvious, since the picture was taken in about 1908, that the youngest person in the group would now be at least ninety. However, the people of South Shields appear to be not only longlived but gifted with long memories, and as recently as the mid-1970s, when the school photograph was published in the *Shields Gazette*, a surprisingly large number of the pupils were recognised and named. They include the owner of the photograph, the late Mrs Eva Oliver — front row, fifth from the left; Aimée Elizabeth Donald, described by Elinor in her dedication to *Heather Leaves School* as 'my oldest friend' — third from the right in the second back row; and Miss Kathleen Page, who supplied the description of Elinor's story-telling sessions on the beach — second from the left in the third row, wearing a saucy bow in her hair.

None of the others named have any special connection with Elinor. But, surprisingly, a girl who is definitely known to have been Elinor's friend has not so far been identified. Her name was Elizabeth Jobling; and since her home was in Winchester Street, just opposite the Dyer family, she and Elinor used always to make the journeys to and from school together. Not in those despised trams: every day Elinor and Elizabeth, as described by Miss Mary Starling, a friend of both, were companions on the 'long walk, up Winchester Street to Fowler

Street along the Westoe Road and so to the Village' and the Misses Stewart's establishment.

Of course there is no way of being certain that their friendship was a specially close one; but it is a safe guess that had the two disliked each other's company they would have contrived in the usual manner of children to avoid it. In any case, there was much about Elizabeth's sad and rather romantic story that would have appealed to Elinor. To begin with, Elizabeth, like so many school-story heroines, was an orphan. Elinor's books were going to be thronged with orphans, right from the first story, *Gerry Goes to School*, where Gerry is an orphan — the first of a long line which includes Joey and Madge Bettany, Juliet Carrick, Robin Humphries, Eustacia Benson, Daisy and Primula Venables, Adrienne Desmoines and the pianist 'genius' Nina Rutherford, among the Chalet School's generous quota. Then Janie Temple and her half-sisters Elizabeth and Anne, central characters of the La Rochelle books, are orphans, and so is Pauline Ozanne. In addition, scores of other people in all the various books are either fatherless or motherless, the latter being perhaps the more usual.

Elizabeth Jobling had something else in common with Janie Temple of La Rochelle: her father, too, had been a sailor. But whereas Captain Temple, RN, dies peacefully at home, somewhere near the beginning of *The Maids of La Rochelle*, Elizabeth's father suffered a more dramatic death having been drowned at sea (as had, of course, Elinor's grandfather, William Dyer). At that time Elizabeth was still quite a small child and she had already lost her mother (who died at the time of Elizabeth's birth). And so, following her father's death, Elizabeth came to live in Winchester Street with her cousins the Hutchinsons. It was then that the two girls, who were much the same age, became acquainted, for Mrs Hutchinson was a friend of Elinor's mother; hence it might well have been Nelly Dyer who recommended the Misses Stewart's school.

Almost nothing can be told about Elizabeth's career at St Nicholas's, only that it was not to be a very long one; for Elizabeth was one of the many unfortunate people at that time who contracted tuberculosis. Perhaps ill-health kept her away from school on the day that group photograph was taken.

The disease may already have been established before Elizabeth came to live in Winchester Street — it would hardly be possible to discover this now. Nor is it known whether her illness was prolonged, or took the form that was grimly known as 'galloping consumption'. All that can be stated for certain is that, at the age of sixteen, poor Elizabeth died.

And it is a sobering thought that Elinor's school-friend Elizabeth Jobling was only one among thousands of people, in all age groups and all parts of Britain, who died from tuberculosis during that one year, nineteen hundred and eleven. In South Shields alone the disease caused many hundreds of deaths. No wonder that the whole subject of tuberculosis became so important to Elinor, and was to play a significant part in many of her stories.

CHAPTER VI

'JOEY WILL GET WELL'

In the summer of 1911 when Elizabeth Jobling died Elinor was only seventeen. Yet it is highly unlikely that Elizabeth's was the first death to have occurred among her youthful acquaintances. At that time it was still a common enough fate to die young; a quick look through the contemporary death registers gives melancholy confirmation of this. An instance at random: in the column where Elizabeth's death is recorded, considerably more than half the total of seventy-five entries refer to people *under the age of fourteen*; and with this in mind it becomes easier to understand why there are so many death-bed scenes in Elinor's books.

Her own first experience of a death in her immediate family circle had come as early as January 1901, when her grandmother, Hannah Rutherford, died after a fortnight's illness during which she had been nursed at home.

Hannah's death must have had a shattering effect on the household at 52 Winchester Street. Through it Nelly Dyer lost the mother who had always been her guide and support, and more specially so after Charles's departure. The two children, Elinor and Henzell, then six and five years old, lost the grandmother who had been there in the background ever since, literally, the first moments of their lives; who had helped to look after them and no doubt also to 'bring them up in the way they should go'.

The immediate cause of Hannah's death had been pneumonia with pleurisy — something else that plainly made a deep impression on Elinor, and was to appear frequently in her stories. In particular, her Chalet School books of the twenties and thirties contain many references to Joey Bettany's having had 'severe pleuro-pneumonia' — the latter being the name Elinor always uses in her early writings.

Nowadays the term 'pleuro-pneumonia' is far more often used in a veterinary context: and a present-day reader might even wonder why Joey should be afflicted with (as described in the *Shorter Oxford English Dictionary*) 'a contagious febrile malady peculiar to horned cattle'. But at the time when Elinor wrote these stories her readers would have been all too familiar both with this often fatal disease and with that particular name for it. That the name should now have become so unfamiliar to most people must be a tribute to modern antibiotic drugs, which have made the illness itself both much rarer and far less serious.

Elinor's books make plain that she did herself know something about the illness. Here, from *The Rivals of the Chalet School* (1929), is her picture of an eight-year-old girl, Robin Humphries, entering the room where Joey is lying dangerously ill with the aforesaid pleuro-pneumonia:

> Everything [in the room] was very spotless. A queer kind of bottle — that was what Robin called it [in her mind] — stood near, and a nurse in fresh uniform was at the fire. By the bed sat Madge . . . one slim hand holding Joey's. Her lips were moving, though no sound came from them, and, baby as she was, the Robin realised that . . . [Madge] was praying. Then her eyes wandered past to the bed and its occupant. Joey lay propped up with pillows to make it easier for her to breathe. Her black eyes were half-open, and her

> cheeks were scarlet, as the Robin had never seen Joey's cheeks before. A tearing rusty sound came through her parted lips, and she was muttering to herself in low tones.

That reads very much as though Elinor were looking back, perhaps to the time of Hannah Rutherford's last illness, and remembering things she had seen and heard herself at the age of six-and-three-quarters. And this imparts a feeling of authenticity which carries the reader along. It is a pity that this is not fully maintained in the scene which follows, where the Robin recalls Joey from the brink of death by her singing of a favourite Russian folk-song. This is perhaps one of the best-known passages in the whole series; and one, it must be acknowledged, that was often singled out for special praise in fan letters. But today the account seems rather contrived. Perhaps it is all too like the typical Victorian death-bed scene — or something from the *Sunday Companion*. Perhaps the reader simply feels too sure that Joey is not going to die.

In an earlier book, *The School at the Chalet* (1925), Elinor had dealt far more convincingly and movingly with a similar situation. Here, too, it is Joey who is gravely ill. She is lying unconscious, while the doctor and Frau Mensch, a kind friend, keep watch at her bedside. Madge, carrying out her duties as headmistress, is downstairs in one of the classrooms.

> At about three o'clock, as Madge was wearily trying to help Amy Stevens disentangle . . . her map of Asia, word came . . . [from] the doctor . . . Literally flinging the map at the astonished Amy, [Madge] . . . fled up the stairs to her bedroom. The doctor was standing by the bedside, one hand on

Joey's wrist. He looked up as her sister entered.

'Ah, *mein Fräulein* . . . I think she is beginning to arouse. Please stand just there, where she can see you.'

Madge . . . stood, her eyes fixed on Joey's face. There was no doubt that she was coming out of the stupor. Her lashes flickered more than once, her lips were parted. The only question was, Would she wake up the old Joey, or would it be to the babbling delirium of fever?

. . . The only sound to be heard was the breathing of the four people . . . and the ticking of the doctor's watch. Then, slowly, slowly, the long black lashes lifted, and Joey looked full at her sister.

'Hullo!' she murmured. 'I'm awfully tired!' . . . with a little yawn [she] turned slightly, snuggling down into the pillow, and fell asleep.

'*Gott sei dankt*!' said the doctor, quietly. 'She will do now; there is no further danger. Hush, *mein Kind*,' for Madge had begun to cry, 'It is well now!'

'I know,' sobbed Madge. 'But oh, Herr Doktor, the relief' . . .

When, finally, the tears were all dried . . . Frau Mensch suggested bed.

'I must tell the girls first,' said Madge. 'I will make myself tidy, and go and tell them.'

Ten minutes later Miss Bettany, who looked like herself once more, entered the room where they were all anxiously awaiting her news. She looked at them, but no words would come to her lips. It was Bernhilda the quiet who helped her out.

'Ah, Madame,' she said, 'there is no need to say anything. Joey will get well.'

And that last phrase may provide the essential clue to understanding why Elinor did have this obsession with death-bed scenes. The point surely is that, with few exceptions, they are not death scenes at all, but describe last-minute miraculous recoveries. And Elinor's continual assertion in fiction that 'Joey will get well' was almost certainly her way of compensating for a loss she had suffered at the age of eighteen, when someone very close to her was taken ill with dramatic suddenness — and did not 'get well'.

This tragedy is recorded concisely and impersonally by the Medical Officer for South Shields in his report for the year 1912: 'Cerebro-spinal fever became notifiable within the Borough in 1912. One case was notified and was removed to the Isolation Hospital, where death occurred. No secondary cases developed.'

The official wording strikes cold. But then no doctor could allow himself to mourn for every individual death; and in this case, as far as concerned his borough of South Shields, one death was plainly less important than the fact that a possible epidemic of cerebro-spinal fever had been averted. This was a killer-disease: sometimes known as Spotted Fever, or cerebro-spinal meningitis, it had been rife during previous centuries; but by 1912 the disease was becoming less and less common; and there must have been general relief among the medical fraternity in South Shields when no further cases followed the first.

The name of that one unfortunate victim appears in the deaths column of the *Shields Gazette* published on Wednesday 25 September 1912. The announcement is of the briefest: 'DYER. At Denes Hospital, on 24th inst., Henzell Watson Dyer, aged 17. No flowers.' But it needs little imagination to picture the grief and stricken numbness that lay behind those few words. Moreover, for Elinor, the sudden death of her brother followed little more than a year after the death of her school-friend, Elizabeth.

Henzell's illness, however contracted, had lasted for barely five days; and probably he did not spend many of them at home, for the moment the illness was diagnosed he would instantly have been removed to the Fever Hospital in Dean Street, which was known as 'the Denes'.

Perhaps it was better that way. Obviously it was distressing for Henzell's mother and sister to see him removed from his home, while they had to remain there unable to help in any way. But cerebro-spinal meningitis is an illness that can be attended by much pain; it could have been even more distressing for them to have witnessed this.

As it was, they were probably not allowed to see Henzell at all after he entered the hospital, unless through a glass panel, since this was the usual regulation laid down at isolation hospitals. The rules might not have permitted Nelly and Elinor even to remain in the building while awaiting news of Henzell's condition. Especially as it was no great distance from Winchester Street to 'the Denes', only about twenty minutes' walk. So most likely the two continued through those anxious days to live at home; and, since they would have had no telephone, to visit the hospital several times each day.

Henzell's mother may have felt unable to manage even this. Certainly it was not Nelly Dyer, but the eighteen-year-old Elinor who finally collected Henzell's death certificate from the hospital and took it to the Registrar. And the ban on flowers that is included in the newspaper announcement does suggest that no one was encouraged to make gestures, still less visits, of sympathy.

The full effects on Nelly and Elinor of their tragic loss can only be guessed. In Elinor's case much was to emerge in her writing. But this was almost certainly an unconscious process. Indeed it appears that after Henzell's death Elinor and her mother seldom talked about him, or even mentioned his existence. At college, only three years later, none of Elinor's fellow students ever knew that she had had a brother; and many people who met her only in later years were also unaware of it.

One friend who was a child of about nine or ten when she first got to know Elinor did learn the bare outline of Henzell's story from her parents; but she still recalls how strongly they impressed on her 'never to ask anything about him', for fear it might upset Elinor's mother. She grew up thinking that his death must have taken place only a short time previously. In fact this was in 1922. Henzell had died in 1912.

Probably it was only to a few friends who knew her really well that Elinor ever again spoke of Henzell — the brother who had been so close to her that she couldn't 'remember a time when he wasn't there'. And it was not until twenty years had gone by that she felt able to dedicate one of her books — *The Little Marie-José* (1932): 'To the memory of my brother.'

CHAPTER VII

TANGLED WEBS

Looking at Elinor's life with the wisdom of hindsight, it seems clear that in some ways she never fully recovered from the shock of Henzell's death. True, certain qualities must always have been latent in her character; in particular a tendency to take refuge from harsh reality in fiction. But the loss of her brother and earliest companion, which severed the links with her real childhood, may also have contributed to an almost indefinite prolonging of her adolescence.

According to the conventions of the day she had become technically speaking a grown-up on her eighteenth birthday, more than five months before her brother died. This event would have been marked in the traditional ways: skirt hemlines down, and hair up. The latter was obviously important to Elinor, for right through the thirties, forties and even into the fifties, her Chalet schoolgirls are anachronistically preoccupied with the question of putting up their hair.

Not that an eighteen-year-old was considered 'of age' at that time. Nor was the attainment of her majority at twenty-one going to bring Elinor the vote: for this right, even after the Act passed in 1918, she would have had to wait until her thirtieth birthday in April 1924; and Elinor was to have reached the age of thirty-four when in 1928 the franchise was finally extended to women over twenty-one. But then, many people today seem unaware that, until 1918 — a time still within living memory for some — even *men* of twenty-one did not all have the vote; while in Northern Ireland there was no universal suffrage until after 1968.

For Elinor, her eighteenth birthday brought another important change, apart from those in her garments and hair-style. On that day, 6 April 1912, she became, according to the records of the Department of Education and Science, 'an unqualified teacher'. And that snippet of information provides the only available evidence about when Elinor's own schooldays ended. It has been impossible to discover anything definite about her last years at school, or to resolve a particular mystery which surrounds them. This concerns the impression she gave when interviewed on television in January 1964 that she had been at Dame Allan's Girls' School in Newcastle upon Tyne.

All existing information points to Elinor's having been educated only at the Misses Stewart's school in Westoe Village. Several people, including a fellow student of Elinor's at college, are convinced of this. However, the late Brian Redhead, who was her television interviewer in January 1964, understood that Elinor had attended Dame Allan's (then, as now, one of the leading schools in the north-east), as did some of those who watched the interview.

The school was unable to help much, although they were anxious to do so. But unfortunately they no longer hold records of admissions to Dame Allan's in the years before the Great War. And so, after patient searching, all they could say for certain was that Elinor had never been a member of their *staff* which had seemed a possibility worth investigating. They did point out that their library contained a surprising number of books by Elinor — 'almost everything she ever wrote' — which might suggest a personal connection with the school. But that was all.

Even the enthusiastic co-operation of an eighty-three-year-old member of the Dame Allan's Old Girls' Association failed to bring anything to light. Neither she, nor any of the friends among whom she made tireless enquiries, could remember anything about Elinor under any of her different names. And since these helpful ladies would have been Elinor's exact contemporaries at Dame Allan's, it does seem unlikely that all were unaware of her presence — noticeable as she was.

So, did Elinor deliberately make a false claim? Or could the whole thing have arisen through a misunderstanding of some kind? There seems no chance now that these questions can be answered. However it does have to be faced that Elinor had an oddly ambivalent attitude to the whole matter of telling the truth. From her books no one could fail to get the impression that honesty was a most highly esteemed virtue. Her schoolgirl heroines all share the infant Washington's renowned and total incapacity. And yet Elinor herself was seldom honest about her real age. Possibly, like many other women, she felt this form of deception to be harmless and justified. But Elinor went occasionally to the length of entering a false date of birth on an official form (one has survived). And her lifelong habit of romancing often caused her to mix fact and fiction (for example, her statement about the story 'Jack's Revenge', mentioned in Chapter IV), and to make extravagant claims.

Most of her friends learnt to disregard these. One, who confesses to having rather enjoyed Elinor's tall stories, added: 'But I always kept the salt-cellar handy'. Unfortunately, though, people who are prone to inexactitude often end up being unjustly disbelieved. And this did happen from time to time with Elinor: for example, her oft-repeated and perfectly correct claim that her father had been a naval officer was always dismissed by one acquaintance with a brusque 'We all knew he'd only been in the Merchant Navy'.

Hence it is possible that another claim Elinor made, which met the same kind of sceptical response, just might have been founded on fact. This was to the effect that she had been much attached, engaged even, to a young man in the Army who was killed in the Great War. His first name, she stated, had been Hugh, but no surname was ever mentioned. Today it seems unlikely there can be proof, either way. But in view of Elinor's personality, it is more probable that Hugh was a myth, in the sense that he was an embodiment or synthesis of various people and circumstances. For there really was a man who was important in Elinor's life during the period beginning about three years before the 1914-18 war. And although his name was not Hugh, he did have one thing in common with that elusive Army officer.

There is ample evidence in the Chalet School series to be found of the lasting impression this man made on Elinor. Many of her Chalet books contain veiled allusions to him, his first 'appearance' being in *Jo of the Chalet School* (1926).

> Presently the girls found themselves looking at another song . . . — one entitled 'Brittany' . . .
>
> These two songs, both by the same composer — an Englishman . . . were totally unlike anything they had ever done.

Then in *Eustacia Goes to the Chalet School* (1930) a singing class is working at 'a setting of "Abou ben Adhem," by an English composer . . . It was modern, but with a wonderful flow and grace.'

And for a concert in *The Exploits of the Chalet Girls* (1933) '[Jo] had chosen a very favourite song of the School's . . . Ernest Farrar's "Knight of Bethlehem".'

Ten years later, in *Lavender Laughs in the Chalet School* (1943): ' "Sing Ernest Farrar's 'Brittany'." coaxed Kitty. "I do so love it, and you sing it toppingly, Jo." '

And again, a further seventeen years on (*Joey and Co. in Tirol*, 1960): ' "Sing that *Brittany* thing we love so," Con coaxed . . . as they climbed upwards . . . [Jo] sang the song.' Incidentally quite a remarkable feat that, since the melody in question is characterised by wide leaps, taxing even for a singer who is *not* climbing a 1 in 3 mountain path.

This song, 'Brittany' could almost be called the Chalet School's signature tune, for it recurs in book after book throughout the series. And yet, oddly enough, many readers have remained unaware that 'Brittany' really does exist, and that Ernest Farrar, its composer, was a real person (see the photograph on page 99). Perhaps this happens partly because, in the books, he is often described as a friend of the entirely fictional Mr Denny. And Elinor mentions his name on few occasions, usually preferring to give only an anonymous description. Just once or twice she lets slip a few more details; as, for instance, in the passage which follows the lines quoted above from *Lavender Laughs*:

> On the way home, Kitty told the rest that 'Brittany' had been composed by a young English composer who had been killed in the . . . [1914-18] war. He had known their own somewhat eccentric singing-master, Mr Denny, who had declared that if he had lived, he would have done great things.

> As it was, he had been shot down before his great gift had had time to mature, and England was the poorer by it.

Strong words. And obviously it is Elinor speaking here, through her schoolgirl character. But in fact there is independent backing for the claims put forward. Musicians of repute, including Dr Herbert Howells and Sir Ernest Bullock (who was a personal friend and had been Ernest's best man at his wedding), have paid tribute to Farrar's gifts; and the composer Frank Bridge (teacher of Benjamin Britten) dedicated a piano sonata 'To the memory of Ernest Bristow Farrar'. Grove's *Dictionary of Music and Musicians* also accords him a respectful entry. And earlier editions of *The Oxford Companion to Music* state that 'the little music he left . . . is delicate in texture, and points to the existence of real talent'.

Nor is it in doubt that the real-life Ernest Farrar was a highly romantic figure. Tall, pleasant-looking, likeable and outstandingly talented, he would have made an ideal hero for any novelist, for his whole career reads rather like a novel.

Born in 1885, the son of a country vicar in Yorkshire, Ernest Farrar had won his own way by scholarships to the Royal College of Music. (This was more than forty years before student grants were generally available.) At the college he gained several important prizes and another scholarship, which enabled him to spend a further period of study in Germany.

His first love was composition, but he was also a gifted organist. And when he returned to England it happened that his first appointment was as organist at the parish church of St Hilda in South Shields. Here he remained for about two years, before moving on to a similar post in Harrogate. Thus, although there is no absolute proof that he and Elinor were acquainted, there is every probability that they were.

It would be tempting to draw all sorts of conclusions from Elinor's enduring devotion to Ernest Farrar's music, as expressed in her books. But, despite indications that there was an element of romantic attachment on her side, it is highly unlikely that anything beyond a possible friendship existed between the two. For when Ernest Farrar arrived in South Shields he was already well acquainted with, if not actually engaged to, the girl he was to marry three years later. And it is virtually certain that any tender feelings Elinor might have cherished for this talented young man would have been kept strictly to herself.

Quite apart from other considerations, she knew Ernest's fiancée, had known her in fact long before Ernest appeared on the scene. For, by one of those odd coincidences that do occur in real life, Ernest Farrar's bride-to-be was Olive Mason — that same Olive whom Elinor had admired so much in her early days at the Misses Stewart's school.

Elinor for many reasons, in particular the gap between their ages and backgrounds, was never an intimate friend of Olive Mason's. Nevertheless she might well have been present at her wedding, among the large congregation which attended St Hilda's Church on 8 January 1913. (If so, surely her thoughts must have turned for a moment to another couple who had been married in that same church, nearly twenty years before.)

After their wedding the Farrars settled down in Harrogate, where Ernest had already moved some months previously; and he was fortunate here in finding the opportunity to compose for, and hear his works performed by, the Kursaal Orchestra under its conductor Julian Clifford. But with the Great War just around the corner the couple were to have only a short time together. In 1915 Ernest was one of those who responded to the appeal 'Your King and Country need you!' He volunteered and, being apparently a very tall man, was selected for one of the Guards regiments. And that he looked extremely handsome in uniform can be judged from a photograph which, to the end of Mrs Olive Farrar's life, was still displayed in her sitting-room.

Oddly enough, in view of the desperate situation at the Front, Ernest's regiment was not sent out of England until September 1918, when they were ordered to France. Before departing Ernest confided to a very old friend his deep conviction that he would never return. The friend, who was on leave from France at the time and had survived for more than three years on the Western Front, tried to reassure him. But it was barely a week after his arrival at the Front when Ernest Farrar was killed in action. The date was 18 September 1918. And by another of life's strange coincidences, Ernest's widow, Olive, was to die on exactly the same date, sixty years later.

Some of Ernest Farrar's music, including 'Brittany', had been published at various times, beginning in his student days. And after his death the Carnegie Trust sponsored the publication of other works; among them a full-scale setting for soloists, chorus and orchestra of *The Blessed Damozel*. Farrar's name and music were still widely known in the years between the wars. Today both have fallen into obscurity. And there is no doubt that Elinor's frequent references to Ernest Farrar in her Chalet School books now constitute his chief memorial.

CHAPTER VIII

STEP-RELATIONS AND SISTERS-BY-MARRIAGE

It had been in January 1913 that Ernest Farrar married Olive Mason. And Elinor's feelings on this occasion remain her secret. But it can be said with assurance that her reactions were mainly unfavourable on 12 June that same year when another marriage took place: that between her mother, now genuinely widowed, and a Mr Septimus Ainsley.

Elinor seems always to have disliked Mr Ainsley. And to have made no great secret of this. One old lady recalled with some disapproval how Elinor used often to declaim, 'I hate my stepfather'. However, in fairness to Mr Ainsley, it should be said that Elinor would probably have reacted in the same way to any man who became her stepfather.

Not that notions of loyalty to her own father would have entered into things at the time of the wedding: in 1913 Elinor can have known few of the facts about Charles Dyer. But where step-relationships were concerned, she had got off to a bad start with the trouble over her half-brother, Charles Arnold Lloyd Dyer. That had always been in the background of her childhood. And however little she was told, and whatever may have been the rights and wrongs of the case, Elinor must have felt the repercussions from it; and have been influenced unconsciously in her attitudes.

The surprising thing is that step-parents mostly emerge quite well in her books. Far more often it is the stepchildren who cause trouble. But there is an indication in the stories that Elinor did have an inner reservation about step-relationships. For it must be significant that in describing one that is exceptionally happy she never allows the actual word 'step' to be used. Two of her characters, anyway, go to extraordinary lengths to avoid it.

'I must go and rout out that . . . sister-by-marriage of mine, Verity Carey' [Mary-Lou Trelawney announces in *A Problem for the Chalet School* (1956). Adding helpfully] 'Her dad married Mother, you know, and that's the nearest relationship we can come to.'

And, in *The Chalet School Wins the Trick* (1961) the same Mary-Lou astounds a new girl, Audrey Everett, by using this particular expression:

> 'Your sister-by-marriage?' Audrey gasped.
>
> 'Yes; her dad married my mother. We aren't real sisters and *we're not stepsisters, of course* [HMcC's italics]. That was as near to it as we could come. See?'
>
> 'Yes, I think so.'

Well — Audrey may have seen. But for most of us it remains a puzzle; because in the circumstances that Mary-Lou describes she and Verity quite clearly *were* stepsisters. So the inference must be that Elinor herself found something off-putting about the word.

And Elinor certainly managed to create one exceedingly unpleasant step-parent in the Chalet School series — that stepmother of Grizel Cochrane's who 'had never forgiven her husband for not telling her of Grizel's existence' (see Chapter I).

Admittedly the second Mrs Cochrane had been much wronged. In real life it seems she might have had a legal right to get the marriage annulled. But the impression conveyed of her character makes it hard to believe that she would ever have treated a stepchild with much warmth, even had her husband not deceived her. 'Mrs Cochrane was never actively unkind, but she possessed a sharp tongue, and . . . the wilful, high-spirited [Grizel] . . . gradually became a frightened, nervous creature, who did as she was bidden with a painful readiness.' (*The School at the Chalet*, 1925.)

Nor was Grizel alone in dreading Mrs Cochrane's ill-temper. 'Now you'd better go, Miss Grizel', warns the kindly 'Cookie', the one person to treat Grizel with any affection at home. 'The mistress only went down to the butcher's, and she won't like it if she finds you here.'

Grizel nodded. 'Too well she knew the scolding that would be the portion of both of them if her stepmother caught her in the kitchen.'

And into the bargain Mrs Cochrane was two-faced: 'she was always gracious in public'. So that, although grown-ups in the little town were 'beginning to conjecture at the causes for . . . [Grizel's] loss of spirit,' two schoolgirls are flabbergasted when Grizel announces her delight at being sent to boarding-school in Austria:

> 'Grizel!' gasped Rosalie. 'Glad to leave home and go right away!'
>
> ' 'Tisn't like your home,' replied Grizel sombrely. 'You've a mother!'
>
> 'Well, but you have Mrs Cochrane, and I'm sure she's awfully sweet to you.'
>
> 'Yes, when there's anyone there to see it,' replied Grizel recklessly. (Now, somehow, it didn't seem to matter [their knowing]. She would not come home for more than a year.)
>
> The two schoolgirls stood in horrified silence.

Not a likeable person, Mrs Cochrane. But perhaps she was a reaction from the second Mrs Temple, who makes a brief but sweet appearance in *The Maids of La Rochelle*. This was published in 1924, and Mrs Temple thus ante-dates Mrs Cochrane by a year. Agnes Temple really is too selfless and understanding to be true. And she does not have a tenth of Mrs Cochrane's impact.

On the other hand, Sigrid, the Norwegian-born second wife of Sir Piers Willoughby in *Seven Scamps* (1927), represents a genuine attempt on Elinor's part to portray realistically a young stepmother and her problems. Sigrid starts off with an extra disadvantage in bringing her own daughter, Britta, into the family circle. And Britta, not one of Elinor's 'angel-children', at first proves most unpopular with the seven young Willoughbys. Inevitably Sigrid is allowed in the end to win her step-family round; but it is by gradual and quite convincing stages.

Mr Ainsley, on the other hand, does not appear ever to have won Elinor round; at least not completely. And it is difficult to know how far his own personality entered into this, especially as there is no one living now who knew him well. A very much younger friend of Elinor's can just remember from her childhood that Elinor's stepfather was 'very big and solemn', and that Elinor 'didn't like him much'. Neither did *she*.

Her description fits with that given by a business acquaintance of Mr Ainsley's, who used the phrase 'a big, dark, saturnine-looking man'. Altogether, size and darkness seem to be part of most people's recollections, adding up to a rather sombre impression.

All the same, it is not hard to see that in material and social terms Mr Ainsley had much to offer. He belonged to a family that was highly respected in South Shields. Moreover his father, Thomas Liddle

Ainsley, had owned a flourishing optician's business in the town, as well as two similar firms in Wales and various other successful enterprises. Thus the estate shared by the Ainsley family following their father's death had been considerable. And although Septimus was literally the seventh child, his portion was eventually much increased by the early deaths of several brothers and sisters.

Understandably then Mr Ainsley never appears to have worked regularly in any trade or profession, although he was qualified as an optician and may for a time have joined the family firm. But the description that usually follows his name in street directories is simply 'Gentleman' — a term reserved for those without gainful occupation. Obviously there had been no pressing need for him to work. And it does seem also that Septimus Ainsley had poor health. Many people confirm this. Ironically though, as often happens with those accounted delicate, Mr Ainsley was to outlive many of his heartier-seeming contemporaries and to reach his seventies.

At the time of his marriage to Nelly Dyer, Septimus was forty-seven years old, and still a bachelor. Had he perhaps been waiting for a long time to marry Nelly? Certainly he had known her since childhood, when his family had lived just round the corner from the Isaac Rutherfords.

Since those far-off days the Ainsleys had moved many times. Septimus himself had lived at several different addresses in both North and South Shields. But during the years immediately preceding the wedding he had once again been close at hand, living in a pleasant house only a few roads away from Winchester Street. He could well have considered installing his wife and stepdaughter here. Most likely, though, both he and Nelly thought it preferable to begin their married life somewhere that had no associations with the past.

Accordingly, after the wedding, Elinor and her mother said goodbye to 52 Winchester Street with its patchwork of memories, and moved into a house Mr Ainsley had recently acquired, 5 Belgrave Terrace.

This really was mounting several notches up the ladder. Belgrave Terrace may not have been quite as grand as the name somehow suggests, but it was a highly superior road, definitely on the right side of the tracks. And number 5 had just the right air of quiet middle-class respectability. Nelly and her daughter had really arrived.

CHAPTER IX

'A VERY ECCENTRIC AND DIFFERENT SORT OF PERSON'

Today Winchester Street has all but disappeared and the area surrounding Elinor's first home is covered by a car-park and a large council housing estate. Belgrave Terrace, on the other hand, is still there, and, although a little run-down in appearance nowadays, is still recognisably the same street as in the days when the Ainsleys lived at number 5. Their house, like the others, stands back discreetly from the road and has gardens at back and front. All rather different from Winchester Street, where the front doorsteps often led straight on to the pavement. Inside there were changes too, and for the better. Even in 1913 the Belgrave Terrace houses would have had both inside lavatories and bathrooms. Thus in terms of comfort, let alone social status, Nelly Ainsley and her daughter were now better off than they had ever been.

Understandably, though, Elinor did not relish her position here; for not only was she the stepdaughter of a man she disliked, she was also largely his dependant. Of course she did earn some money of her own, but her salary as an unqualified teacher was small; and any writing she did at this time — stories for the *Sunday Companion* and the like — cannot have brought in much, either.

All the same, by present-day thinking it is hard to see why Elinor stayed. She had good health, did not lack ability and she was nineteen years old. Girls younger than that are leaving home every day in the 1990s to make their own lives; some succeed very well. However in 1913 things were different. Then, a middle-class girl in Elinor's position had few chances to achieve independence. In order to take up any career or job she needed not only her parents' approval, but usually their financial backing as well. And this was to remain true long after the Great War.

Elinor personally cannot have found her opportunities greatly extended by the war. Her character and tastes make it hard to visualise her working, for instance, in a munitions factory — not that the Ainsleys would have allowed it. And although they might have reacted more favourably to the idea of nursing, Elinor never seems to have shown any leanings in this direction, nor towards any of the women's services. Nevertheless a majority of the men in her stories were to be doctors; and many others in the services, most often the Navy.

Of course getting married had always been the classic escape route for girls. Elinor, however, was neither pretty nor well-off; she was hardly the type to make an early marriage. And later she was to join the 'two million surplus women', so many of whom were condemned to involuntary spinsterhood.

Altogether it is perhaps less surprising that Elinor stayed at home, than that she did twice get herself away, and for considerable periods. The first and shorter of these began in September 1915, when she temporarily gave up her various teaching jobs in South Shields and entered the City of Leeds Training College. By this time she had gained more than three years' experience of teaching. And unquestionably she had natural gifts as a teacher: a genuine love of children — which remained with her to the end of her life; tireless energy and enthusiasm; and, something her severest critic could not deny, a lively imagination. Oddly enough Elinor, who in many ways was old-fashioned, might well have fitted better into the present-day teaching world with its less formal approach. For those long-ago days her methods were decidedly unconventional. Two former pupils, now husband and wife, who were both taught by Elinor, 'remember her as a very eccentric and different sort of person'. Another recalls that:

> Miss Dyer was no end of a character, very unlike other teachers. She would go wandering round the classroom and sitting on the desks while talking to us. And one incident I will never forget was when she sat down on an inkwell and ruined the cream tailored dress she wore. You can imagine the hilarity and the joy of lessons coming to an end.

That particular episode with the inkwell was something Elinor apparently did not forget, either. Her school stories are dripping with spilled ink and similar disasters. One of the messiest of these occurs in *The School at the Chalet* (1925). Here Bernhilda, the prefect in charge of stationery, is seated on the top of a step-ladder tidying the higher reaches of the stationery cupboard when Grizel Cochrane, 'in her capacity as ink monitress', arrives to collect the week's supply for the classrooms.

> Grizel had very nearly finished, when Bernhilda gave a sudden shriek, and dived forward, nearly collapsing on to Grizel, who echoed her shriek. At the same time there was a crash as the large pint bottle of red ink fell heavily against the step-ladder, and smashed, sending a fountain of red ink in every direction. Bernhilda's tunic suffered, but the one who came off worst was Grizel . . . the

> ink deluged her — hair, frock, hands, even her legs were dripping with it.

Poor old Grizel — but at least her tunic was brown, and it probably survived better than Elinor's cream-coloured dress can have done.

Another character who spills ink is Jennifer Craddock, in the little-known and almost unobtainable *School by the River* (1930). Her experience is comparatively trivial, though.

> 'Come Jennifer! . . . Where have you been all this time?'
>
> 'Mopping up my ink. I caught the bottle with my arm, and it wasn't corked, and went in every direction. You never saw such a mess!'

However in other books plenty of people do see similar and worse messes. And it is not only ink that gets spilled. In *The Chalet School and Jo* (1931) various girls are swamped with paste. And in a later book, *Lavender Laughs in the Chalet School* (1943), Jo, now grown-up and married, manages to dislodge from some high shelf a bowl full of extremely fast green dyc, and is needless to say drenched by the contents. (Elinor's editor at Chambers, Mr Thomas Collocott, claimed — perhaps not too seriously — to see a Freudian significance in Elinor's timing of this incident, which takes place when Jo is on the point of producing her eldest son.)

Such disasters are of course part of the school-story tradition, which Elinor was faithfully following. In real life she seems to have been far less prone to follow tradition, as witnessed by Miss Mary Starling, whose descriptions and comments have been quoted in several earlier chapters. Miss Starling, who like Elinor had chosen a teaching career, writes at some length of their acquaintance.

> When I came out of Training College and returned home to South Shields, I was posted to Baring Street School (which is built on part of the Roman Camp of Arbeia). To my surprise I found that May Dyer was on the staff of the Boys' Department. We renewed our acquaintance [originally they had met through Elizabeth Jobling, Elinor's school-friend and neighbour]; and as our paths to and from school lay in the same direction we had many happy journeys together. I found her a most interesting and cheerful companion. Altogether a very remarkable person whom I remember with pleasure.
>
> Her imagination was inexhaustible. And some of our conversations I can still easily recall. On one occasion she began to pour forth as soon as we met: 'Last night I was at the Ingham Infirmary Ball' (a big event in the social life of South Shields . . .) 'and, what do you think, three men proposed to me.' (No names mentioned.) I replied: 'How nice. And who is the lucky man? . . . 'Oh, I refused all three,' she replied. (By this time I always kept the salt handy.) . . .
>
> Another day she suddenly stopped and turned round, saying reproachfully 'Oh, Miss Starling, how could you?' . . . . 'Why, what have I done?' I asked. 'You split an infinitive' was the answer. (I had done honours English at College so realised my transgression.) [Chalet readers will note with amusement that the split infinitive was already a bugbear of Elinor's; and all readers that, although the two friends were only around twenty-three years of age, they did not use each other's first names.]
>
> Yet another time she came up the Baring Street

> bank panting after me. I remarked that she was late. 'Yes,' she said. "You see, I could not make up my mind which camisole to put on.' (Around this time the 'New Look' many-gored and calf-length skirt was replacing the ankle-length hobble skirt. And most blouses were 'see-through', of Jap silk, crepe-de-chine, nun's veiling, delaine, etc.; and under them girls wore coloured camisoles of crepe-de-chine with satin ribbon straps.) 'First I chose a blue one,' she continued. 'It wouldn't do. So I threw it out of the window on to the lawn. Then I threw out a green and a pink one as well. So I have chosen this.'
>
> I wondered what her neighbours can have said to see these pretty parachutes floating down — IF they saw them.

Well, Elinor's neighbours in Belgrave Terrace did include the chief constable of the borough and the vicar of St Thomas's Church (now demolished). So they may not have looked on the eccentric Miss Dyer with as much humour and affection as Miss Mary Starling obviously did.

At the City of Leeds Training College her fellow-students mostly viewed Elinor with a good-natured tolerance. There was a general tendency to laugh at her strange behaviour and unlikely tales, but the laughter was not unkind. However it undoubtedly was sometimes embarrassed, for Elinor, free from any restraining home influence, really did let down her hair during the time she was at the college.

It was at this period in her life that she took to calling herself Patricia Maraquita — the latter name being one she could have learnt from the books of Mrs De Horne Vaizey, although there seems no obvious reason for this particular choice. Possibly Elinor took the name in an attempt to create an entirely different personality for herself. Possibly it made her feel more remote from Mr Ainsley and Belgrave Terrace. Not that it really can have helped much, for in the end Patricia Maraquita Dyer was little different from the May Dyer who had preceded her, or the Elinor Brent-Dyer who eventually followed.

At any rate the new name did not induce more sober behaviour in Elinor, rather the reverse. And she certainly left an enduring impression on her companions. There was one particularly famous occasion: at the time Elinor had been been been suffering from 'a perfectly ordinary cold', but had suddenly caused great alarm by taking to her bed and exhibiting all the symptoms of delirium. A former student of the college, the late Mrs Isabel Miller, remembered volunteering to sit at her bedside, and being convinced even at the time that Elinor — or, rather, Pat — 'was no more delirious than the Archbishop of Canterbury'. (But could she, just possibly, have been acting out events connected with Henzell's last illness?)

This same kind-hearted but realistic contemporary also recalled having been frequently scandalised by Elinor's personal untidiness; in particular that 'her underclothing was tied up with string'. Shades of the Chalet School . . . where girls suffer the most dire penalties if they have so much as a button missing, and are strictly trained by Matron in the most perfect tidiness. Perhaps 'Matey', that dragon for order and method, embodied for Elinor a kind of wish-fulfilment.

Apart from untidiness and tall stories Elinor was chiefly renowned at college for the way in which she took violent crushes on other students. And here one thing is of particular interest: there was no slightest hint of anything that was not (as described) 'perfectly harmless'. Indeed 'Pat' was considered rather undemonstrative and 'certainly not the kind to be always wanting to hug and kiss you'. It seems that Elinor at twenty-one used much the same ways of showing affection as when she was a six-year-old schoolgirl, and 'always under the feet' of her adored Olive Mason. Only now the presents that she offered, with real if embarrassing generosity, were rather more elaborate than wild flowers; and the compliments which accompanied them were more extravagently phrased.

> To Isabel la Belle, With all the affection that she merits, from Patricia Maraquita. R.I.P.

runs the handwritten dedication in a book presented in December 1915 to the current recipient of Elinor's admiration.

And this effusive way of behaving towards other girls must have been specially noticeable at the City of Leeds College since it was, rather surprisingly for the period, a mixed college. True, the male side was much depleted during those war years. But there was still a number of men among the students, so it could be significant that Elinor's name was apparently never linked with any of them.

Elinor's true attitude to men remains obscure. Not that her books show any lack of male characters, numerically speaking, for the incidence of marriage among the staff and old girls of the Chalet School is high. However these men are nearly all versions of one basic type. Dick Bettany, Jem Russell and Jack Maynard, the three most important males in the Chalet School series, all fall into this same category: tall, fair-haired, pleasant-looking Englishmen; upright, kind, with a twinkle in the eye and a compulsion to tease. Probably much the same type as Elinor's brother. The few men in her books who deviate from the pattern are usually found among the older age group; these, always peripheral figures, are often quite convincing.

However if Elinor's books are only limitedly revealing on the subject of men, they are clear about another matter: that of schoolgirl crushes — or 'pashes', or what the Gemans descriptively name *Schwärmerei*. At the Chalet School, swooning around is definitely out. Elinor's schoolgirls inhabit a different world from those of Angela Brazil, who often protest their undying love for each other in passionate terms. And although Chalet girls may occupy less time, and fewer pages, in crusading against soppiness than do Miss Fairlie Bruce's at the Jane Willard Foundation, they are no less 'Anti-Soppist' in spirit.

> 'I don't think she'd do a thing like that . . . she'd know that Len would be down on her like a ton of bricks. . . . Jack [female, short for Jacynth] wouldn't risk that. The sun seems to set and rise on young Len so far as she's concerned!'
>
> 'What? Len! You surely don't mean — '
>
> 'Don't be such an ass! Of course I don't! Len would never allow anything like that to happen.' (*The Chalet School Wins the Trick,* 1961)

Nor would any true Chalet girl have allowed it. 'Sentimental *grande passions* were severely sat on at the Chalet School, which had contrived to remain remarkably free from such silliness.' (*A Problem for the Chalet School*, 1956). And even before the Chalet School came into existence Elinor had dealt at some length with this question in *A Head Girl's Difficulties* (1923). This on the whole is just a very ordinary school story, but it contains a lively account of how the prefects deal with an epidemic of sentimental letter-writing among the juniors.

> 'Look here, you've got to collect all the idiotic notes you can find. When we've got, say, twenty, we'll call a meeting of the whole school in the hall, and make the people to whom they are addressed read them aloud from the platform. How's that for a scheme?' The prefects were almost overcome by the thought.

And the unhappy children are totally overcome when forced to read out such effusions as:

> You are my dearest friend, and I just love you. But you mustn't be jealous if I tell you that I love Rosamund even better . . . You are lucky to be her sister. She kisses you good-night, I expect. I should almost die for happiness if she would kiss me.

And so it continued. 'One by one the wretched recipients of the notes followed [each other] . . . reading aloud such utter rubbish as startled even themselves.' Elinor's books leave no room for doubt that she was against 'all that sort of thing'. But whether this was simply because she — as a teacher — deplored the silliness it induced, or whether she had deeper feelings on the subject, is not clear.

Today it has become almost impossible to believe in the existence of any adult woman so innocent — and ignorant — that all sexual or homosexual undercurrents flow past her unnoticed. Yet such women did exist. Moreover it seems probable that they numbered among them many of those who wrote schoolgirl fiction in the pre-war days.

Elinor, in a private handwritten book of her own

poems, reveals enough to prove that she was at least not totally ignorant about sex. But she also shows in this oddly sad little collection how essentially innocent she remained.

This emerges strikingly in a poem called 'Wedding Eve'. Here the opening already poses a problem:

> Lie closer; in your arms let me forget,
> Just for one sweet brief hour, my joy to come . . .

For, since this is Wedding Eve and not Wedding Night, who is being addressed? But it is in verse four that perplexity becomes astonishment:

> Dear understanding heart that holds me close,
> Oh woman friend, that never failed me yet,
> Say, do you blame me for the part I chose?
> Can your most faithful heart bear with me yet?

Nowadays any schoolgirl would see that, in this particular context, the meaning of these four lines could be ambiguous — to say the least. However, after careful study of the whole poem, it eventually becomes clear that the girl here is speaking to her mother. And in fact Elinor's poem bears an interesting resemblance to the German words set by Schumann, in a beautiful song Elinor could well have known. Here the verses by the minor 19th-century poet, F. Rückert, describe a bride's outpouring of love and gratitude to her mother — to whom she owes the gift of life itself; and since the first words of the song are 'Mutter, Mutter', the entire situation is clear.

But then, in Elinor's case, the thought that her lines could be interpreted in any other way presumably never even crossed her mind. And yet, she was twenty-five years old when she wrote 'Wedding Eve'.

CHAPTER X

WAITING TO BEGIN

SQUARE ONE AGAIN

Back in September 1915, when the newly created Patricia Maraquita first arrived in college, a rumour about her had been whispered among the students: this was to the effect that Miss Dyer's school (the Misses Stewart's?) had classified her as 'not really suitable material for a teacher'.

That rumour may or may not have been well founded but, considering certain aspects of Elinor's personality, it cannot be ruled out that a school report on those lines existed. Especially if the head teacher who furnished it really was one of the formidable Miss Stewarts. However no proof is available either way, since all relevant papers belonging to the City of Leeds Training College were destroyed in an air-raid during World War II.

This means too that the final reports by the college on Elinor's work, and her potential as a teacher, have vanished as well. Here, though, it is possible to deduce that the authorities must have thought Miss Dyer's teaching at least satisfactory, because one of her first appointments on leaving College was to the boys' high school in South Shields, a post which carried a certain prestige. True this was at a stage in the war when men of all ages right up to the fifties were being conscripted; but, even so, a student who had received a bad report could never have gained such a position.

Thus the autumn of 1917 saw Elinor enjoying

promotion in her teaching career, and also the better pay to which her qualified status entitled her. But in other respects her life must have had a rather dreary back-to-square-one feeling. She was back to South Shields and teaching. Back to 5 Belgrave Terrace.

Once again it is impossible not to wonder in passing why Elinor, having tasted comparative independence for a couple of years, did not make an attempt now to launch out on her own. Perhaps she did try. And of course she would probably have been obliged, following her training, to teach locally for a time. At any rate the fact remains that about four years were to pass before she again left home.

From the biographer's point of view this period represents the second largest gap in Elinor's life. The other lies between 1927 and 1933; and although wider that gap is less barren. Of the years between 1917 and 1921 all that can be said for certain is that Elinor continued with her teaching; and was a regular member of the congregation at St Jude's C. of E. Church in the Laygate.

Nor is it possible to discover much about her writings prior to 1921. The only manuscripts to have survived are the collections of poems mentioned in the previous chapter. Anything else she may have written at this time has now disappeared. However in view of her later record — an average of two books a year sustained over nearly half a century — it is almost incredible that Elinor did not, at the very least, attempt a book of some kind. For one thing, she always showed throughout her life a sheer enjoyment of writing. And undeniably she possessed great natural facility as a writer — too great, perhaps, for her own good.

Something that does seem clear is that Elinor had not yet found her bent as a writer for schoolgirls.

The stories she reportedly sent to magazines like the *Sunday Companion* are remembered as 'not school stories but more of a romantic nature'. And many of the poems she wrote are also highly romantic in character.

It could be that her writing energies at this time were mainly directed towards poetry. There is some evidence in the various notebooks to suggest that she considered making a selection from her verses: one page contains a list of titles in two columns, headed respectively 'Lullabies' and 'Love Songs' (the proposed name of the collection); and the poems listed are marked in the manuscript with asterisks, while others are crossed out. So perhaps Elinor may have hoped to interest a publisher in some kind of anthology of lyrical verse. Not that all the poems she wrote were of a romantic kind. Several were inspired by the 1914-18 war, and a few of these show a surprisingly stark realism.

In any case, quite apart from all this activity, which may have delayed her start in fiction-writing, there could have been another reason for the tardy arrival of her first book: a very old friend of hers put forward a theory that 'although Elinor managed to write all those books, and it may sound odd to say this about her, she did in a funny way lack persistence'.

Initially surprising, this idea nevertheless fits in with remarks Elinor made in some of the Chalet Club newsletters. Here, in giving advice to would-be authors, she often emphasises the need for perseverance; and on at least a couple of occasions she confesses to having lacked this virtue herself. 'To those who claim they find it easy to begin, but difficult to continue, I can only say "Stick to it!" I've been through all that myself in my time, so I speak from experience,' she writes in the issue for

September 1966. And she is even more explicit in an earlier number, that for November 1963, where she describes the publication of her first book, *Gerry Goes to Schoo*l, and how excited she felt: 'For one thing . . . though I'd *begun* quite a number of stories before, I always got tired of them and left them unfinished. *Gerry* was the first I really wrote to the bitter end.'

Perhaps the use here of the last cliché is significant: plainly Elinor recalled that it had been a real struggle to get through a full-length book (incidentally quite an undertaking then in terms of sheer length, for at that time children's novels were commonly expected to contain a good 60,000 words). And it is possible that even *Gerry Goes to School* might never have been finished if the Bainbridge family had not come to live in South Shields. Elinor had needed some incentive, something in her own phrase to make her 'stick to it'. The Bainbridges, and in particular their small daughter Hazel, were to provide exactly the stimulus that was required. And in this way they were so important in Elinor's career as a writer that it is worthwhile to describe them in some detail.

A STORYBOOK FAMILY

Edith and Julian Bainbridge, and Hazel their talented only child, might have walked straight from some children's novel of the theatre by, perhaps, Noel Streatfeild. Edith came of an established theatrical family: she represented the third generation; Hazel, who by nine years old was already quite an experienced actress, represented the fourth; and today the fifth and sixth generations of this remarkable family are carrying on the theatrical traditions, for the well-known actresses

The composer Ernest Farrar (1885-1918) whose work is so often mentioned in the Chalet books. Taken in 1916.

Elinor (second from left) and some of her colleagues at Western House School, Fareham, Taken *c.* 1925.

Hazel Bainbridge (to whom Elinor's first book was dedicated), with her parents Julian and Edith who later owned the Marina Theatre.

Kate O'Mara and Belinda Carroll are Hazel Bainbridge's daughters, while Kate's son, Dickon, is an actor-producer.

Hazel's father also belonged to the theatre world. He, on the other hand, had not been born into it; in fact his family had been rather less than delighted when Julian, a couple of years after leaving school, had announced his intention of going on the stage. It did turn out though that Julian had some talent: and not only for acting but as producer and manager; later also as playwright. And by the time he first met Edith Boughton, his future wife, he could claim a fair amount of success in all these capacities — even if financially he was only just keeping his head above water.

Oddly enough Edith at this time had done no acting at all. Her father (Hazel's grandfather) had for personal reasons been fiercely determined that none of his seven children was to enter the theatrical profession. Thus, although the theatre was in her bones, Edith was past twenty and a married woman when she first took part in a professional production. Then her success was immediate. 'But of course, of the two, it was my mother who had the real acting talent' — Hazel recalls about her parents.

Once started, Edith found plenty of opportunities to continue acting, since nearly ten years were to elapse between her marriage and Hazel's birth. And it was just as well that Edith did have real ability: for when the Great War came Julian Bainbridge joined up almost at once, and he was then sent off to the Middle East, where he was kept for the best part of four years. During all this time his wife and daughter — little more than a baby when the war began had to remain on their own in England; and most of the family's financial responsibilities now fell on Edith. Because of her undoubted gifts she was offered enough engagements to keep things going. But it was a tough life. Certainly for her, and perhaps also for the small Hazel, who until 1917 went everywhere with her mother. Not surprisingly, most of Hazel's earliest memories are of continual touring round provincial theatres and living in theatrical digs.

Hazel's own first appearance on the stage was made in true storybook fashion, when at the tender age of five she went on as Little Willie in *East Lynne*. But this event, unlike those in stories, was not a great success. At least not from Hazel's point of view: she found Little Willie 'altogether too soppy' and 'hated the whole thing'. With the result that she flatly refused to take part in any other play. Her mother wisely made no attempt to persuade her; and two or three years were to pass before Hazel changed her mind.

By that time the war was over; Hazel, at about seven, had gone off to a boarding-school near Portsmouth; and Julian Bainbridge was back in England trying to pick up the threads of his career. He had got himself the job of managing a small repertory company; and, because they suffered from the usual lack of funds, Julian decided to put on a play he himself had written some years previously, called *The Little Witness*. His motives were primarily economic: no royalties had to be paid on his own play. But just possibly Hazel's father had something else in the back of his mind, for this play did contain a most important part for a child actor. And Ned, the 'Little Witness' of the title, was a very different matter from Little Willie. He was a tough child, a real little cockney urchin. Something about him appealed greatly to Hazel; and her parents had no difficulty in getting her to take the part. The play was a great success. So was Hazel. And from then onwards, quite literally from that day to this, she was to be heart and soul in the theatre.

This particular play appears always to have been a sure winner with audiences. So it is no surprise to learn that when the Bainbridges' company began their season in South Shields, around the middle of April 1921, they chose to open with — as advertised in the *Shields Gazette*: '*The Little Witness*. Written by Captain Julian Bainbridge. The leading part being taken by little Hazel Bainbridge.'

And it is more than likely that Elinor had her first glimpse of Hazel and her parents during a performance of this play. Certainly Elinor and her mother, and also more unexpectedly her stepfather, were great theatre-goers. However this is to anticipate. First of all, back for a moment to 1919 in order to discover why the Bainbridges — who had no local connections — should have chosen to set up a company in South Shields in the first place.

THE MARINA THEATRE

It had always been Julian Bainbridge's ambition to have his own theatre, and to manage there a repertory company of his own, in which he and his wife would both appear. His daughter too, of course. Edith Bainbridge had sympathised with and even shared his dream. But they had both felt that the plan was unlikely ever to be realised. For one thing they had no capital. And, money apart, the task of finding a theatre was certain to prove lengthy and time-consuming. In the mean time there was always the urgent necessity of earning a living, not to mention putting aside enough to pay for Hazel's school-fees.

Then suddenly, in 1920, everything was changed.

Edith came into a legacy, and although by no means a fortune it was enough for them to be able to get Julian's project off the ground at last. All that now remained was to find a theatre; and here again they were to be lucky. Julian at this time had been touring with the Frank Marriott Watson Company; and early in 1920, while the company was playing at the Theatre Royal in South Shields, he learnt that the new Under the Clock Pavilion was going to be available. It was only a tiny little place, not suited to anything but concert parties; nevertheless it offered a starting-point.

So in June 1920 Julian and a friend became joint-lessees of the Clock, as it was known locally. And perhaps it does provide an indication of how much times have changed that the first concert party to appear in their theatre was named simply the Queers.

The venture at the Clock seems to have run successfully, but Julian was still far from having reached his goal. For one thing, the Clock did not on its own provide a living, which meant that he and his wife had often to be working with different companies, and Hazel had to spend all her holidays living out of suitcases.

So it must have appeared the most splendid piece of good luck when, in March 1921, the opportunity arose for Julian to take over another and far more suitable theatre, conveniently close at hand in South Shields. This was the newly converted Marina Theatre, which stood then on the South Pier (on the site of the present-day Majestic Ballroom).

Of course there had to be some snags. Outwardly the Marina was not very attractive: a large, gaunt-looking building, it had originally been used as an indoor sea water swimming bath. For that purpose its situation on the pier had no doubt been extremely healthy and suitable. For a theatre the position was rather on the exposed side. And complaints from the audiences about the cold, especially in winter, were to cause recurrent trouble that even the installation of 'A New and Efficient Boiler' was unable to cure altogether.

All the same, the conversion had provided an adequate little theatre. In addition there was plenty of living accommodation available in the rooms above. This latter particularly attracted the Bainbridges. Now at last their small daughter could have something approaching a permanent home. It was too good a chance to miss. And in April 1921 the Bainbridge family took over the Marina and settled down to the luxury of an extended season in one place.

Hazel's parents threw themselves and their capital into the new venture with huge enthusiasm. In only one matter did they remain cautious: Hazel, who of course would now spend all her holidays in the flat above the Marina, was to continue at her boarding-school in Southsea — at least for the time being.

Hazel herself was happy enough with this arrangement. On the whole she enjoyed school, the only drawback being that it restricted her opportunities for professional acting. However, each holiday her father did contrive to choose for the company several plays which involved her. And everyone at the school took a great interest in Hazel's stage career. The headmistress, according to the memory Hazel still retains today, was a remarkably understanding woman and ready to provide her gifted pupil with every kind of encouragement. The girls too, were always eager to hear details of life in the theatre and about Hazel's latest roles. They seem to have regarded Hazel with only a romantic kind of envy, quite unmixed with any real jealousy. And that her schoolfellows did accept her in this way suggests that Hazel must have been an unspoilt and likeable child.

There is no doubt at all that Elinor found her so. Nor that between Elinor and Hazel, despite the wide gap in age that separated them, a genuine friendship was to grow.

A STAGE-STRUCK YEAR

No one can remember exactly how or where the Bainbridges and Elinor first became acquainted. It seems they could have met at the house of a local lady, a Mrs Jessie Anne Fisher, who regularly held Sunday tea-parties. (Did the unusual name of Jesanne, borne by the heroine of *The Lost Staircase*, perhaps originate with Mrs Fisher?) Or their first meeting might have occurred quite casually at the Marina Theatre. Julian Bainbridge, according to his daughter, was a very sociable man who considered it part of a theatre manager's job to be around after the performances and to talk to the patrons as they left: 'rather like the vicar after church, you know'.

In any case, however the friendship may have begun, it certainly grew fast. Both sides found the other attractive. The Bainbridges enjoyed Elinor's vitality and enthusiasm. Elinor enjoyed their society and felt at home in their world of the theatre, where her extravagant manner and general excitability could be accepted with hardly a raised eyebrow.

Most of all though it was Hazel who captivated Elinor. And looking at the photograph of a charmingly grave little girl seated between her parents, with one arm clasped around her mother, it is not hard to understand Elinor's reaction. Especially since Hazel was to offer a warmth of affection and an unstinted admiration that would bring out all the very best in Elinor.

To Hazel 'Len', as she always called Elinor, was quite simply everything that was wonderful. Not only was she endlessly kind, she was so entertaining, so interesting; she had so much to talk about — books and poetry and history; famous people and countries on the far side of the world (not that Elinor had as yet been out of Britain, but that made no difference to her imagination). Above all, Elinor, in the phrase used by an eight-year-old Chalet schoolgirl about Joey Bettany, could tell 'the most gorgeousest stories'.

Before those Easter holidays of 1921 drew to their close Hazel had become a regular and much welcomed visitor to 5 Belgrave Terrace. And she still retains a memory of childhood clarity about the house and its inhabitants. Mrs Ainsley was 'delightful and so nice-looking'. Of Mr Ainsley she always stood in considerable awe: not that he was actually disagreeable to her, just generally taciturn; and Hazel was continually aware that Elinor disliked him, which tended to make things uncomfortable during the formal tea that began each afternoon visit. 'We always had tea in the drawing-room. That was upstairs on the first floor, like it usually is in those houses.' And Nelly Ainsley, who had now come a long way from Winchester Street, always liked everything 'to be done just so — with pretty china and silver, and all that sort of thing'.

Hazel grew to be very fond of Mrs Ainsley, who not only returned the affection but was to mark her approval in a significant way. On this particular occasion Hazel was acting in a schoolboy role at the Marina Theatre, and when Mrs Ainsley learnt that the company possessed no suitable clothes, she immediately offered to lend a grey flannel suit of

Henzell's, which was then ceremonially unwrapped from the tissue-paper and mothballs in which it had been preserved through the years.

Nevertheless, Hazel always found it was nicest when the formal tea was over and she and Len could escape to Len's own room. This during the earliest days of their acquaintance was only a small bedroom. But later Elinor was allotted a room right at the top of the house where, although the ceilings sloped, there was plenty of space and she was able to arrange herself a proper bed-sitting-room (quite a progressive notion for the early twenties). In one corner there was a large divan bed; but it was disguised as a sofa with cushions during the daytime; and there was a minimum of other bedroom furniture. A couple of cats were often to be found snuggled up in some nook or other. Books were everywhere; and not only on the shelves, although these covered 'the whole wall behind the door, from floor to ceiling'.

In addition to those books, of which many hundreds would accompany Elinor to the end of her life, there was always a vast quantity of papers lying around the room, for it was here that Elinor did her writing. Hazel knew all about that. Quite early on she had been told of Len's intention to 'become an authoress'. Julian Bainbridge also had learnt of this ambition with considerable interest; and soon he was able to provide practical encouragement. With the result that when Hazel returned home after the summer term of 1921 she found that exciting plans were being made. Len had written a play; it had parts specially tailor-made for her mother and herself; and at the end of August her father was going to produce it with the company at the Marina Theatre.

Whether this idea had originally been Julian

Bainbridge's or Elinor's, it is obvious that the plan held advantages for both of them. It gave Julian the chance to offer the public 'An entirely new play by Miss Eleanor Dyer, a resident of South Shields', which with luck would attract local interest. It gave Elinor the chance to write for a professional company; and, almost more important, with an actual performance date in view there was a built-in compulsion for her to get the thing finished. Which was exactly what she needed.

Nor can there be any doubt that she enjoyed it all immensely; and must have learnt a great deal in the process. Many years later, in *Jane and the Chalet School* (1964), Elinor was to describe just how differently a seasoned professional and an amateur may react when considering the same play. In this story Jane Carew has been asked to take part in a play written by some of her schoolfellows. Jane's parents (like Hazel's) are both actors, and Jane has grown up in the theatre.

> For schoolgirls, *The Little Germaine* was quite a good effort, but some of the stage directions struck [Jane] . . . as funny and once or twice she murmured, 'Oh, *no*! That's not good theatre!'
>
> 'I can learn it all right,' she decided when she had [read] . . . to the end . . . 'But I wonder if I dare suggest some alterations. That speech of Germaine's won't do here. It ought to come much earlier. And I'm sure she ought to begin crying before *this* one.'
>
> . . . Finally she decided that she had better wait for a rehearsal before she said anything.
>
> 'And then only if I see a good chance,' she thought. 'It's their play, after all. It's all very well for Father to insist on changes in the script.'

And it would be hard to believe that Elinor was not recalling here the various occasions more than forty years earlier when Julian Bainbridge had insisted, though no doubt with great tact, on having alterations made in *her* script.

All in all her writing must certainly have benefited from her experience of the theatre, brief as it was. And in many of the earlier Chalet School books, where her quality — always uneven — is often at its best, Elinor does show herself able to produce natural-sounding schoolgirl dialogue, something she could well have learnt from writing plays.

Not that her plays (either of those she wrote for the Bainbridges) had anything to do with schoolgirls. For her first attempt she had chosen a historical subject. *My Lady Caprice* was, in fact, billed as 'A Costume Drama' and was set in the reign of George III — a favourite period of Elinor's (and also of the grown-up Joey Bettany's when she turned authoress). Hazel still has a poster showing her mother in costume as the heroine, and wearing a high powdered wig. Hazel's own part was that of a small boy ('I nearly always did have to play boys. I got dreadfully bored with it sometimes'). This particular boy was called Hugh; but whether the name was inspired by that probably mythical wartime friend of Elinor's cannot be said.

Nor is it possible to say much about the public's reception of *My Lady Caprice*. In those days the local paper did carry a weekly column on plays and films, but this usually gave no more than a bald report. In the case of Elinor's *My Lady Caprice* it has nothing of interest to say.

However the play itself, against all odds, has survived, the script having been unexpectedly run to earth in 1994, when Miss Janet Backhouse of the

British Library had the brain-wave of searching for a copy among the plays submitted for licence to the Lord Chamberlain's Office. And, according to Miss Backhouse, *My Lady Caprice* could be well worth resurrecting since it might prove a useful play for a school or amateur dramatic club.

At the time of the production in South Shields, Hazel was still too small for her to have kept any detailed memory of the performances. She does recall that it was all enormous fun; and that on the last night her mother was presented by Len and the company with a minute puppy, who had been named George after either the monarch or the play's leading male character.

(George deserves a short paragraph to himself. A small black mongrel, he grew up to become what is known as a character. For years he went everywhere with the Bainbridges and appeared regularly on stage. The height of his fame was probably reached during a season in Berwick, when George became so well-known in the town that policemen would salute him as he crossed the road.)

Looked at in absolute terms Elinor's achievement with *My Lady Caprice* was modest. But from her own point of view the play marked a turning-point. Above all it had shown her that she really was capable, if she tried, of completing something longer than a short story — something full-scale. Moreover she now had a purpose to sustain her. Hazel always enjoyed her stories. She would write a book specially for Hazel. And this one would not be left unfinished.

CHAPTER XI

MY OWN DARLING LITTLE SISTER

That Elinor should turn now to the girls' school story was natural enough. In the early twenties the genre was high fashion; shoals of the stories were being published each year; and with the demand increasing steadily any number of writers were kept busy.

Probably the best known today, apart from Angela Brazil the all-time Head Girl of the School Story, are Elsie J. Oxenham and Dorita Fairlie Bruce. Elinor much admired these two; but it can be inferred from her writings that she did not care for Angela Brazil. More of this later. Other writers whose tales of school life enjoyed considerable popularity during this pre-war period included Christine Chaundler, Dorothea Moore, May Wynne, Brenda Girvin, Josephine Elder, Winifred Darch, Evelyn Smith, Katherine Oldmeadow, Ethel Talbot and, of course, May Baldwin — she, as mentioned in an earlier chapter, had been hard at work since Elinor's own childhood.

For the most part, the successful and prolific ladies named above wrote about boarding-schools. Elinor however, and wisely in view of the fact that she had no personal experience of residential schools, chose to begin with a day-school story. And it would seem just possible that St Peter's High School, the setting of this first book *Gerry Goes to School* and of its sequel, was based on Dame Allan's Girls School in Newcastle. After all, even if she herself did not ever attend this school, Elinor could well have known girls who did; and she might have visited the school on speech days, or for concerts or plays.

Be that as it may, St Peter's appears to be quite an authentic establishment. On the other hand no one could pretend that *Gerry Goes to School* is a very good book. Even Elinor, who was not greatly given to self-criticism, wrote to a fan in the 1960s that 'Gerry was a very long time ago; I doubt if anyone would be interested in her now'.

In fact *Gerry* does still have a certain interest today, simply because it marks Elinor's starting-point, thus providing a useful yardstick. And certainly a comparison of *Gerry* with the first Chalet School book, written only three years later, makes clear what a remarkable rate of progress Elinor, once launched, was to achieve.

Gerry also shows the early emergence of many themes that would recur throughout Elinor's books. Jealousy and rivalry, for instance; the iniquities of old-fashioned teaching methods — as discussed in Chapter III; the attractions of a large closely knit family; illnesses, and especially those following as a direct result of disobedient or imprudent behaviour.

Music, too, is given great importance in this first book of Elinor's. The Trevennor family, with whom Gerry comes to live, are all musical in various degrees, and Gerry herself outshines them all: she is even able to take over the piano part in Schumann's E flat major quintet, which certainly argues unusual ability in a child of twelve.

Of course *Gerry Goes to School* was written expressly for ten-year-old Hazel Bainbridge, and the heroine has a good deal in common with Hazel. Gerry also is an only child (in her case, an orphan) with precocious talent, and she too has lived most of her early years among adults. There, however, any resemblance ends for there is no suggestion that Elinor used Hazel as a model for Gerry. Undoubtedly her affection for Hazel was a powerful influence in Elinor's writing, but interestingly this is discernible less in the specially written *Gerry Goes to School* than in the early Chalet School books. Here, the affectionate comradeship between Madge and Joey Bettany, who are sisters but separated by an age difference of twelve years, must surely have been coloured by Elinor's feelings towards Hazel. And this accurately observed relationship between the Bettany sisters contributes to making Madge Bettany of the early Chalet books into quite a convincing adult, one of the few to appear in any school stories of the period.

Then again, in creating the character of Cecilia Marya Humphries, known as the Robin, who first comes on the scene in *Jo of the Chalet School* (1926), Elinor clearly owed much to Hazel. Not that the Robin is based directly on Hazel any more than Gerry was. But there is no room for doubt that the special affection, which grows between Joey Bettany and the six-years-younger Robin, sprang from the real-life equally warm affection between Elinor and Hazel.

One thing in particular underlines this parallel: the Robin, very shortly after her arrival at the Chalet School, becomes Joey's 'little adopted sister', and is often referred to thus throughout the series. And the handwritten dedication in Hazel's original copy of *Gerry Goes to School* reads: 'To my own little sister, Hazel Mary Bainbridge'. Altogether it seems indicated that a connection did exist in Elinor's mind between Robin Humphries and Hazel. Whether this was conscious or not is less certain. But either way the results were beneficial, for the Robin was destined to become one of Elinor's most successful and best-loved characters.

It is difficult though to pin down the reasons for this. And equally hard to quote, out of context, anything which really conveys the Robin's personality. The key to her charm does not lie in the directly descriptive passages, for in these Elinor is apt to use such phrases as 'an almost angelic loveliness' which fall uncomfortably on a present-day ear. On the other hand the child's appearance, so well recaptured in some of Nina K.Brisley's charming illustrations, is undoubtedly part of her spell; and from time to time Elinor does succeed admirably in conveying this to the reader. Here, for instance, from a chapter in *Jo of the Chalet School* about Christmas in Innsbruck — incidentally one of the most effective sequences in the whole series — is the Robin pictured on Christmas morning:

> The Robin's frock . . . was [made of] a warm crimson [silk], and had holly leaves embroidered round the hems of skirt, sleeves, and neck in very dark green. Madge had tied up her hair with a big dark-green bow, and with her rosy face and velvety eyes she looked like a Christmas fairy.

But more important than her looks is her attractive disposition. 'The whole of the . . . day [after her arrival] was devoted by the children to the Robin, with whom they all fell in love at once. She was a dear little girl, very happy and sunshiny . . . and not at all shy.'

Perhaps Elinor does cheat a little in making the child's situation so intrinsically romantic: when first introduced to the Chalet School the Robin, a tiny six-year-old, has just lost her Polish mother (who died from Elinor's pet bogy, tuberculosis), and her father has gone to take up some post in Russia (further than the back of beyond to a 1926 child reader). The devices to evoke sympathy are a little obvious; but there is genuine feeling shown in a scene like the following from *Jo of the Chalet School*: here an end-of-term concert is under discussion, and the Robin volunteers to sing 'The Red Sarafan' in Russian.

> The Robin danced forward, curls dancing, cheeks crimson with excitement . . . and promptly lifted up a sweet baby voice in the well-known Russian folk-song.
>
> They all clapped her, laughing at the pretty picture she made. She nodded her head at them joyously. Then suddenly the little voice quivered and broke, and she buried her face in her dimpled hands in a perfect storm of tears. '*Maman! Maman!*' she sobbed . . . '*Viens, je te prie! Maman!*'
>
> [Joey dashed from the room] nearly in tears herself — for there was something so desolate in the baby's little wail [and fetched her sister, who] . . . bore her off to be cuddled back to serenity, while the girls finished their *Kaffee* rather more soberly.
>
> 'She is so happy always,' said Gisela [the head girl], 'that one forgets how short a time it is since the little mother left her.'
>
> 'I suppose *she* used to sing that song,' added Juliet [another of the older girls]. 'Poor baby!'

Nowadays, of course, someone would point out to Elinor that the words 'danced' and 'dancing' (in line one) follow each other too closely; and might suggest that another phrase be substituted for 'lifted up a sweet baby voice'. But provided that the whole passage is read in context, and with an eye to the period and genre, it certainly makes its point.

To return from the days of Robin Humphries and

the Chalet School to the time when Elinor was still struggling with her first book: the untidy heap of manuscript which contained the draft of *Gerry Goes to School* had grown to an impressive size by the time that Hazel arrived home in South Shields for Christmas 1921. And, all through those holidays, whenever she visited 5 Belgrave Terrace, she and Len would retire to that attic bed-sitter where Len would read aloud the latest instalment of Gerry's adventures.

These, when set beside the happenings in many school stories of the period, were unusually sober. Indeed it might seem that Gerry Challoner had a less exciting life than did Hazel herself. Gerry though had some experiences that Hazel had never shared, including that of coming to live with a big family (there are ten Trevennors), and Hazel found this fascinating. To her, Gerry and all her friends and enemies were real people. And to Elinor too, it seems: 'She would talk about the different characters in the story, and describe what they were doing at that moment — just exactly as if they were really there'. Something Elinor continued to do all her life.

Of course Hazel was much aware that to have a book specially written, and a heroine specially created, just for her, was the most enormous compliment. And she found it easy to identify with Gerry in her various predicaments, major and minor, although apparently none of these were borrowed from real life.

On the other hand, a small adventure that happened to Hazel around this time was almost certainly stored in Elinor's memory for future use. Certainly it is hard not to think of the Chalet School when Hazel describes the incident:

> I think my parents must have been away that night because I was there in the flat above the theatre with just a friend looking after me — baby-sitting as we'd call it. It was quite late, and pitch dark outside of course, and our friend-cum-housekeeper who'd been out somewhere arrived back and rang the bell. I was sent downstairs to let her in. I wasn't awfully fond of having to go down in the dark, and there was no light on the stairs of any kind. So I made my way very slowly down the stairs, carrying a lighted candle.
>
> When I got to the first landing I thought I'd take a look through the window there that overlooked the front door; just to make sure it really was our friend ringing. Well, there she was below, and she was gesticulating and throwing her hands around and making a tremendous carry-on. I can remember thinking 'All right! All right! — I'm coming as fast as I can'. And while I was standing there at the window my candle must have been gradually leaning over; and the next moment the muslin curtains had caught fire and were blazing up beside me.

Well, that was real life — and fortunately Hazel was unhurt. Here are two rather similar incidents from the Chalet School series. The first takes place during the presentation of a tableau showing the 1812 siege of Moscow:

> Crimson and yellow lighting added to the effectiveness of the scene . . . There came a sudden creaking followed by a sharp cry as the tower suddenly swayed and from it poured a stream of crimson smoke, accompanied by a flame that was all too real . . . Janet . . . in [her] muslin dress . . . tried to spring off the stage. The inflammable

> muslin had caught and was already flaming around her.
> (*Adrienne and the Chalet School*, 1965)

In the second, two girls are helping Miss Cochrane (Grizel of the early stories, now a member of staff) to tidy up after a sale of work. They are still wearing fancy dress.

> [As they worked Grizel] took a cigarette . . . struck a match and lit up . . . [Absent-mindedly] she tossed the match in the direction of the fireplace. She threw short, and it fell, still burning, into the reed basket Len was holding. The tinder stuff caught fire at once and flared up. The flame caught the flimsy material of Len's Chinese dress and in an instant the sleeve was a mass of flames.
> (*Carola Storms the Chalet School*, 1951)

It would of course be foolish to assume that all the fires in Elinor's books were ignited by that episode of Hazel and the candle. Fires, like spilled ink and floods, were considered an obligatory ingredient of the school story. Elinor supplied her readers lavishly, beginning in her second book, *A Head Girl's Difficulties* (1923); here the blaze causes much devastation in the drawing-room of the heroine's home. Then in *The Maids of La Rochelle* (1924) there is a cliff-fire: 'A lurid glow lit up the skies and the dark, tranquil water of the bay'. (A sentence that seems more Brazil than Brent-Dyer in style.)

The School at the Chalet (1925) also contains its fire, this one following a train crash; and in *The Princess of the Chalet School* (1927) a thunderbolt sets fire to the playing-fields which are tinder-dry after the long hot summer.

All the above are rather routine affairs, but in *The*

Head Girl of the Chalet School (1928) there is quite a hair-raising description of four girls descending the fire-escape from the top floor of a blazing hotel in Salzburg. Elinor may never have produced a fire sequence as powerful as that in Angela Brazil's *A Fourth Form Friendship*, but here she does manage to create a genuine atmosphere of excitment and suspense as a panic-stricken woman flings herself down the high narrow stairway, all but pushing the children off it. 'Those railings [on the stairs] were as open as anything,' one of the girls remarks afterwards.

Altogether Elinor's first dozen books seem more often than not to contain a conflagration of some kind. To us it all seems rather ridiculous; but Elinor was of course only giving her readers what they wanted. Or, at least, what she and a great many other writers thought they wanted. Apparently there was another side to the matter even at that time, for in November 1926 *The Times Literary Supplement* reviewer mentions a 'schoolgirl critic' who longed to read of 'just one school . . . that did not often [sic] catch fire'.

At least *Gerry Goes to School* could have passed muster on that score. So perhaps that youthful critic had never come across it; although by the autumn of 1926 it had been on sale for exactly four years, and had enjoyed a modest success.

The story had eventually been finished at some time during February 1922, and it is not difficult to imagine Elinor's triumphant rejoicings. Something of her feelings can be gathered from the chapter in *Jo Returns to the Chalet School* (written fourteen years later) where Jo has almost completed '*her* first book:

> 'And I've done it myself,' she murmured as she turned over the closely written sheets. 'Goodness knows I've *begun* piles in my time; but this is the first I've ever *finished*.' . . .
>
> She glanced through it. It was not a really long book. Joey religiously counted the number of words on every sheet [Elinor, too, used to do this], and she knew that it would finish somewhere in the neighbourhood of forty thousand words. But it would be a *book*, even if it never found a publisher, and if she could write one, she could write another. Already her brain was teeming with ideas.

On the question of publishers Elinor seems to have decided straight away on trying her luck with W. & R. Chambers, who were then of course one of the leading publishers of school stories. There followed the inevitable period of suspense after the book had been parcelled up and posted. But it does not look as though Elinor can have waited very long to hear the firm's favourable verdict, since by the autumn of that same year (1922), *Gerry Goes to School* had been published, complete with four illustrations and a coloured dust wrapper, and was actually appearing in the book shops. Plainly things in the publishing world were able to move faster then than they sometimes do nowadays.

CHAPTER XII

NEW FRIENDS AND OLD

TWO PARTINGS FROM SOUTH SHIELDS

The month of January 1922 must have been a crowded one for Elinor. Not only was she busy with *Gerry Goes to School*, she was at work on another play for the Bainbridges' Stock Theatre Company.

This second play of hers received quite a lot of publicity. '*Polly Danvers — Heiress*. Special Production of a New Play by Miss Eleanor Dyer, a resident of South Shields' announced the local daily paper; adding that Miss Dyer, besides her residential qualification, was the 'Authoress of *My Lady Caprice*', and that it would be well to 'Book your seats early'.

Hazel on this occasion was not in the cast, having the previous week made 'her last appearance before returning to school'; 'in *The Stepmother* the role of Danny the son [was] ably sustained by Miss Hazel Bainbridge'.

But she did see the play in rehearsal and can remember that it was 'a comedy about a North Country working girl who unexpectedly inherits a fortune'. And this scrap of information makes it likely that *Polly Danvers* had one feature that was unusual for its author. It is not that Elinor's books lack a fair quota of broad-spoken folk — from Yorkshire and Scotland, for instance; but these are always subsidiary characters, and most often cast in such roles as faithful domestic servant, or understanding shopkeeper. Even where a leading character — Jacynth Hardy in *Gay from China at the Chalet School* (1944) — is allowed to have lived 'all her life in a little coal-mining town in the industrial north', she is no working-class girl but comes from a background of impoverished gentility. So Polly Danvers would appear to have been unique among Elinor's heroines.

The play was produced at the Marina Theatre during the last week of January 1922, and seems to have gone down well. But it was to be the last play that Elinor would write for the Bainbridges' company; for, sad to say, Julian and Edith's venture, on which they had embarked with such verve, was to collapse barely a year after its beginning.

The reasons were many and complicated; but in the end everything came round to the question of money. Artistically the company had achieved an undoubted success, as witnessed by the local paper where the critic often rose from the normal humdrum of rapportage to heights of lyrical praise. The public too, those who attended the productions, had been enthusiastic. But unfortunately the audiences had often been small. Here the cold was much to blame: it took more than notices in the paper about the New Boiler to convince people that the hopeful statement 'This theatre is now warm and comfortable' was literally true.

One way and another, Edith Bainbridge's capital had dwindled to the point where it was no longer possible for the enterprise to continue. It was a bitter ending to the dream. For all of them, but most of all perhaps for Julian; since the fact that it was not his own but his wife's money which had been swallowed up can only have made matters worse.

The Bainbridges did make a gallant effort to keep their Stock Company going. And they did not immediately forsake South Shields. Right up to the middle of July 1922 they continued to play in the town, appearing now at the Theatre Royal, and living in rented accommodation. But after that there was nothing for it but a return to the old life of touring.

Elinor's feelings when the Bainbridges finally left South Shields can be imagined. Quite apart from her tremendous affection for Hazel, she had found in Julian and Edith two most congenial friends — perhaps the most congenial she had ever had. And it seems possible that her decision to continue teaching in the south of England was connected with her friends' departure.

However, at this point it becomes impossible for a time to find exact information about Elinor's movements. It has now been established that during the period between the autumn term of 1921 and the summer of 1923, she was teaching at the well-known St Helen's School in Northwood, Middlesex. Few details are available, but the school magazine, *St Helen's Own*, contains several mentions of Elinor's having organised various dramatic performances, including a masque which she both wrote and produced in the summer of 1922; and Elinor herself contributed to the magazine on at least a couple of occasions. Apart from these snippets in the magazine, only two other things have come to light about her time at St Helen's and both are speculative. The first is a suggestion that Elinor could have gleaned the idea of the 'No Spot Supper' (featured in *Excitements for the Chalet School*, 1957) from St Helen's, where it was apparently a tradition. The second, which is more important, will find its proper place in a later chapter.

After leaving St Helen's, probably in July 1923, it seems likely that Elinor spent at least part of that summer holiday in the Channel Island of Guernsey. Her *Maids of La Rochelle* (see page 99), which is set mainly in Guernsey, was published in October 1924 but must have been completed many months earlier; and the detailed descriptions in this book indicate that the author had actually visited the Channel Islands before writing the story. Unfortunately, though, no details have survived about her visit, so nothing definite can be stated.

However it is known that by the autumn term of 1923 she had joined the staff of Western House — a girls' school at Fareham in Hampshire. (The school still exists but is known today as Wykeham House.) Here Elinor taught mainly English, with some history and geography; and also, from time to time, coached hockey — an experience that may well have helped with her school-story writing.

And an interesting question arises at this point, concerning Elinor's decision to go and teach at this particular school. Western House was a far smaller and less prestigious school than St Helen's, and, from a career point of view, the move seems an odd one. But could Elinor's choice have been influenced by the fact that Fareham is so close to Portsmouth? And Portsmouth was the place where Elinor's father and a number of his forebears had come from, and where in all probability many of his relatives were still living. They were her relatives too. So did she perhaps feel a sudden urge — or even not so sudden — to go and make some contact with them? It would seem highly likely that she did.

How far she succeeded in doing so is another matter. There were more than twenty Dyers listed in the Portsmouth street directories of that period: some were almost certainly related to Elinor, for her father's family had roots in Portsmouth extending back at least to the mid-19th century, quite possibly much further. There was plenty of scope for research. And all in all it would be hard to believe that Elinor, during the three or four years she spent in Hampshire, was not impelled by curiosity, if nothing else, to try and find some of her unknown kindred. There is also a possibility that some of her father's relatives could have made contact with her.

Speculation apart, there is one piece of real evidence that Elinor's thoughts had turned at this stage towards her father: it was in the course of 1922 that she decided to adopt the surname Brent-Dyer; and Brent came of course from her father, Charles Morris Brent Dyer. Charles had in fact been named after a Captain Brent (possibly Charles Morris Brent), who had commanded the ship in which William Dyer (Elinor's paternal grandfather) was serving at the time of her father's birth. Captain Brent had consented to be the baby's godfather. And clearly he took his responsibilities very seriously, for, when William Dyer was drowned at sea at quite an early age, it was Captain Brent who financed Charles's education and training for the Royal Navy. If Elinor perhaps learnt this from her paternal relatives (it is hard to imagine that she heard it from her mother) it could have influenced her decision to include Brent in her surname. In any case, the implications of this particular decision are clear. The new version of name linked her immediately with her father; and may have represented also a kind of anti-stepfather gesture. On the other hand, her reasons for changing the spelling of Eleanor to Elinor are obscure. One friend was told at the time that the name was now to be spelt like Elinor in *Sense and Sensibility*. Another suggested that the idea may have come from Elinor's publishers, although no one at W. & R. Chambers could confirm this. The point is not really important:

for, whatever Elinor's motives were, with the publication in October 1922 of *Gerry Goes to School* the name Elinor Mary Brent-Dyer had come to stay.

NEW SURROUNDINGS

The first definite information about Elinor's time in Hampshire dates from the autumn of 1923. By this time she had long ago completed her second book, *A Head Girl's Difficulties*, which was just about to appear; she had spent the holiday in Guernsey that would provide material for her third story (*The Maids of La Rochelle*) and had already begun work on it; she had settled into her teaching at Western House School; she had made a number of friends, but had fallen foul of her landlady.

The latter, on independent testimony, was not a pleasant person. Elinor disliked her extremely. In fact there is a distinct possibility that horrid Matron Webb, who sets everyone by the ears in *The Princess of the Chalet School*, did not spring entirely from Elinor's imagination. Moreover the landlady — in a well-used Chalet School phrase returned Elinor's dislike with interest. To make matters worse the house was small, which meant that the two incompatibles were continually thrown on top of one another. Which suited neither of them.

Soon Elinor was grabbing any pretext to get outside the house. And she discovered that an excellent opportunity to do this was being offered by the Fareham Philharmonic Choir. That autumn they were just beginning to work on Bach's St Matthew Passion. Bach was of course her favourite composer, and the rehearsals would fill up an evening each week in an altogether pleasant fashion. So Elinor decided to go along and join the choir.

Thus, in a roundabout sort of way, the disagreeable landlady had done her lodger a good turn. For not only did Elinor enjoy her membership of the choir, it also led her to a valued friendship.

At that time a young pianist, Marjorie Jewell, used always to play for the Philharmonic Choir's rehearsals. She was about seventeen then, the elder of two musical sisters, and she was working seriously at the piano with a view to taking up music professionally. This in itself would have caught Elinor's interest; and presumably she asked someone in the choir for an introduction to Marjorie. At any rate it was not long before Marjorie was inviting Elinor to visit her home, and to meet her mother and her younger sister Vivien. Also, and very important, the Jewell family's cats, which were as much loved and nearly as numerous as those in Elinor's own home.

After that Elinor was to spend much of her free time with the Jewells. Marjorie and Vivien's mother took a great liking to her; although also sizing her up realistically: 'Elinor' — she remarked after an occasion when there had been some misunderstanding between her daughters and their friend — 'may be a clever writer but she doesn't *really* know much about girls'. And throughout the years that Elinor lived in Fareham, Mrs Jewell was kind enough to offer a regular refuge from that landlady's clutches.

It turned out, too, that they all had interests in common. Not only in the musical field: the Jewells shared Elinor's love of reading, and Mrs Jewell was also an avid book collector. 'The two of them would sally forth on a tour of the secondhand bookshops in Portsmouth, and return quite bowed down with books.' Later Elinor would pay a special tribute to Mrs Jewell in her dedication to *Stepsisters for Lorna*

(1948); and in fiction Joey Bettany was to patronise those very same bookshops:

> Miss Maynard turned to Joey and asked her . . . about the books she had come to buy [in Portsmouth].
>
> 'Got three of them,' replied the girl. 'The Francis Thompson was five bob [25p], but worth it — I've wanted him for ages! The Green's history was five too. The other thing was sixpence [2½p].' (*The Head Girl of the Chalet School*, 1928)

At the time when Elinor first got to know the Jewells, Vivien (later Mrs Pass) was about fifteen. She was obviously an observant girl, with a retentive memory, for she was able to supply detailed descriptions of Elinor, both as regards character and appearance.

> She was tall [or seemed so to Vivien: probably not more than five feet six inches], and far from thin. She had brown bobbed hair — straight; rather large features, nose and chin being both very prominent. Blue eyes [other people however have suggested grey, or hazel], and very strongly marked eyebrows. Not at all pretty, but she did have a very mobile and expressive countenance. Her appearance was always dreadfully untidy, and she didn't seem to care much about clothes, but enjoyed wearing bold colours.

Something that stands out from the memories of those days is that Elinor gave the impression of being considerably younger than she was. The Jewells, for example, had always thought of her as being then around or less than twenty-five; whereas in that autumn of 1923 she was only six months short of thirty. Most probably it was Elinor's remarkable vitality that made her seem youthful. It also made her at times a rather tiring companion.

> She was extremely excitable, and full of enthusiasms. A compulsive talker, too, with a distinctly loud voice; and she always laughed a great deal — rather a loud laugh. [Perhaps the landlady did have her side of the case.] Like many imaginative people, she could be up in the heights and down in the depths within the same hour. Her imagination really was amazing. And, exhausting and tiresome as she could sometimes be, she had a tremendous sense of the dramatic, and enjoyed so much of life.

Altogether the impression given is hardly that of a sober schoolmistress. Making it hard to picture Elinor fitting in well at Western House, which was a conventional enough establishment. She and the headmistress there do appear to have got across each other, and this may well have had less to do with Elinor's work (in her own way she was a most effective teacher) than with her personality. There is no doubt that Elinor lacked discretion; and she often referred to her principal as 'the fat white slug', a phrase that must have given mortal offence if — or more likely, when — it reached that lady's ears.

However, although Elinor's relations with the head of Western House appear to have been strained, she did become very friendly with one of the other mistresses, a Miss Edith Le Poidevin, who taught French and had joined the staff not long after Elinor did. Miss Le Poidevin is described as 'a delightful person . . . very bonny and friendly'. She came from the island of Guernsey, something of which she was extremely proud. And this would certainly have interested Elinor, who retained a lifelong affection for Guernsey. Undoubtedly her Channel Islands holiday must, with hindsight, be judged less important in her writing career than was her subsequent visit to the Tyrol, but its effects were nevertheless both perceptible and enduring. Moreover it was to furnish her with background material for five of her La Rochelle series (family stories, of which many are set in Guernsey and with remarkably accurate topographical details); as well as for parts of two wartime Chalet School books (*The Chalet School in Exile* and *The Chalet School Goes to It*).

Elinor and her colleague at Western House had quite a close friendship. So at one time it seemed odd that Miss Le Poidevin had quickly vanished from Elinor's life. More recently, it has emerged that there was a simple explanation. Edith Le Poidevin had not stayed long at Western House; she had married at quite an early age and had gone with her husband to live in India where she had remained until the mid-1980s. This makes it easy to see why, in this particular case, the two lost touch. On the other hand, something that becomes increasingly plain is that Elinor often tended to blow very hot in the early days of a friendship but to cool off very suddenly later on. More than likely she was unaware of this. Her most important Chalet School characters still have the same 'best friends' at forty-odd as they did in their middle-school days; and this is obviously something of which Elinor approves whole-heartedly. Nor, clearly, does she consider it any bar to Joey's acquiring — and keeping — hosts of new friends. The fact remains that a number of the friends Elinor herself made along the way dropped out of sight and out of mind altogether.

NEW INTERESTS

Her friendship with the seventeen-year-old Marjorie Jewell was one of those that had got off the ground at a great rate. 'She was extremely kind to me at first,' Marjorie recalls; 'I liked her a great deal; and I really think that in her own way she was fond of me and of us all'. Then one holiday, probably during the summer of 1926, Elinor invited Marjorie to go with her to one of the holiday courses held by the English Folk Dance Society. Marjorie was delighted, perhaps a little flattered too, and looked forward greatly to the holiday. The two arrived at the Summer School together; but, from that moment, 'Elinor was so completely swept away with all the new people, and so absorbed by the whole Folk Dance set-up' that she completely dropped the younger girl.

And that she was simply unaware of Marjorie's reactions is suggested by the fact that, the following year, Elinor actually invited Marjorie to accompany her on another folk dancing course. What is more, she was most offended when Marjorie refused. A definite break in the friendship ensued. And although later this was patched up, and in 1934 Elinor dedicated a book, *Carnation of the Upper Fourth*, to the Jewell sisters, things were never to be quite the same again.

Ironically it had been through the Jewells that Elinor first encountered the English folk dance movement, which for a while became one of her great crazes. And it was also to Marjorie and Vivien that she owed her introduction to the writer Elsie Oxenham, whom she had long admired from the distance. She possessed all Miss Oxenham's books, and had presented copies of several to Hazel Bainbridge.

Elsie Jeanette Oxenham had an enormous enthusiasm for everything connected with English folk dancing. Moreover, and far more unusually, she was a real expert on the subject. And, as anyone who has ever come across her books will know, folk dancing often plays an important part in her stories. Many of these books appeared during the early twenties, when Vivien Jewell had been among the vast number of schoolgirls who devoured them. And Vivien did not see why the 'Abbey Girls' should have all the fun. She herself joined a folk dancing group; and was enterprising enough, when this group entered for a national folk dancing contest, to write and ask Miss Elsie Oxenham for her advice.

This can hardly have been the only request of its kind to reach Miss Oxenham at that period. But perhaps there was something out of the ordinary about Vivien's letter; Vivien herself thought it might have been connected with her great fondness for cats, which had somehow spilled over into the letter. But, whatever the reason, Elsie Oxenham not only replied most kindly, but offered to come over to Fareham and coach the group herself. 'That,' as Vivien Pass recalled, 'was a real thrill. And what's more, thanks to her our group got into the finals at the Albert Hall.' Real storybook stuff, in fact.

This incident shows Miss Oxenham in a pleasant light; and the impression that she was a genuinely kind person is strengthened by her friendly treatment of Elinor, who was introduced to her during one visit to Fareham.

It must be remembered in order to get the right perspective that Elinor was then all but unknown in the world of schoolgirl fiction. Miss Oxenham, with about twenty published books to her credit, was near the top of the league. Yet she was neither too preoccupied nor too grand to take an interest in Elinor, and to encourage her in her writing. And that Elinor appreciated this can be seen from the dedication of *Seven Scamps* (1927): 'To Elsie Jeanette Oxenham, whose friendship and books have given me such pleasure, and to whom I owe so much.' A friendly contact between the two writers was to continue until Elsie Oxenham's death in 1960. It never became a specially close friendship and the number of their meetings must necessarily have been limited, but the two corresponded at intervals and often sent each other copies of their books. Those from Elinor always contained some special handwritten message on the fly-leaf. And it may have given Miss Oxenham a little gentle amusement — if she recalled their first meeting at Fareham — to read the one written in *Judy the Guide* (1928) which concludes 'From one writer to another'.

Probably by the end of 1928, when *Judy* was published, Elinor felt sufficiently well-established in her career to make the claim. Certainly she had advanced by nine books during the four years since that spring of 1924, when her third story, *The Maids of La Rochelle* was still not quite completed.

AN IMPORTANT MILESTONE

The Maids of La Rochelle had been in many ways an important book for Elinor, marking as it did a number of 'firsts' in her career. It was the first of her books that was not a school story; it was the first where the setting plays an integral part in the story: *The Maids of La Rochelle* could hardly take place anywhere but the Channel Islands, whereas in Elinor's first two books the events could happen in any number of places. It was the first book to introduce Janie Temple (later Janie Lucy), who is the first of Elinor's non-beautiful heroines. And it was the first of her stories to receive favourable notice from the national papers. The *Times Literary Supplement*, for instance, wrote:

> *The Maids of La Rochelle* lead quite a quiet life in comparison to some of their peers; [And since the story contains a fire, several deaths — one of them violent — two marriages, a witch, an escape from an angry mob, and a number of severe scarlet-fever cases, this tells much about *Elinor's* peers.] . . . but Miss Elinor Brent-Dyer makes full use of the legends of the Channel Islands . . . she is really more concerned with character than with incident and has given to her three orphans a happy youthful grace.

And if that seems only moderately enthusiastic, a glance further up the column reveals that authors far more established than Elinor was in 1924 are far less appreciatively treated. Many are upbraided for the impossibility of their plots, the monotony of their writing and the unlikeliness of their characters — one heroine being dismissed as 'a particularly tiresome person, who talks stage Irish of the 1890s'. Into the bargain, one of the best-known writers is accused of having 'filled the prescribed three hundred pages with folly, which, though not actually harmful, is folly'. After which Elinor's review reads like a panegyric.

All in all, *The Maids of La Rochelle* marked a milestone in Elinor's life. But it was only a milestone. The important turning-point was still to come. By the spring of 1924 it was just round the corner.

CHAPTER XIII

'IT ALL GREW FROM ONE HOLIDAY IN THE TYROL'

In real life a decision with far-reaching consequences may appear unremarkable at the time. Thus when Elinor chose to spend her 1924 summer holiday in Austria she can have had no inkling that this choice would affect quite literally the whole future course of her life. Yet it is no exaggeration to state that it did.

That year she had passed her thirtieth birthday on 6 April. And however little she allowed herself to remember this (her official age was still around twenty-five) she can hardly have escaped an occasional awareness that time was rushing past and leaving her without a great deal to show for it.

Viewed in terms of career, her life at this point offered little to make her feel complacent. True, there were her books: two published and a third on the way. But by now the first thrill of getting into print must have faded a little, and neither *Gerry Goes to School* nor *A Head Girl's Difficulties* had attracted much notice; they had been just two more small fish in the teeming pond of the school story.

However, at least her writing was making some progress. Her teaching career, on the other hand, showed signs of becoming stuck in a backwater; for Western House, described in its advertisement as 'An independent day school for girls and little boys', was not an establishment of importance in the educational world.

Elinor could of course have looked for another job. But, as she once confided to Marjorie Jewell, her qualifications were simply not good enough to gain her a top-class appointment, so her prospects for advancement in teaching were poor. Not to mention that her personality and social background would have been against her in the boarding-school world, as she may well have been aware.

Financially, too, things cannot have been easy for Elinor at this time. Her salary as a teacher was modest: quite possibly no more than £150 per annum for someone in her position in 1924. And, as a comparatively unknown author, she did not earn much from her writing, either. On this point reliable figures were hard to find, but a possible clue exists in *Jo Returns to the Chalet School* (1936). Here part of the story concerns the writing of Joey Bettany's first completed book (like Elinor, Jo has got many unfinished efforts behind her). The manuscript of this story has been posted to 'a well-known firm'. Then one day a typewritten letter arrives for Jo:

> Two seconds later Madge Russell was startled . . . by a wild yell from her sister.
>
> '*Joey*! What on earth is the matter? . . . What's wrong? Tell me this instant! . . . at once before I shake you!'
>
> 'Oh, Madge!' Joey was stammering in her excitement. 'It — it's from those people I sent . . . [my book] to Madge! They *like* it — they say so. They say their reader has reported favourably on it! And they offer me thirty-five pounds for the copyright! Think of it, Madge! *Thirty-five pounds*!'

Now that was 1936. Elinor's own first book had appeared fourteen years earlier. And it does seem unlikely that in 1922 Elinor would have been paid *more* than the £35 Joey is offered here. At this stage she might well have received less; but, since the contracts for her first three books have all disappeared, there is no way of being certain. It has now emerged that, three years later, Elinor was paid £40 for *The School at the Chalet*, and this was probably the going rate in 1925. But it does seem a little odd that in 1940, when *The Chalet School in Exile* was published, Elinor, despite having by this point nearly thirty books behind her, was still being paid only £40 for the copyright.

Of course £40 was quite a handsome sum in the 1920s. It could, for instance, have provided a term's fees for a girl at boarding-school. £120 a year is 'only what most decent schools charge,' Madge Bettany points out to her brother — in *The School at the Chalet* (1925). And Madge had 'got some prospectuses to see'. So, probably, had Elinor; among them no doubt that of St Helen's School, where the fees at this time were £120 per annum.

All the same, even making allowances for the greater value of the pound in 1924, Elinor was undoubtedly not well off. And very probably one of the reasons she chose the Tyrol for her summer holiday was that Austria then was an extremely cheap country for British people to visit.

Nowadays this seems hard to believe. But during the early twenties inflation had reduced the value of Austrian currency in an almost unimaginable way: by 1924, 10,000 Kronen — the equivalent of more than £435 before the Great War — was worth only about 2½ pence. And, as one result, foreign visitors were able to tour Austria for incredibly little. Full board, for example, was offered by many of the best hotels for a 100,000 Kronen a day — which sounds staggering but meant less than five shillings in English money (25p). In pensions it could have been found for very much less, particularly in small places.

Other prices were equally low. 'Oh, look at those plums!' Grizel Cochrane says excitedly to Joey as they stand waiting outside a shop in Innsbruck (*The School at the Chalet*); 'Only *six* hundred Kronen the kilo! I must buy some!' And with 'those plums' costing less than a farthing a pound her enthusiasm is understandable.

Grizel's remark is enlightening in another way, for it contains a reference to Kronen — and the early Chalet School books do frequently mention this form of Austrian money. Elinor, it is obvious, had failed to notice an important change which took place in Austria about four months after her visit. Then, on 1 January 1925, the now familiar Schilling was introduced to replace the Krone, which thereafter vanished from the scene.

It took Elinor three years and four Chalet books to catch up with this change: only in *The Head Girl of the Chalet School*, published in 1928, do her characters begin using Schillings. But at least this small anachronism is helpful in one way, since it establishes definitely that Elinor's own visit to Austria must have taken place no later than 1924.

Any such confirmation is welcome for, as might be expected, there is little written evidence to be found about the holiday. Elinor never seems to have kept a diary; and if she sent either letters or postcards from the Tyrol they have long ago disappeared.

However in this instance a wealth of information is given indirectly by the early Chalet School books; and with their help it is possible to learn a great deal about that momentous visit.

First of all, the journey to the Tyrol. It seems a reasonable guess that Elinor would have travelled by the same route, and with the same strict economy, as the Bettanys and Grizel Cochrane do in *The School at the Chalet*. Not that an author is obliged to make her characters do exactly what she did herself. But it is noticeable in the Chalet School series that anyone going to Austria by public transport *always* travels in one particular way; which suggests that to Elinor this was indeed the one and only way. And it became so fixed in her ideas that even in the sixties, when the Chalet School was established in Switzerland, her school-girls are still travelling from England by boat and train, although by this time in real life, with the ready availability of student air-fares, they would more probably have gone by plane.

The School at the Chalet provides a blue-print for the Journey, and certain details can be filled in from other books. It begins at London's Victoria Station. Here Grizel Cochrane's father, suffering a belated 'feeling of regret that he meant so little to his only child', gives Grizel 'into Madge Bettany's charge'; and Madge, Joey and Grizel proceed to the coast and thence across the Channel to France. 'Even the draughty, prosaic *douane* of Boulogne, where everyone had to go in queue with their cases, was invested with a certain pleasure glamour for [Grizel]', who 'had never been out of England in her life before'. Neither, perhaps, had Elinor, with the exception of her visit to Guernsey the previous year; although, since her one and only passport was applied for in July 1922, there is at least a possibility that she had already travelled somewhere abroad that year.

Once through the customs 'they settled down in their second-class carriage'; Grizel is intrigued by 'the unusual trains with their funny, high engines and little steps up into the carriages'. 'A little later they produced sandwiches and milk.' Never any dining-car meals in those pre-war days.

'It was five o'clock — or seventeen, if you cared to

take French time — by the time they had arrived [in Paris]'; and on this occasion they go to an hotel, 'a quiet one, not far from the Madeleine'. However a stay in Paris is not an obligatory part of the proceedings, and Elinor may or may not have made one.

'Half-past eight saw them at the Gare de l'Est, climbing into the Paris-Wien train express.' Or — to take another version (T*he Head Girl of the Chalet School*) — 'It was nearly nine at night . . . [as they] walked down the long platform of the Gare de l'Est, where the Paris-Wien express was standing, and quickly found the carriage.' Second-class, naturally. And no question of sleepers: 'Joey and Grizel did as they were told . . . rolling themselves in rugs, and curling up on the seats which had been widened by the pulling out of a kind of underseat.' A detail that surely was learnt from experience,

' "We shall be in Switzerland, I hope, when you wake tomorrow . . . we reach Basle about six in the morning." . . . And . . . before long all three were fast asleep, while the great train hurled onwards through the darkness.'

'It was half-past seven on . . . [the following] evening when the Vienna express slackened speed before entering the Innsbrück Station . . . an hour late", observed Madge . . . "We've missed the last train of the mountain railway, so we'll have to go to an hotel somewhere for the night." '

And that presents no problem, for Madge's brother Dick Bettany is there to meet them, and he has got 'rooms booked at the Europe'.

Outside the station then, and 'into the big square, where carriages intended for two horses, but drawn by one only [presumably no one could afford the second horse], were waiting for hire; while the coachmen . . . in their short open jackets, full skirts, and little green Tyrolese hats with the inevitable feather at the back, leaned up against the wheels, shouting chaff to each other, or smoking their long china-bowled pipes. Beyond, they could see the great snow-capped mountains, towering up on all sides.'

And so at last, after a day of sight-seeing in Innsbrück, to the final stages of the Journey: up into the mountains above the Inn valley, to the beautiful Achen See and the village of Pertisau. In the books this is to be renamed 'Briesau', while the lake becomes the 'Tiern See'. Here, Elinor would spend the holiday of her lifetime; and in fiction Madge Bettany would open the Chalet School.

'The journey from Innsbrück to Spärtz [Elinor's name for Jenbach] is of no particular interest, with the one exception of the old-world town of Hall, famous for its salt mines now, though in olden days it had a great reputation as the centre of plots and wars.' True about Hall — or Solbad Hall, as it is sometimes known. But apparently no one had told Elinor that a few miles short of Jenbach/Spärtz a dramatic glimpse may be caught of the monastery of St Georgenberg, unbelievably perched above a ravine at a height of more than 2,000 feet. However, anyone would agree with the next part of her description:

> The little mountain railway, which carries you up to a height of three thousand feet and more above the sea-level, is something to remember. Higher and higher they climbed, now and then stopping at a tiny wayside station, till at last they reached the great Alp, or rather Alm, as they are called in the Tyrol, and there before them, dark, beautiful, and clear as a mirror, spread the Tiern [Achen] See, with its three tiny hamlets and two little

> villages round its shores; and towering round on all sides the mighty limestone crags and peaks of the mountains.
>
> The railway terminus is known as Seespitz, and here the steamer was waiting for the passengers. Dick was there too, ready to help with the parcels.
>
> 'It's a jolly walk round the lake,' he said, 'but tonight I think we'll take the steamer. It's about a quarter of a mile nearer from the [Pertisau] landing-stage than it is from here . . . '
>
> The little steamer waited ten minutes, then her whistle blew, and off she went — first to Buchau at the opposite side of the lake, and then to . . . [Pertisau] . . . From the landing-stage to the Chalet was a good ten minutes' walk, and then they saw the welcoming lights . . . They were . . . [there] at last.

Naturally there can never be proof that the above synthesis provides an accurate picture of Elinor's own journey to the Tyrol. But the first Chalet School story, from which most of the quotations come, was begun, at a guess, within a few weeks of her return to England and was certainly completed by Easter 1925, only seven months later. It would be impossible to believe that, with everything so fresh in her memory, her own experiences were not incorporated in her writing. There is, too, something about the type of details supplied in all the early Chalet School books which proclaims their origin in real life. And later, when Elinor began to fall back on guide-books for local colour, the difference is unmistakable.

The sheer quantity of small details is bound to strike a reader of today; and now any writer would hesitate to include so many. Here, however, Elinor was accurately gauging her audience: the schoolgirls of that pre-television era possessed a fair amount of reading muscle; and there is plenty of evidence that they actually enjoyed having every little detail spelt out. In particular anything to do with foreign lands was fascinating, for it was then only the tiniest minority of children who ever went abroad themselves.

School-story writers were obviously aware of this; and many of them sent their characters off to the Continent or the far-flung Empire. Angela Brazil in *The School in the South* (1922) chose Naples as the destination for the Beverley family; and the differences between their mode of travel and Elinor's Standard Chalet School Journey exactly reflect the difference in financial status between the two authors. It is implicit, though not stated in so many words, that Angela Brazil's characters travel First Class; they 'sit in comfortable padded armchairs, eating fish or ham and eggs, and watching . . . the deft-handed waiters nipping about with trays or teacups'; and for the 'thirty-eight hours' journey from Paris to Rome [Curious how anyone in schoolgirl fiction travelling to any place abroad always seems to go via Paris — perhaps something to do with all foreigners being Frenchmen?] . . . they had engaged two sleeping compartments, wagons-lits as they are called on the Continental express.' (Readers will note that Miss Brazil works into her stories just as many informative details as Elinor into hers.)

Angela herself always travelled in comfort, according to her biographer (Mrs Gillian Freeman, *The Schoolgirl Ethic*), and stayed at good hotels. Elinor, on the other hand, almost certainly chose somewhere cheap for her stay in Pertisau — not that any of the hotels there would have been expensive at this time. But, true to form, she never revealed exactly where she had stayed; and her short account, written for the first Chalet Club newsletter, refers only to 'a Chalet beside the lake'. And this description, with its implication of a private house, is probably a piece of poetic licence. Old photographs of Pertisau show clearly that there were then (as now) only two houses, as distinct from hotels, directly on the lakeside; both have been working farms for many generations back. And although it is not absolutely impossible that Elinor stayed as a paying-guest in one or other of these houses, living conditions there would have been so primitive at the time as to make this quite unlikely.

On balance, it is safe to assume that she stayed in one of the hotels along the waterfront: perhaps the Stephanie, or the Post Hotel, or the Alpenhof. Any of these would fit the description and all were there, indeed long-established, in Elinor's day; moreover, at that time their buildings were much simpler than now, and were in the traditional style which could loosely be covered by the word 'chalet'.

The Post Hotel and the Stephanie are frequently mentioned in Elinor's books. The Alpenhof, hardly ever; which may be significant for, in the opinion of many 'Chalet experts', this hotel has the situation most nearly corresponding with that of the Chalet School, as described in the stories — a matter that has given rise to much discussion among readers. The early books do supply a remarkable number of details about the school's exact location in 'Briesau'/Pertisau; and these details are so precise and, for Elinor, so unusually consistent that it seems she really did have a specific place in mind. And a careful study of the books will reveal the following six points of identification.

(1) The school was near, but — unlike many of the

important hotels — not directly on the lakeside.
(2) It commanded splendid views, in one direction of the lake, in the other of the valley and mountains behind the village.
(3) It was on slightly higher ground than the waterfront (an important point during the flood in *Jo of the Chalet School*).
(4) It was 'a good ten minutes' walk' from the steamers' landing stage, going in the direction of Seespitz — in other words, southwards.
(5) It was even further south along the lakeside than the Post Hotel — hence well to the Seespitz end of the village.
(6) It was surrounded by a garden — something quite unusual in Pertisau.

Bearing in mind all these points, there is only one site in Pertisau that fulfils every requirement: that of the Alpenhof Hotel. Not that the Alpenhof building, either today or in 1920s pictures, bears much resemblance to the actual chalet described in the books. But then Elinor, like other writers of fiction, clearly enjoyed using a mixture of real life and imagination when describing places. And more often than not in her books she proceeds, after giving minute and topographically accurate details about an identifiable site, to place there an entirely different house — or in this case, chalet — from that occupying the site in real life. (Later this emerges frequently in the seven books which are set in Herefordshire.) That Elinor herself may actually have stayed at the Alpenhof is a possibility, although it is unlikely now this could ever be proved.The hotel was apparently a favourite with English visitors in those days, and, according to Baedeker, its tariff would have been modest in terms of British currency. The Alpenhof was in fact to remain a popular hotel right up to the 1970s. But since then, following the death of the owner, there have unfortunately been endless legal wrangles among the family about the future of the site — unquestionably one of the most desirable in Pertisau. Sadly, there seems no end to the quarrels, with the result that the hotel was closed many years ago, while the building has become more and more dilapidated. No chance now of holding a Chalet School Reunion there.

Of course the other place Elinor could well have stayed was 'the big white-washed hotel which stood near the boat-landing'. This, the 'Kron Prinz Karl' of the stories, is in real life the Fürstenhaus, the oldest hotel in Pertisau. Its name dates back to the days when the Fürsten, or Princes, had a hunting-lodge on the site; and a very old engraving shows the Fürstenhaus looking much the same as it did until the rebuilding operations in the late 1970s. The Princes had also their own private chapel, a simple but charming little building, with carved wooden pews and some quaint frescoes around the walls. This was the original of 'the little white-washed chapel' which stood near the Kron Prinz Karl, where the Chalet School Catholics went on Sundays; and where Elinor almost certainly went too during her visit, for at that time there was no form of Protestant worship in Pertisau — nor, probably, in any place nearer than Innsbruck. Until the early 1970s this chapel could still be seen, but now it has sadly been demolished to make way for a car-park.

In general their regulations about preserving old buildings, and about the construction and style of new ones, have been so strict that Pertisau has changed far less than might be expected during the seven decades since Elinor's visit. There are of course a great many new houses and hotels, for the tourist trade is booming. There is a new Catholic church at the top of the village, a pleasant enough building which successfully combines traditional and modern elements. (And in 1994 a plaque commemorating Elinor's visit to Pertisau was placed on the wall of the library which stands beside the church.) Then today the pine-woods, which cluster over the mountain slopes all around Pertisau, and where in the stories the Chalet girls loved to wander, have as it were retreated in various places, having been cut back either to make room for ski runs or to allow more hay to grow; nowadays it is reaped on slopes that would appear to the uninitiated impossibly steep. And another change since Elinor's time: today both a chair-lift and a cable-car are waiting to haul the less energetic up to the Bärenbad Alm. Her Chalet girls were of course to walk up there and back in an hour or two, without blinking an eyelash.

On the whole, though, building in the village has been restricted to the inland areas; and as a result the view of Pertisau from the lake — comparing old and new postcards — still looks recognisably the same as it did to Elinor.

And nothing can really alter the Achen See itself, or the surrounding mountains. Indeed this region is so spectacularly beautiful that it is difficult to write anything about it that does not sound like the lush paragraphs of some romantic novel. Even Baedeker's Guide does not manage to keep its usual cool approach: at least, the 1911 edition (which was among Elinor's books), after dutifully informing its readers that the Achen See is 3,045 feet above sea level, five-and-a-half miles long, about half-a-mile broad, and 436 feet deep, goes on to say that it is 'a dark-blue lake, the largest and finest in Tyrol' (which for Baedeker amounts almost to purple

Pertisau-am-Achensee, Tyrol, taken in the early 1950s but little changed from the time of Elinor's visit in 1924.

The Alpenhof Hotel in Pertisau in the 1970s. Was this the inspiration for the Chalet School site?

prose).

This opinion of the lake is backed by a far more recent publication, a guide produced locally in 1975; but this goes further than Baedeker, claiming that 'The Achensee ranks beside the Vierwaldstättersee [Lake of Lucerne] and the Königssee [in Bavaria] among the most beautiful Alpine lakes.'

Elinor goes further still, writing, at the beginning of *Jo of the Chalet School*, that 'the . . . [Achen] See in the North Tyrol is surely one of the loveliest places in the world'.

Thus, in the midst of all the uncertainty and speculation that surround many aspects of Elinor, her books make it possible to be absolutely certain about one thing. Until the end of her life she was to go on thinking of the Achen See as the loveliest place in the world.

WHAT BECAME OF LILIAN?

The early Chalet School books do clearly contain much that is autobiographical; but they offer no help whatsoever towards a solution of one particular mystery, that surrounding Elinor's companion on her Tyrolean holiday. Her first name was Lilian; but at the time this book was first published no other information about her could be found.

Elinor herself mentions this friend in the inaugural *Chalet Club News Letter* (of May 1959) referred to above:

> Years ago, I was spending a holiday in Tirol and the friend who was with me and I made our headquarters at a chalet by the shore of the beautiful lake you know as the Tiern See. We met two other . . . friends and made many expeditions together, though they were there for only three

> weeks and my friend and I stayed for nearly eight. If you want to know their names, you will find them in the dedication of *The School at the Chalet* which was the first of the series to be written.

And, sure enough, there in the dedication are the three names: 'TO LILIAN, JEAN, AND FLO — BUT ESPECIALLY TO LILIAN IN MEMORY OF OUR JOLLY TIME TOGETHER IN THE TYROL'.

Nothing could be clearer: Lilian was Elinor's friend; Jean and Flo the two who were 'staying in another chalet'. But who exactly was Lilian? In the circumstances it would be reasonable to expect that she was a friend of some standing — perhaps one of Elinor's teaching colleagues. And yet no one could remember that Elinor ever had a friend with that particular name. Lilian had vanished completely. Or so it seemed — and for many years.

Then, in the spring of 1995, a Chalet fan, Mrs Gillian Hill, who was working in the library at St Helen's School in Northwood, just happened to come across a reference to Elinor in the school's magazine, *St Helen's Own*. Intrigued by this, she searched further and found not only that Elinor's name appeared on several other occasions (as already mentioned in Chapter XII), but that another contributor to *St Helen's Own* during the early 1920s was a Miss Kirkby, whose first name was Lilian. Moreover it turned out that Lilian Kirkby had been at St Helen's during exactly the same two-year period as Elinor, and that during this time she had been the magazine's editor. Of course this in itself provides no proof that the Lilian Kirkby who taught at St Helen's between 1921 and 1923 was the same person as the Lilian of Elinor's dedication. But it does seem highly probable that she was. Especially in view of the fact that Lilian Kirkby's contributions to the magazine include a piece describing her experiences during a visit to the Austrian Tyrol in 1922 or 1923. Making it a strong possibility that it was she who influenced Elinor's choice of Pertisau for her momentous Tyrolean holiday, and that she did indeed become her companion on that visit.

Today it would be hard to discover any personal details about Lilian. The registers at St Catherine's House in London record the births of only two Lilian Kirkbys who would have been of a suitable age during the relevant period. And of these two the more likely is a 'Constance Lilian Kirkby', who was born in Kensington in the spring of 1900. This would have made her between twenty-one and twenty-three during the years that Elinor was at St Helen's, and twenty-four at the time of the Tyrolean holiday. And the particular name, Constance Lilian, is interesting in itself. Elinor always stated that she never based her characters on friends, and this may well have been true as regards the actual personalities of her fictional people. But there can be no question that Elinor was often influenced unconsciously in her choice of their names. No prominent character in the Chalet series is called Lilian; but it could be significant that Miss Stewart, who teaches history in the early stories and becomes a close enough friend of Jo Maynard's to be chosen as godmother for the second of the Maynard triplets, is in fact called Constance. What's more, Miss Stewart's god-daughter is then named Constance after her. And this does suggest that the name had personal resonances for Elinor. Even in the late 1920s, when she bestowed it on Miss Stewart, 'Constance' was becoming old-fashioned; and by the time of the triplets' birth (*The Chalet School in Exile*, 1940) it would have been quite anachronistic.

Whereas Elinor's schoolgirls are for the most part given names that are typical of their period.

One other point about Lilian is thought-provoking. She and Elinor must surely have known each other well to have embarked on an eight-week holiday together. But did the prolonged period of being thrown continuously into each other's company prove too great a strain on the friendship? Otherwise it seems odd that Lilian should have vanished so completely from Elinor's life. At least, it would be odd with someone other than Elinor. In her case, numerous people among her friends and acquaintances seem to have disappeared. Edith Le Poidevin, for one — although there was never the least mystery about Miss Le Poidevin's existence; plenty of people remembered her, and spoke warmly of her pleasant appearance and friendly personality. And anyway there could have been reasons, as mentioned earlier, why she and Elinor lost contact. Lilian, on the other hand, seems to have left no trace in Elinor's life apart from her name in the dedication. She might almost not have existed.

But then others, too, on the long list of people to whom Elinor dedicated books, have disappeared. Notably Madge Russell — not the fictional Madge, née Bettany, Joey's much older sister who founds the Chalet School, but a real-life friend to whom Elinor dedicated *The Maids of La Rochelle* in 1924, *Jo of the Chalet School* in 1926, and *The Princess of the Chalet School* in 1927. This Madge would appear to have been a special friend not only to receive three dedications in as many years, but also to have her name bestowed on one of Elinor's important and very special characters. And yet, after 1927 nothing further is heard of the real-life Madge Russell. At one time it had seemed possible that Madge Halliwell, the dedicatee of *Changes for the Chalet*

School (1953), could be the same person, but this now seems unlikely. For although her son, David Russell Halliwell, to whom Elinor dedicated *Condor Crags* in 1954, has confirmed the odd coincidence that his late mother's maiden name was indeed Madge Russell, he seems clear that she and Elinor only became acquainted in 1940. And, to date, no trace of the 1920s Madge Russell can be found.

However, in spite of all this, it would be wrong to assume that Elinor always dropped her old friends and acquaintances. To the end of her life she did keep in touch, in different ways and perhaps only at wide intervals, with many of them; including the Jewells, Miss Elsie Oxenham and Hazel Bainbridge. Also of course with Phyllis Matthewman, in whose house she eventually went to live.

Returning for a moment to Lilian — her disappearance was particularly frustrating at the time this book was first being written, for plainly she could have related much of interest about that Tyrolean holiday. As matters stood, the only thing was to make use of guesswork, the snippets of information (not always reliable) contained in the Chalet Club newsletters; and above all those early Chalet books where Elinor is remembering her own experiences. And it is at this point that one can be grateful that Elinor included such a profusion of small, everyday details in her stories; and that she presented them with such obvious affection. For in reading the books it becomes possible to picture everything: the beauty of the scenery; the house where Elinor and the elusive Lilian stayed; some of the different ways in which they occupied their time; the meals they enjoyed; and their reactions to some of the people whom they met.

In the chapter which follows, most of the material has been provided by Elinor herself.

CHAPTER XIV

'WRITE IN YOUR OWN WORDS . . .'

(An impression of the holiday as Elinor saw it)

The Chalet was a very large wooden building which had been designed for a hotel . . . There were no carpets on the floors but they were brought to a fine polish with beeswax and hard rubbing. The furniture . . . was all old.

[In the salon] was the inevitable sofa with its little table before it [and] in an alcove . . . stood a beautifully carved *Brautkasten*, or bridal-chest . . .

[In the dining-room, at breakfast time, baskets] piled high with brown rolls and dishes full of amber honey gave colour to the cloth-less table. The big, hand-made cups and plates, with their cheerful decoration of unknown flowers painted in vivid colours, which stood at each place, had come from Tiern Kirch [Achen Kirch]. The table looked un-English in the extreme, but very pleasant and inviting. Presently [the maid] . . . came in bearing a huge earthenware jug in which steamed delicious coffee such as one rarely gets in England. She filled the cups by the simple method of dipping a mug into the boiling liquid and pouring its contents into each cup.

[The coffee had come from] the long kitchen situated at the back of the house, where [the cook] . . . reigned, with a younger sister and a cousin to help her, while . . . [her brother] cleaned shoes and knives, and attended to the huge porcelain stoves which warmed the place throughout.

Of course the stoves can hardly have been in use during Elinor's stay in Pertisau, for summers there are warm. As she herself often points out: 'Heat in the Tyrol can mean something that England may experience once in a century.' The temperature in August and September probably seemed remarkable to anyone brought up in South Shields, for it can be hot enough even at the Achen See, which 'is 3,000 feet above sea level . . . [and where there is usually] a delightful breeze from the lake'. Most days 'there . . . [wouldn't] be a breath of air in the valley [and] it . . . [would] be stewing hot in Innsbruck'.

All the same, those tiled porcelain stoves are mentioned so frequently that it seems they must have made a big impression on Elinor. And another thing that plainly impressed her was the continental quilt, or duvet as it would probably be called now. In the stories this article is always referred to as a 'plumeau', sometimes spelt 'plumeaux' even when in the singular: 'When she came back . . . her bed [N.B. one bed] had been stripped and the *plumeaux* hung over the balcony'.

Today, this usage of 'plumeau' seems to have been dropped in the Tyrol — or at any rate in Pertisau. Obviously the word must first have come to Austria from France, along with various other words and expressions: 'Das ist mir ganz *egal*', is one that can be heard many times a day — meaning literally 'It's all the same to me' and often used with an implication of 'I don't give a damn'. But nowadays, even in French, 'un plumeau' is more often used to mean a feather duster rather than a quilt, while most ordinary-sized German/English dictionaries do not appear to include the word at all. However, in support of Elinor, Langenscheidt's eneyclopaedic volume does give 'eiderdown or quilt' as possible translations of 'das plumeau (plural -s)'. So Elinor was evidently using the word, if not the 'x', correctly.

Anyhow, whatever its proper name, this piece of bedding was later to appear on every Chalet School bed. And naturally there is one in the bedroom of which Elinor supplies a detailed description in *Jo of the Chalet School* (1926):

> It was a typical Tyrolean room . . . with walls and floor of polished pine-wood. There were a couple of mats on the floor, and in one corner was a huge wooden bed, with its big puffy *plumeau*, and pillows in pillow-cases edged with exquisite handmade lace. Two tiny wooden wash-stands stood side by side, with the usual baby bowls and pitchers on them [on another occasion Joey Bertany complains that 'They never do give you more than a pudding-basin to wash in']; . . . A tall wardrobe, a chest of drawers with a mirror [above], and three chairs made up most of the furniture. At the foot of the bed . . . hung a 'beautiful copy of Guido's 'Blue Madonna'.

Now for the outside of the Chalet:

'The building was [made] of wood and plaster, like most buildings in the . . . [Achen] thal'. A 'fresco . . . adorned the walls'; and a 'balcony . . . ran all round the house . . . about ten feet above the ground'. At the windows were 'window-boxes full of geraniums and marguerites'. Today, such window-boxes are still a feature of the houses in Pertisau. On the other hand, it is now impossible to wander at will 'across the flower-sprinkled grass that . . . [lies] between . . . [the Chalet] and the trees which cluster at the foot of Bärenbad', since all the meadows are either fenced off or have properly surfaced paths. Nor could a present-day visitor find quite 'such a wealth of bloom' in 'the stretch of meadow that lies between Seespitz and Torteswald', or for that matter in any place nearer to Pertisau than the nature reserve in the mountains behind the village.

In any case most wild plants are protected nowadays. But in Elinor's time it was possible, apparently, to gather in the fields quite near the Chalet 'armfuls of gentian, anemone, hepaticae, heartsease, narcissi, and daisies'. Nor should anyone raise an eyebrow at the simultaneous presence of narcissi and gentian: this particular passage refers to 'mid-May' and, although the more common gentians are summer-flowering, at least a couple of species can be seen in flower from April onwards.

The early books are in fact pretty accurate in their presentation of local details; allowing, that is, that from the beginning Elinor did make changes, not only in place names but in topography. These were deliberate. The names were altered in order to disguise the identity of the 'Tiern See' — which Elinor was successful in doing for many years. The topographical changes were made to fit the requirements of the stories, and they are the result mainly of a scaling down in size of the district. For example, 'the Tiern See is only three miles long', because this allows Chalet girls on foot a wider and more varied territory than they could have covered had the lake, like the real Achen See, been five-and-a-half miles in length.

All this is perfectly understandable. It is only in the later books that the alterations sometimes get rather wild: as when the Bärenbad mountain, which the early books clearly establish in its proper place to the south of Briesau/Pertisau, is suddenly required by the demands of the ninth story to be situated on the opposite (Gaisalm) side of the village. (See *Exploits of the Chalet Girls*, Chapter

VII, and compare with map.)

Of course by the time that book was being written nine years had passed since Elinor's visit to Pertisau, and her memories may have faded a little. In the early stories she still recalled everything so vividly that she was able to present what amounts to a guide-book of Pertisau/Briesau; and moreover, as one of her fans points out, 'A guide-book in the right way, making one want to see the places for oneself'.

The fictional Chalet School was to face the lake — 'the loveliest of all the Austrian lakes'; for doubtless the front windows of the chalet where Elinor and Lilian stayed had 'a glorious view of the [Achen] . . . See'; and perhaps from those at the back they 'could see right up the valley toward the great "Tiern" Pass'; the latter being a semi-fictional amalgamation of the three different valleys which in real life stand behind Pertisau.

The position in the village of her Chalet is also clear. On leaving it and turning right, 'once past the white fencing that [enclosed Pertisau] . . . the lake path . . . led to Seespitz at the lower end of the lake . . . The lake-road at this point was narrow, the wall of the mountain-side rising not three yards from the margin of the lake'. (Today, with the aid of modern engineering, the road has been made much wider.)

From Seespitz, one possible route 'lay round the south end of the lake, across the water meadows . . . and then . . . to Buchau, a tiny hamlet on the opposite side of the lake from Briesau [Pertisau]'. Another was to take 'the mountain-path [leading] to Spärtz [Jenbach] by the banks of the little stream which frolics gaily down to the Inn, and supplies power for the saw-mills half-way down the mountain-side'.

Back once more to the Chalet, and then off again,

but this time turning left, 'down the road in the direction of the Post Hotel, one of the largest in Briesau [Pertisau]'. (It still is.) Here, a 'little shop [was] situated beneath the hotel entrance — the only shop in the district'. And the shop remained there until 1977, although latterly it became a kind of boutique, selling expensive knitwear and the like, for the village now has a fair number of shops, including at least two supermarkets. In Elinor's day, the Post Hotel shop 'served the purpose of post-office and general stores to the lake-folk'; and it sold a variety of things in addition to such obvious items as stamps and picture postcards. Oranges and chocolate are specifically mentioned.

Now to range further abroad — still with Elinor as a faithful guide. 'It was a hot Sunday, and . . . once she had left the fields, she turned towards the grateful shade of the pine-trees that grow up the slopes of the Bärenbad Alpe . . . [Soon] she had arrived at the foot of the path that led up to the *Gasthaus*, where . . . [they] often went to have saucers of cream and wild strawberries' (*The Chalet School and Jo*, 1931). The cream cost only 'three-pence a saucer' then — 3d. being the equivalent of $1\frac{1}{4}$ new pence. Today, what with inflation and an exchange rate notably unfavourable to the sterling, the price might well be over a pound.

'It was too hot even for this climb . . . so she turned aside, and went along a narrow byway that led . . . to a point from which it was possible to get a glorious view of the lake.' Signposts now direct the panting tourist to this 'Aussichtsbank' — literally, viewpoint bench.

So far, so good: all of this is basic stuff, simply if rather prosaically presented. But Elinor, like other school-story writers, was sometimes unable to resist the temptations of would-be fine writing:

> Across the path, beaten hard by the tread of many generations of feet, bright-hued beetles ran, intent on their business; a scarlet-winged butterfly paused on the wing, and then darted off again as . . . [she] approached; . . . somewhere overhead a bird was carolling gaily; a faint breeze stirred the short grass, starred with gentian, heartsease and a hundred other flowers. On one bush the alpenroses were glowing with their warm fire.

Well . . . in fairness to Elinor it must be said that her descriptions very rarely have this contrived, over-lush quality. The above comes from the seventh book in the series, and perhaps a romantic haze was beginning to cloud the original memories. But in any case Elinor is always much better when the demands of the action leave her no time for carolling birds and the fire — warm or otherwise — of alpenroses. One example is her account (mentioned in Chapter V) of Joey and Elisaveta 'scrambling and slipping down . . . [a] bare rock slope' with nothing to catch hold of except 'one or two naked tree-trunks'. Underlying the narrative here is a feeling that Elinor really knew what it felt like to skid precariously down a mountain slope, uncertain how, or even if, you would reach the bottom.

Perhaps she did know. In the terrain round Pertisau such hazardous descents can happen in real life, as witnessed by one of Elinor's readers who once spent a holiday in the district with her family. They were making their way down through the woods high above Pertisau when they had an experience that recalls Joey and Elisaveta's.

> We thought we were on the proper way but we must have taken a wrong turning somewhere and

> the path just petered out. The trees grew so thickly that we couldn't see ahead, and once we'd gone wrong we couldn't find anything like a path again. The only thing seemed to be just to go on downwards. The next half-hour I shall never forget. We had to crawl down this awful slope that felt like the side of a house, and cling on to the tree trunks to stop ourselves sliding out of control. The children were really frightened and I don't mind confessing my heart was in my mouth until at last we reached the bottom, shaking all over but safe. I used to think that maybe all those bits about the Chalet girls getting into difficulties on the mountains were only put in to make the stories more exciting. Now I know how easily these things can happen.

So possibly Elinor too had discovered how easily these things happen. However, the girls in her stories do occasionally go for more or less peaceful mountain climbs; and, on these expeditions also, it is clear that she herself had been there before them. Her description of a day's outing to the 'Mondschein-spitze' could almost have come from the diary she never wrote.

'The climb up the Mondscheinspitze is remarkably easy.' This in fact is misleading, for Elinor here is applying the name Mondscheinspitze — which presumably appealed to her — to quite a different mountain: perhaps the Feilkopf, which more or less fits the bill. The real Mondscheinspitze is an awkward, even dangerous climb, far more like Elinor's Tiernjoch and categorised in the local guide-book as 'only for the very experienced'.

> There is a well-defined path, which winds in and out among the dark pine trees, every now and

> then coming out into narrow — very narrow — grassy ledges. Presently, however, it left the woods, and . . . [the party] climbed up the bare limestone face of the mountain beneath the glare of the July sun. Tufts of grass, with wild scabious and white marguerites, punctuated the way, and gorgeous butterflies, brown and orange and scarlet and yellow, fluttered round them, so little afraid that often they settled on hat or frock.
> (*The School at the Chalet*, 1925)

Arrived on the alm they turn and look down.

> At their feet lay the valley they had crossed that morning, cool and green, with the empty river-bed stretching like a white ribbon down its length. In the distance they could see Briesau [Pertisau], lying like a toy village some giant child had set out; and beyond it . . . the Tiern [Achen] See, a living sapphire, gleamed beneath the sun. (ibid.)

Here everything apart from one or two names is exactly true to life. And the same can be said of the passage in *The Chalet School and Jo* where a party of climbers look back towards Pertisau from the top of 'a narrow rocky path' on the Buchau side of the lake. 'Opposite them were the mighty peaks of the Bärendbad Alpe, the Mondscheinspitze, the Tiernjoch and Bärenkopf . . . Away to the north they could see blue hills fading into the blue of the sky. To the south lay other and mightier peaks [the Zillerthal Alps], some still covered with snow, silent testimony to their height.'

Altogether, Elinor leaves no room for doubt that she and Lilian — with or without Jean and Flo — did a lot of walking in the district all round the Achen See. Many features of the real-life landscape are mentioned in the books, including the somewhat vertiginous path to Gaisalm, and the 'Dripping Rock'. And Elinor probably found time for several excursions further afield: certainly to Jenbach/Spärtz, the Zillerthal, the Stubaithal and to Innsbrück, for her descriptions of all these places contain small personal touches. Possibly to Salzburg, although without a car it is difficult to get there and back in a day from Pertisau; and in the two books where Elinor writes about Salzburg there is nothing that could not have been gleaned from guide-books.

Nearer base, the four holiday friends probably enjoyed 'rowing over the lake in one of the clumsy but serviceable boats . . . kept [by the hotel] for the use of the many tourists who came . . . during the summer months'.

And Elinor, if not the other three, may have been hardy enough to swim in the lake; after all, she had been accustomed to the sea at South Shields, so might not have been daunted by the Achen See, although it 'is fed partly by [underwater] springs . . . [which] tend to keep it very cold' and make bathing advisable only 'during the day when the sun . . . [is] on the water'. One thing though, if the water was cold, at least the air was always wonderfully pure and clear; there are endless references to the 'dry health-giving atmosphere of the Tyrolean Alps'.

Then there were plenty of less active occupations. Perhaps, sitting on the Fürstenhaus terrace at one of 'the tables with their huge scarlet umbrellas' and listening to 'the Tzigane bands who frequently come up to the lake on summer Sundays' to play their gipsy music with its 'peculiar haunting wildness'.

That happened only on Sundays, of course. But every day there was the pleasant task of finding somewhere to have *Kaffee und Kuchen*, that delightful tea-time meal. This usually meant 'milky coffee and delicious cakes, all nuts and cream'; but sometimes the cakes were replaced by equally 'delicious little fancy-bread twists'. When food is described in the books, and it very frequently is, the word 'delicious' is almost done to death. Tea, as a beverage rather than as a meal, occurs very seldom. Perhaps Elinor had been nonplussed early in her visit (as Joey was) by a request to choose between 'Thee mit Citron, oder mit Rhum?'! 'She hated the one, and had no idea of taking the other' — unlike the Tyroleans who are partial to tea with rum in it.

Menus for other meals are often given in exhaustive detail. They vary in style and scope. On Madge, Joey and Grizel's first evening there was 'Nothing really exciting,' said Dick. 'Only *Kalbsbraten* — all right, Grizel! That's German for roast veal! — and *Kartoffeln*, otherwise spuds, and *Apfelntorte*, which isn't apple-tart, although it sounds like it.' Soon Grizel, and incidentally the reader, learns that it is in fact a kind 'of cake with cooked apples on it'.

There are several appearance of 'hot thick soup into which are ladled little sausages, very savoury and delicious' — a dish that often is served today in the small mountain-huts around Pertisau.

One of Elinor's more exotic menus includes first 'soup with eggs in it . . . ('They just let the eggs *look* at the soup, and they are so light they are *gluey*') . . . followed by pink boiled ham served with prunes: . . . and then plates of something that looked, and tasted, not unlike porridge . . . [accompanied by] cherries steeped in spirits. The whole was topped off by excellent coffee, and rolls split and spread with jam of some kind.'

Even picnickers are seldom condemned to eat the humble sandwich. On a trip to the Zillerthal they have a 'gorgeous feast: there were rolls, buttered, and with hard-boiled eggs beaten up with butter and cream and shredded lettuce; . . . There were delicious little cakes . . . from Vienna; . . . there were piles of apricots and plums and greengages [no doubt of incredible cheapness], and there were two huge melons.'

Meals are served by 'smiling waitresses', often in Tyrolean costume. Maids also wear national dress: Gertlieb, the maid-of-all-work at a house visited in Innsbruck, is 'a rosy, smiling girl, wearing a full white blouse, short blue skirt, and wonderfully embroidered apron'. Incidentally, Gertlieb 'had been at work since half-past five [a.m. naturally], and [by breakfast time had] much of the ordinary housework . . . finished'. Moreover, after working all over Christmas, apart from 'two hours off to go and see her mother', she was nevertheless deeply grateful to be getting, the 'next week, . . . a whole half-day and a gift of money'. This made Madge (and no doubt Elinor) think of 'their own maid in England, who had demanded Christmas and Boxing Day in addition to her Sunday and weekly half-day; but . . . she knew that Gertlieb considered herself very fortunate.'

Elinor was plainly struck by the remarkable amount of work the Tyroleans did; also by the warmth of their kindness and friendliness. And it is interesting that in 1924, with the Great War not yet far behind, the English apparently were welcomed with special warmth: 'We [Austrians] are grateful to you, . . . for . . . it is the great loans that England has made to Austria that are making it possible for us to become a nation once more' — so Joey Bettany is told by a Tyrolean friend. And presumably someone must have made this same remark to Elinor, for it would be such an unlikely thing for her to have made up.

Another thing that struck Elinor, and with great force, was the poverty of the ordinary Tyrolean people. Her visit to 'the . . . [Achen] valley had taught her how pitiably poor the peasantry were'; and time after time this is emphasised in the stories. Examples are easily found:

> Most of . . . the people round about the lake . . . [depended] on the summer season for their livelihood. [Others] . . . were herdsmen, who watched the cattle up on the high alms or alpes during the summer months, but had to come down with them when the cold weather came. The cattle were housed in great byres and sheds, and only one man was required to care for them in place of two [or more] . . . The rest had to manage as best they could . . .
>
> Starvation was never very far from the door when winter came early.
>
> (*Rivals of the Chalet School*, 1929)

When that happened, as one of the herdsmen on the 'Mondscheinspitze' explains to Madge Bettany 'in his curiously hoarse tones, . . ."We all go to our homes and pray . . . for an early spring. Last winter it did not come, and some of us went hungry for a time. [But] it will be as *der liebe Gott* wills." '

The attitude implied in the last phrase — 'the curious fatalism' of people in the Tyrol — is also mentioned over and over again. And this is something not restricted to herdsmen, or farming people, or others who might be described as peasants. Herr Marani, a business man from Innsbruck (his actual occupation is in doubt, for it changes at one point between books), had 'like all his race . . . a simplicity of faith which could understand [a] . . . child's own belief'. And Elinor always lays great emphasis on the simple piety and strong religious feelings of all Tyroleans. Nor would many visitors to the Tyrol disagree with her. Even today the ordinary Tyrolean people do seem to possess these unfashionable qualities to an outstanding degree; and in the past this has often been remarked upon by writers. The latter include two very different ladies, one 19th and one 20th century, who both published books about journeys to the Tyrol.

The first was an intrepid character, Miss R. H. Busk, who in the 1870s travelled extensively in Europe and the Far East to gather the legends of many nations. In her book *The Valleys of Tirol* (1874), which was one of Elinor's treasured possessions, Miss Busk writes that, although 'the description of . . . [engineering and hydraulic works] does not come within the sphere of my present undertaking, it does, however, to observe that over this, as over everything in Tirol, religion shed its halo'.

The second, Miss Nina Murdoch, whose *Tyrolean June* (1936; an interesting if rather over-written account of 'A Summer in Austrian Tyrol') appeared sixty-two years later, says at one point that the Tyrolese are a 'people who seem really to know the secret of weaving the philosophy of Christ into the fabric of their everyday life'. And she comments on their innocent cheerfulness and their gifts of being 'quietly industrious, extraordinarily gentle, and . . . kind (amazingly kind!) . . . and [yet] shrewd, as the intelligent should be'.

Nina Murdoch, in fact, appears to agree with Elinor on every point about the Tyrolean character. And Elinor's own attitude is surely being expressed when Madge Bettany affirms: 'As for the Tyrolese, I cannot say how much I like them'.

This chapter, with its ragbag of quotations, torn out of context, does inevitably give an unbalanced impression of the books concerned. To Elinor's readers everything looked different, for they were able to absorb the information over a period, in the course of incident and dialogue. And although Elinor's descriptions can sometimes be flat or, at the other extreme, over-written, it cannot be denied that she was often most successful in recreating the scenery and special atmosphere of the Tyrol. Nor that — as put by one of Elinor's most loyal fans, Judith Humphrey — 'Miss Brent-Dyer certainly captured the imagination of vast numbers of girls to an incredible degree'.

An anecdote may serve to illustrate this point — if only in a lighthearted way. It was related by another reader, in this case not a special fan, who visited the Achen See district some years ago. She recalled with amusement that on one occasion, when the 'little white steamer' crammed with tourists was approaching Pertisau, she heard an unknown fellow-passenger exclaim to her companion 'There, look — that must be where Joey Bettany fell into the lake'.

How delighted Elinor would have been. And Lilian too might have found the incident amusing. Unfortunately, though, there can be little chance now of learning anything about her possible reactions.

CHAPTER XV

OUR LOCAL AUTHORESS

According to Elinor, in the Chalet Club's first newsletter, her idea of writing about a school beside the renamed Achen See came to her at some time following her return to England: 'Later on in the year [she explains], I decided that . . . [Pertisau] would be a lovely setting for a school story.' And maybe it did happen like that. However, in view of the extraordinary precision of the topographical details given in the early books, it seems more likely that she was still there on the spot when the plan first began forming in her mind.

She could then have talked over her plan with Lilian; and perhaps discussed with her a possible location for the Chalet School during some of their daily walks around Pertisau. To do this would have been quite in her character; for although Elinor was reserved, not to say secretive, about her personal life, it appears that she was always ready to pour forth about her books and their characters. It might even have been that Lilian unconsciously started the Chalet School rolling with some chance remark — 'Wouldn't it be lovely (or topping, or ripping) to be at a school here?' — or 'Why don't you write your next book about a school in this gorgeous place?'

The notion of placing an English school abroad was not altogether unusual in schoolgirl literature of the day. In the two years preceding Elinor's Tyrolean holiday Angela Brazil had written of a school in Italy (*The School in the South*, 1922 — mentioned in Chapter XIII) and of studies in France

(*Schoolgirl Kitty*, 1923). France is also the setting of Katherine Oldmeadow's *Princess Prunella*. And May Baldwin had for many years been establishing fictional schools all over the place; two of her earlier stories, about Germany (1901) and France (1905), were mentioned in Chapter IV; and *The School in the Wilds*, set in Kenya, was to appear at the same time as Elinor's first Chalet School book. Elsie Oxenham, too, had published several stories with continental settings: they include *Expelled from School*, *The Two Form Captains* (1921) and *The Captain of the Fifth* (1922), which all use Switzerland for their background. (And many Oxenham fans do point out, with some feeling, that when Elinor eventually linked her Chalet School with a nearby sanatorium the idea was not original, having already been used by Miss Oxenham in a number of the 'Swiss' books.)

However no one prior to Elinor seems to have chosen the Tyrol. Thus *The School at the Chalet* added an element of novelty to the proven advantages enjoyed by all fictional schools in foreign lands. One of these advantages is commented upon by the *Times Literary Supplement* critic in the issue for 26 November 1925 — where *The School at the Chalet* and a May Baldwin story share the honours. 'Adventures . . . ', according to this reviewer, 'seem more probable when they happen in Tyrol and in Kenya Colony than in Sussex, and those in these books arise naturally out of the circumstances.' Although that sentence would win no prizes for its syntax, its meaning is clear enough and the point made is an important one. Often disbelief *is* more easily suspended when a story revolves around characters in an unfamiliar setting.

The attitude of this 1925 reviewer to the whole enterprise of the Chalet School is strikingly different from that adopted in 1976 by Mary Cadogan and Patricia Craig, in their sometimes entertaining but always heavily slanted survey *You're a Brick, Angela!*

Cadogan/Craig dismiss Madge Bettany's multi-national 'non-denominational school in the Alpine Tirol' as a 'preposterous undertaking'; and by 1970s thinking they may be right. But that was not how it struck people at the time. To quote again from the *Times Literary Supplement* review:

> [Finally] we have two delightful stories of small schools in foreign lands, started by Englishwomen who are left with children dependent on them, and who feel, as so many of their like have done from the days of Mary Wollstonecraft onwards, that school-keeping is the only way open to them of at once earning for their dependents and giving them a home. These are *The School at the Chalet* by Elinor Brent-Dyer, and *The School in the Wilds* by May Baldwin, both published by Chambers at 3s. 6d. net each . . . The chief characters . . . are well described; and these [two] books will, we think, be found interesting by some parents and teachers as well as by girls.

In fact it is just possible that, given the special circumstances, a school like the Chalet School might have existed in the mid-twenties. No doubt it would have had a tougher struggle to survive in real life, and its success might have been far less spectacular. But there was after all a real school launched at about the same time as the Chalet School, which grew from an equally modest beginning in an equally astonishing fashion, and this school has now become known throughout Britain and far beyond.

The ladies who founded this establishment

started off, like Madge Bettany, with very little money (incredible as it may seem now), and also in a large, sparsely furnished house in the country — in their case, in Kent. Fifty years later, on 23 June 1973, their school celebrated its Golden Jubilee, and one of the three founders recalled the early days in words which often underline the parallel with the Chalet School:

> We started with faith and hope and very little else. We wanted to create a happy school, with personal integrity and service for others always in mind; and where everyone would be given the chance to follow her own bent, whether it was in academic or physical activities, or in the creative arts, such as drama, music, art and embroidery, or in the more practical side of life, the domestic arts.

This extract might easily come from some speech made by Madge Russell or Mademoiselle Lepattre, the co-founders of the Chalet School. But here the words were being pronounced by Miss Anne Hindle, who, with her two friends Miss Sheldon and Miss Bird, had begun the now famous Benenden School for girls half a century earlier.

Of course the remarkable and undisputed success of Benenden gives no warrant that the Chalet School, too, would have succeeded in real life; but it does provide a heartening example of one 'preposterous undertaking' that thrived against all odds.

In any case it hardly mattered to Elinor at the time whether the Chalet School was really a practical proposition or not, just so long as her readers accepted that it was. *The School at the Chalet* seems to have found an immediate welcome, being well received both by the press and — more important — by the schoolgirl audience to whom it was addressed.

Favourable comments began to arrive at the publishers; and Elinor was encouraged to plunge straight into a sequel. In fact this idea must already have been at the back of her mind, to judge from the last sentences of *The School at the Chalet*: ' "I expect we'll have some more adventures presently," said Joey. And so they did. But that, as Mr Kipling says, is another story.' Naturally it is impossible even to guess Elinor's reactions could she, at that moment, have been told there would be not just 'another story' but fifty-eight others — not to mention several related books. The prospect might well have shaken her a little, even though she was always what could be called series-minded, as shown by her first three books: these all have characters in common, many of whom appear again later in this loosely named 'La Rochelle' series. A number of the La Rochelle characters also turn up eventually in the Chalet School books. But there is one rather odd exception: Gerry Challoner, the heroine of Elinor's first book, vanishes in rather the same way as did Lilian and the real-life Madge Russell. Gerry does play a minor role in the second book, *A Head Girl's Difficulties*, but from then onwards, apart from one tiny appearance in *The Rivals of the Chalet School* (1929), she is lost to view.

Possibly Elinor felt that Gerry's character was not strong enough to stand expansion. Perhaps she simply got bored with her. And of course she did soon become much involved with, first, Janie Temple (later Mrs Lucy), the quaint-looking, quaintly spoken little heroine of *The Maids of La Rochelle*, and then with Joey Bettany, later Maynard.

In fact Joey, from near the beginning of her

existence, was to absorb the greater part of Elinor's interest and to come first in her affections; unquestionably first in so far as her writings were concerned, and to a certain extent in real life, for with Elinor the line between fiction and reality was often blurred.

Joey, paradoxically, was to provide both strength and weakness in the Chalet series. As a schoolgirl she is convincing and likeable, with plenty of faults to balance the talents and virtues lavished upon her. Her character, as Margery Fisher remarks in *Who's Who in Children's Books*, is treated in some depth; and the early books contain a leaven of humour which allows her to remain a human schoolgirl.

So long, then, as Joey is of school age, or near it, all is well. Unfortunately by the fourteenth book she has reached the age of twenty-two and is married with three small children. (The grown-up heroines of schoolgirl fiction frequently produce twins but Joey trumps all aces by having triplets.) This by rights should debar her from playing the lead in a school story. Yet because Joey is Elinor's dearest character, and moreover has always been the lynchpin of the stories, she cannot be allowed to go into retirement and get on with producing her own books — and children. With the result, aptly described by the Cadogan/Craig team as the 'artificial prolongation of Joey's connection with the school', that Joey is condemned to spend the next forty-four books as an ever less and less convincing adult.

For many readers Joey, when grown-up, gradually becomes less a character than a collection of stereotypes, designed to evoke admiration: a woman of unusual insight and boundless compassion; an incredibly successful writer and at the same time a wife and mother of inexhaustible patience (she needed to be with eleven children, but nothing in her girlhood would have led one to expect it); a friend of wonderfully sympathetic understanding and steadfast loyalty (which does at least constitute a logical development); a mature adult, though still at heart a schoolgirl with a would-be delicious dottiness and sense of fun. It is all quite simply too good to be true. Or so it might seem; although it does have to be conceded that Joey — and the adult Joey Maynard as well as the schoolgirl Joey Bettany — has remained fantastically popular with Elinor's readers.

But all this is running much too far ahead. At the time of the second Chalet School story — which could be considered among the best of them all — Jo was only thirteen, and still very much a lively and amusing schoolgirl.

This book, *Jo of the Chalet School* (1926), contains less that is obviously autobiographical than its predecessor did; but certain things may plausibly be linked with the author's personal life. For instance, it is during this story that the Chalet School is introduced to folk dancing, still a fairly new hobby of Elinor's at the time. And it is here that the first reference to Ernest Farrar (quoted in Chapter VII) can be found — though not as yet by name.

The book contains also the first mention of Girl Guides, which makes it likely that at this period Elinor was herself beginning to take an interest in the Guide movement. And it could be that during 1925 or 1926 she, like Madge Bettany, attended a course at Foxlease — the Girl Guide training centre in the New Forest. Foxlease was just round the corner from Fareham, and even during term-time Elinor could easily have gone there for a weekend.

Guiding was to be important in one of her books that is unconnected with any series, *Judy the Guide*, published in 1928. It was also to be a regular feature of the earlier Chalet School stories, including some of those written in the 1940s. Later on Elinor seems characteristically to have lost interest in the subject.

How far Elinor was personally involved with the Guide movement, and for how long, is not clear. She writes in one of the Chalet Club newsletters: 'I greatly enjoyed my own Guiding days', which could imply that she had herself been a Girl Guide in her youth. But the Girl Guides did not come into existence until 1909, by which time Elinor was fifteen; and although it is not impossible that South Shields was among the first places in Britain to start a Guide company, it seems unlikely on the whole that Guiding was available locally during Elinor's schooldays.

However it now appears that, following her return to the north-east in or around 1926, Elinor briefly ran a Guide company, connected with St Michael's Church. This information was imparted by an elderly lady in South Shields, who had been in her early teens at the time, and recalled that Elinor had often tried to persuade her into joining the company, but with no sucess because, as a great fan of Elsie Oxenham, she 'wanted only to be a Camp Fire girl'. And later Elinor did also act as Captain of the '1st Herefordshire Lone Ranger Company' — 'Lone Guides' being the branch established for girls living in isolated places, without access to regular meetings, who were sent a monthly circular letter to keep them in touch with Guiding.

Apart from this, Elinor must also have had personal experience of a Guide camp, for underneath one of her poems — 'A Guide Hymn' — appear the words: 'In camp. 6.viii.26'. And this helps to explain why the eighth story in the Chalet School series, *The Chalet Girls in Camp*, succeeds in creating a sufficiently authentic atmosphere to convince many readers who are themselves active and experienced in Guiding.

For the most part, Elinor's books tell little about Girl Guides that could not have been learnt second-hand. Nor do they reveal why, or at what point exactly, she decided that the time had come for her to leave Hampshire and take herself back home to South Shields — for this in fact is what she did, most probably in the autumn of 1926.

Her reasons for leaving Western House are not hard to deduce: by all accounts she had been growing more and more discontented with her job there for some time past. And she must surely have jumped at the chance of bidding her landlady farewell. But it does seem odd that once again she should throw away independence and run back to mother, not to mention stepfather. The conclusion must be that Elinor found certain other things more important than independence: foremost among them, an opportunity to concentrate on her writing, unfettered by the demands of a full-time job.

And this, it appears, she did gain by her return home; for although the evidence is scanty, what there is indicates that, in the period between 1926/27 and 1933, Elinor did no regular teaching. She did apparently undertake occasional supply work in different local schools; and she actually spent a while teaching English, singing and country dancing at her own old school, the Misses Stewart's in Westoe Village. Whether this was an entirely happy experience for either side is questionable. Elinor possibly found some satisfaction, even wry amusement, in returning to St Nicholas's as a 'local-girl-makes-good', with the right to be accepted where before she had perhaps felt something of an outsider. But was she really accepted? By the children, quite probably. One ex-pupil, Lucy Grimes, then about ten years old, who has now become a professional writer herself, remembers being encouraged by Elinor, who awarded her the prize in an essay competition. The subject was 'Kindness to Animals'; the prize, a copy of the latest Chalet book.

Nevertheless even she, young as she was, looked upon Elinor as 'quite a bizarre character'. Nor was she alone in this: another former pupil recalled with great amusement how Elinor used to stand on a chair when conducting their singing class, to the delight of the small boys seated on the floor in front of her, since they were thus afforded a splendid view of her scarlet bloomers . . . And there is no lack of evidence that people in South Shields continued to think of Elinor as 'a very eccentric and different sort of person'. Mrs Olga Hargreaves, who as a schoolgirl was one of the dedicatees of *Rivals of the Chalet School*, retains vivid memories:

> I can see her now, striding into the room, her Alsatian at her heels. [This was 'Bryn', a much loved Alsatian bitch of Elinor's, of whom more in Chapter XIX.] Elinor, with her wandering eye, flamboyant manner and bizarre clothes was often a source of amusement, though never malicious, but also of pride. She was 'our' Authoress. And we didn't expect her, as an authoress, to be 'normal'!

On the other hand, the two Miss Stewarts appear to have had grave reservations about Elinor, which is hardly surprising in view of their circumstances and background. In their eyes it would have mattered little that their former pupil was now a qualified teacher; still less that she had been dubbed by the press 'our local authoress'.

This, at any rate, was the impression conveyed by

a very much younger relative of the two old ladies (she had long ago left South Shields, but was still living there during the twenties and thirties). When asked about Elinor's connection with St Nicholas's, she wrote: 'I'm afraid that I am not able to help you about May Dyer . . . She returned [to the school] for *one term*, I think . . . to teach country dancing . . . But I am sure my aunts would not have considered having her [permanently] on the staff. And she added the somewhat deflating comment: 'I know that she wrote books, but my children did not care about them.'

And that would appear to be that. But then Elinor's methods would hardly have appealed to teachers of the Victorian generation. Although apparently her classroom technique was effective, as an ex-pupil of Western House recalled in the 1970s to Marjorie Jewell: 'My friend did not like Elinor but admired her capacity for dominating a class. As she put it, Elinor did not so much *teach* as act in front of the class.'

Anyway, successful or otherwise, Elinor's days as a teacher at St Nicholas's seem to have extended to only about a term, for there is no doubt that during the late twenties and early thirties most of her time and energies went into her writing (apart from one activity, of which more in a moment). And to Elinor's credit she did at least make good use of all the free hours she gained once re-installed in that attic bedsitter at 5 Belgrave Terrace. The chronological list of her publications shows that until this point she had managed only one book a year, making a total of five published between 1922 and 1926 — no bad effort either, in the midst of a busy teaching career, especially when the shortest contained 248 pages. But now, in 1927 alone, she was to produce three books, all extremely full-length (around

75,000 words); and in 1928 another three. Moreover she was also involved during this period in editing, and frequently writing herself, a column for the *Shields Gazette*, the local daily newspaper. This, rather surprisingly, quite often required her attendance at social functions, such as the annual Ingham Infirmary ball, and the writing of the detailed reports on the ladies' dresses.

Of course the quality of that whirlwind half-dozen books of 1927 and 1928 is uneven. Two of the six are frankly poor (*Judy the Guide* and *The New House-Mistress*); but two are vintage Chalet School examples (*The Princess of the Chalet School* and *The Head Girl of the Chalet School*); and both the others (*Seven Scamps* and *A Thrilling Term at Janeways*) are good average.

The last named, set in a school which Elinor would use again ten years later in *Caroline the Second*, is of passing interest because of its dedication 'To Mother and Dad'. In this context and at this date (1927) 'Dad' can only mean Septimus Ainsley — although in fact Elinor seems always to have spoken of, and to him, as 'Steppy'. So perhaps Elinor at this time had softened the tiniest bit towards her stepfather. Or perhaps, and more likely, she thought this a politic gesture towards the owner of the house where she was now living again.

After all it was undoubtedly due, at least in part, to Septimus Ainsley that Elinor could devote so much time during these years to writing. Not only was she able to produce fifteen published books between 1927 and 1933, she also wrote a full-length novel, *Jean of Storms*, which was serialised during the spring and summer of 1930 in the *Shields Gazette*. This story, which to date has not been published in book form, has several features that are unusual for Elinor. In the first place, it is set in the north-east, in the country around South Shields; and indeed the advance publicity in the paper made much of the fact that this was 'A Local Serial by a Local Writer', and that the author was 'a South Shields Lady, an accomplished writer who has a number of books to her credit'. This novel, they proclaimed, 'has a strong local colouring [and] . . . will make appeal to both young and old'. But perhaps the greatest surprise comes at the end of the advance announcement, which promises that the story has 'AN ABSORBING LOVE INTEREST'.

Jean of Storms is definitely not a children's book. Nor does it, despite its local north-east setting, follow the Catherine Cookson tradition, but is best described as a light romantic novel. It embraces many of Elinor's pet subjects, including folk dancing, Girl Guides, illness (a bout of influenza being apparently regarded as quite a serious event), and a characteristically dramatic cliff-top rescue scene. It is of interest, too, that many of the principal characters have had connections with India; raising the unanswered question of why India held such an extraordinary fascination for Elinor. No personal connection has ever been traced, but the Chalet School stories show frequent mentions of India: Madge, Dick and Joey Bettany, not to mention Juliet Carrick and others, have all been born there, and Dick continues to work in the Indian Forestry Commision until nearly half-way through the series. But this is digressing . . .

Yet another opportunity Elinor enjoyed during this period of the late twenties and early thirties — and once again this opportunity could perhaps be credited to Mr Ainsley — was that of finding time for further study in music, something which had always been one of her castles-in-the-air. There seems no question that Elinor had any great practical abilities in music. According to one of her franker and more musically expert friends, 'she never played at all well. It was always very inaccurate, with faults both in notes and time values'. (A possible link here between Elinor and Joey Bettany, at whom the Chalet School's irascible Herr Anserl 'raved for her lack of a sense of time'.) But Elinor's sheer enthusiasm for music is not in dispute. And it is no surprise that she should now, even at thirty-plus, have embarked on a formal course of music study in Newcastle — which is only eleven miles from South Shields.

At this time there was a rather grandly named institution there, the Newcastle Conservatoire of Music. It was really just a smallish private school of music, but it did have as its director Dr Edgar Bainton, a musician of considerable standing. Under his guidance the school had achieved a good reputation and it can safely be assumed that there were some promising performers among the students in Elinor's day. And it was, in all probability, this rubbing shoulders with the talented young that helped more than anything to open Elinor's eyes musically. Thus, although her studies in singing, cello and of course piano, which she was taught by Edgar Bainton himself, wrought no miracles in her own performances, they did give her far more insight than she could ever have gained in any other way. (See Chapter IV.)

The Newcastle Conservatoire has also a tenuous link with Elinor's books in that one of them, *The School by the River* (1930), is dedicated 'To my music master, Edgar L. Bainton'. And the book itself possibly owes something to Elinor's studies in Newcastle, for it centres round a music school, although in this case a residential one in an imaginary land, the Balkan Kingdom of Mirania.

(This fictional kingdom was to reappear many years later in the Chalet School series, when, in one of the involved link-ups Elinor enjoyed so much, Elisaveta, the Princess of the Chalet School, would marry Raphael Mirolani, a nephew of the Queen of Mirania.)

The School by the River, which has the distinction of being the rarest title among all Elinor's books, relates the fortunes of a gifted young music student, Jennifer Craddock, and of other starry talents at the Collège des Musiciens. Here, in the words of one critic, 'The pupils are too busy practising sonatas to play the usual pranks on Mademoiselle, and it is refreshing to read about a heroine who does *not* save the school from fire or flood, and distinguishes herself on the concert platform instead of the hockey field'. This critic, who was writing in *The Tablet* in the issue of 28 June 1930, obviously liked *The School by the River*, for the review ends 'We recommend this book because it is a story about really nice young folks, and also because of the virtue — rare in modern school tales — that every incident is not only possible but probable.'

But in sharp contrast the *Observer* of 27 June 1930 wrote *The School by the River* . . . is rather silly and rather snobbish but, fortunately, quite improbable'. Which goes to show that it all depends on where you're standing. And Elinor must have appreciated the joke, for she placed the two notices prominently side by side in her book of press cuttings. Probable or improbable, *The School by the River* is now completely unobtainable — partly as a result of air-raids suffered by the publishers during the last war. But this is no great matter, for today the book's only real significance in Elinor's life story is that it appeared during the year 1930. And that, for her, was to be a specially important year.

CHAPTER XVI

'IT'S ONLY ONE OF THE ROADS TO GOD'

The School by the River, which was published in June 1930, was followed two months later by the sixth of the Chalet series, *Eustacia Goes to the Chalet School*. 'This story . . . should receive a warm welcome', said the *Journal of Education*; and *The Spectator* agreed that, 'All who have enjoyed the Chalet School series will welcome [it] . . . '

'Distinctly better than the average school story [said *Scottish Country Life*], for . . . there are real live characters.' And *The Scotsman*, with true Edinburgh briskness, announced that this was 'An exhilarating story in every respect, with plenty of open air about it'.

The *Guardian* (then the *Manchester Guardian*) thought it 'among the best of the [year's] school stories', adding that 'Those unfortunates who have not yet visited the Chalet School are advised to do so without further delay'.

'Miss Elinor Brent-Dyer . . . has given us a book of the high quality we expect from her,' said the *Irish Times*. And certainly Elinor and her publishers could not have complained of any lack of press coverage, for by this time newspapers as far afield as Christchurch, New Zealand, were giving her reviews.

The *Christian World* summed up Elinor's position at the time in saying: 'Quite a number of readers will need nothing more than the mention of the title and authoress to send them flying round to the nearest bookshop'; and this review gives some measure of how fast things had moved for Elinor. It was still not quite eight years since the publication of *Gerry Goes to School*, but she had now travelled from total obscurity to join the best-known writers of schoolgirl fiction. Not, it is true, the most prolific: fifteen books in eight years left her well behind Elsie Oxenham, for instance, who had published twenty-four during the same period. Nor had Elinor yet reached the position she would eventually hold, alongside Angela Brazil, Elsie Oxenham and Dorita Fairlie Bruce, as one of schoolgirl literature's Big Four. Nevertheless, by 1930 she could justifiably have claimed to be in the Top Ten.

There were other ways in which her life had changed since those Christmas holidays of 1922 when she had been writing *Gerry Goes to School* and reading it aloud, chapter by chapter, to the small Hazel Bainbridge. And her thinking, in particular in one important direction, had altered significantly, as proved by the step she took on Friday 12 December 1930. That day, at the Church of St Bede's in Westoe Road, South Shields, she was formally received into the Roman Catholic Church.

Elinor had been brought up in the Church of England and, on the evidence of various friends, had always been a practising member of that Church. And it is not possible to trace with certainty the path she followed in arriving at her decision to change. Nor to say with absolute assurance that the decision was reached, not suddenly, but over a period of some years. However, there are indications in her books that she may have been considering the idea for a long time, possibly ever since her visit to Austria in 1924.

The manner in which she writes of religious matters in her recently discovered adult novel, *Jean of Storms*, conveys a hint that Elinor could at this time have turned against certain more fundamentalist ideas; and this story was of course written during exactly the period when Elinor was finally deciding to become a Roman Catholic. It has also been suggested that during the late 1920s Elinor may have had some contact with the nuns of the La Sagesse convent in Newcastle — perhaps at the time when she was visiting the city regularly in connection with her musical studies. Today this cannot be definitely established, but a personal contact with the La Sagesse nuns would certainly help to explain why, later on in the Chalet School series, Robin Humphries chooses to join this particular order of religious sisters, which has never previously had any connection with the stories.

On one point there can be no doubt: Catholics in the Tyrol must have given Elinor an entirely new impression of their Church. She had grown up as a Protestant in Tyneside, where at the time there was little understanding between Protestants and Catholics. Indeed, bigotry and sheer ill-will often existed on both sides — as may be gathered from some of the books of Catherine Cookson, a best-selling writer — very different from Elinor — who also grew up in South Shields during the early decades of this century.

Mrs Cookson was brought up on the Roman Catholic side of the fence. And probably she would be among those few who can really understand the magnitude of the step that Elinor took when, brought up as she had been, she crossed that fence in the year 1930. For most people of the present time it is difficult to appreciate this fully.

Nowadays the word ecumenical is hard-worked. An Archbishop of Canterbury visits the Pope, and the Pope pays a return visit to Canterbury Cathedral, where a joint Church of England and

Roman Catholic service is held. A Roman Catholic cardinal preaches in Westminster Abbey, and inter-denominational services have now become familiar in most parts of Britain. Hence there is a tendency today to forget that the active, even violent expression of sectarian prejudice has not always been confined to Northern Ireland. Liverpool and Glasgow, for instance, have long records of interdenominational clashes, and in the latter city feelings between the supporters of two famous football clubs, one Protestant, one Catholic, can still run so high that it was considered a remarkable event when a Roman Catholic was appointed to a high office in the Protestant club. And surely it must be significant that football clubs should have religious affiliations at all.

On the other side of the country, in Edinburgh, there was considerable anti-Catholic rioting during the 1930s — only a few years after Elinor joined the Catholic Church. Contemporary newspapers give startling accounts of violence at public meetings; and it appears that, in the summer of 1935, the schoolchildren at a convent in the suburbs of Edinburgh actually had to have police protection during a religious procession through the convent's own private grounds.

Prejudice, of course, works both ways. And that it has not altogether disappeared even in more recent times is the unhappy experience of many. Among them a Roman Catholic nun, Sister Prudence Wilson RSCJ, who, after twenty years teaching in the south of England, went in the 1970s to be head of a college in Elinor's native Tyneside. Here she was 'often astonished and saddened to see the lack of understanding that could be shown by apparently good Catholics towards their Protestant neighbours'.

But perhaps it is hardly surprising that goodwill between the Churches should be slow in growth. After all, until the mid-1960s Roman Catholics were strictly forbidden to attend the services of other denominations — as any Catholic over a certain age will undoubtedly recall. What is more, they were enjoined with much severity that if ever they found themselves obliged to enter a Protestant church, perhaps for the wedding of a relative or close friend, they must hold themselves aloof from the service and let no word of any hymn or prayer — even the Lord's Prayer — escape their lips.

In schools, too, there were invariably barriers set up between Protestant and Catholics; and, today anyone reading *The School at the Chalet* must bear this in mind in order to understand Madge Bettany's dilemma at the opening of the Chalet School. On that morning, the nine girls who then made up the school's entire complement have assembled in 'the first of the big schoolrooms'. And their headmistress, having ' welcomed them all . . . [found that] prayers were something of a difficulty, since all the Tyrolese girls, and also Simone [French], were Roman Catholics, while she and Joey and Grizel were Church of England. For the present, she solved it by a short reading from Thomas à Kempis, and the Lord's Prayer said in Latin. "But I must hurry up and decide what we are going to do about it," she thought.'

Today this particular 'difficulty' would not exist. But, at the time, the only acceptable solution, in real life as well as fiction, would have been to adopt the arrangement that became traditional at the Chalet School, where 'Prayers was always a dual affair . . . As it [the school] had begun in a Catholic country, it had been necessary to separate the girls for religious teaching . . . Miss Wilson, as second-mistress and a Catholic, always took Prayers for the Catholics; while Miss Annersley, the Head, and a staunch member of the Church of England, did the same office for the Protestants.'

This custom was to persist at the Chalet School. And descriptions similar to the above (from *Lavender Laughs in the Chalet School*, 1943) can be found in a majority of the Chalet books up to and including the fifty-seventh of the series, which was published in 1969. But here Elinor betrays a certain failure to move with the times, for by 1969 Catholics and Protestants in a real-life boarding school would probably have been holding joint prayers.

However there is nothing remarkable in anyone of her age (Elinor had reached her seventies in 1964) being slow to change. The unexpected thing in Elinor is that, when younger, she had been quite unusually forward-looking and also tolerant in her own religious outlook. And, interestingly, in this respect her change from Protestant to Catholic brought no discernible change of attitude. At least, it appears to be impossible for anyone to guess from her books alone, even approximately the year in which she became a Catholic.

Nowadays there would probably be widespread agreement with the point of view expressed by Joey Bettany when, during an argument, she defends the Catholic Church although, at the time, still a member herself of the Church of England: ' . . . after all, . . . it's only *one* of the roads to God. If you think that way, then it's best for you. If you think another way, then *that's* best. But they all go to the same end.' Yet in 1930, when Elinor wrote the words for Joey to speak (in *Eustacia Goes to the Chalet School*), the ecumenical idea they embody was years ahead of its time.

And it is because Elinor did have a different

attitude from many of her contemporaries that her school stories differ from others in an important way. Up until the coming of the Chalet School, in 1925, the typical schoolgirl of fiction — or, for that matter, schoolboy — had been a Protestant, and more often than not a member of the Church of England. Angela Brazil's girls, for instance, are Church of England to a man — stroke person. Even when their school is situated in a Catholic country, as happens in *The School in the South*, they still 'On Sundays . . . paraded to the British Church [which] . . . the school liked [although] . . . It was so utterly different from anything to which they had been accustomed in England or America . . . [being] simply a big room in the basement of the Hotel Anglais . . .' (Indeed, where else?)

Thus the whole concept of Elinor's Chalet School, with its high proportion of Roman Catholic girls associating happily and on equal terms with Protestants, must have seemed revolutionary to schoolgirl readers of the time. On the other hand, readers then would have found nothing unusual in the strong religious feeling which, to a greater or lesser degree, permeates all Elinor's books. A religious element was considered an almost obligatory ingredient of pre-war schoolgirl fiction; and all the best-known writers in the genre had their own ways of bringing religion into their stories.

Today some people find this side of Elinor's writings totally off-putting; among them, predictably, Mary Cadogan and Patricia Craig, the authors of *You're a Brick, Angela!* (1976), who declare that: 'A serious weakness of the Chalet School series is the religious sentimentality which [so they inform us] accompanies each episode of physical danger.'

Now the two parts of this pronouncement require

separate consideration. The first can in itself pass muster, even if one disagrees. The second is simply inaccurate. A reader need look no further than the episode (in *The Rivals of the Chalet School*) cited only two pages earlier by these same authors, where Joey '[drags] a foolhardy skater out of an icebound river [sic]'. This rescue is unquestionably fraught with physical danger, but Elinor's paragraphs describing it contain not one sentence that could possibly be construed as religious.

And although Chalet girls in danger do sometimes have audible recourse to prayer (a reaction not absolutely unknown in real life), innumerable hair-raising emergencies occur where they do not. But then neither is it exact that 'In the first five books Joey . . . [comes] near to death herself only *once*'; nor is the Tiern/Achen See a 'river'.

However there is no denying that a vein of sentimentality exists in Elinor's books. Nor that it sometimes comes to the surface in her *manner* of writing about religious matters. But of course it does also in connection with many subjects: friendships, schooldays, families, engagements, marriage, babies, loyalty and patriotism are among them.

Here, it is important once again to remember the passing of time, for certainly Elinor does not exceed in her modes of expression other writers of her type and period. Angela Brazil, for one, whose books are often filled with a far more cloying sentimentality. And both Elsie Oxenham and Dorita Fairlie Bruce were in their different ways capable of greater extremes in sentimental writing. As to the affirmation of religious and moral principles that underlies all Elinor's stories, it is plain that a majority of her readers, past and present, have felt this to be sincere. Further, that many have derived from it a genuine sense of security. Three letters from three different periods may be quoted here as being typical of many others. The first correspondent, who described herself in 1975 as 'now middle-aged', had been a Chalet fan from childhood; she wrote in special praise of the 'sense of deeply held religious views [which is] running through the series, without the books being at all "pi".' The second, also an admirer from her early years, wrote in the 1960s to thank Elinor, not just 'for writing the Chalet books' but specifically for their 'religious aspect'; and she explains that, after 'a long time [when] I . . . suffered from lack of faith, the fact that characters I admired so much in [your books] . . . were Christians inspired me to try to rediscover my faith'. The third, who at the time of writing was in her early thirties, made the point that although 'the verbal expression can sometimes be coy and perhaps sentimental, the underlying faith and trust are not. It is the trust and faith to which . . . [the readers] are responding and in which they find hope and support.'

There is also evidence in letters concerning a particular passage in *The Head Girl of the Chalet School* (1928) where some lines were singled out for unfavourable mention by the writers of *You're a Brick, Angela!* (who were, to be fair, writing in the extremely unsympathetic climate of the mid-1970s, and might perhaps be less severe today).

To put the scene in context: Joey and Grizel, aged fifteen and seventeen at this point, are staying with Joey's sister Madge, whose husband James Russell is a doctor; on this particular evening they have just heard some bad news about a patient of Doctor Russell's; and, as they sit with books in front of them:

> [Joey's] thoughts were all on that mysterious thing that was happening at the sanatorium.

> Madge divined it as soon as she entered the room . . . 'Joey, you need not be sorry for this poor fellow. He has nothing to live for, and he will be joining those he loved best to-night. The priest was here this morning, and he is prepared.'
>
> The two girls came and sat on the floor beside her.
>
> 'Madame, what is death?' asked Grizel suddenly.
>
> 'Just falling asleep with God — to awake in His presence — that's all,' said Madge Russell quietly.
>
> 'Then why are we afraid of it?'
>
> 'Because it means a change, and most of us are afraid of changes that we don't understand. But, Grizel, there is nothing to fear, really, any more than there is anything to fear when we fall asleep at night.'
>
> Grizel sat silent, thinking this over.
>
> 'God is with us through it all?' asked Joey.
>
> 'Yes, Jo. He never leaves us if we have faith in Him.'

It was those lines about 'falling asleep to wake with God' that incurred the censure of the Cadogan/Craig team. And perhaps no one would claim that this description of death, with its echoes of Victorian tombstones, was particularly striking or original. But it should not be forgotten that *The Head Girl of the Chalet School* was written in 1928 and within the conventions of a particular genre. Bearing all this in mind, it must be allowed that the passage quoted above represents an honest attempt by Elinor to grapple with a universal problem: that of facing death.

Even today the particular form of reassurance that Madge offers to the younger girls would not be rejected by everyone. And Elinor's fan mail makes it clear that the phrase about death did in fact make a special appeal to many of her readers. One, who was a young nurse during the World War II air-raids on London wrote that she could remember finding 'comfort for . . . [herself] and others' in the words. And surely nurses working in the Blitz cannot have retained any sentimental illusions about death.

Another fan, the writer of an article about Elinor which appeared in *The Scotsman* in February 1970, voiced particular appreciation of the way that 'in each [book] Miss Brent-Dyer managed to convey her own clear-cut moral values, her belief in loving kindness towards our immediate circle and then outwards into the world beyond'.

On the other hand there were some, right from the beginning, who would not have agreed. One, who is now herself a well-known writer for children, recalls that although in her youth she liked some of the early Chalet School stories, 'even those were too religious for me'.

However she does go on to make an interesting point concerning this over-religious side, as she found it, of certain books — (she mentions also E. J. Oxenham's 'Abbey' series): 'somehow that rolled over me when I was young. I just thought it odd and left it at that.' And this last describes neatly a typical child reader's capacity for selection; something that may well explain why so many children today, including the growing number who have had no formal religious upbringing, continue to enjoy reading Elinor's books.

One thing does not admit of question: despite her sometimes dated phraseology, Elinor herself, whether as a member of the Church of England or as a Roman Catholic, emerges from her writings as a firm believer, and someone to whom religion mattered greatly. No one could read her books with an open mind and fail to be convinced of that.

As an ending to this chapter, mention should be made of another event that took place in the year 1930, since undoubtedly it was important to Elinor and might conceivably have influenced her decision to join the Catholic Church. This was the world-famous Passion Play at Oberammergau.

A visit by the Chalet School to Oberammergau forms a central part of *The Chalet School and Jo*, which was published in 1931. And in this seventh Chalet School story Elinor gives detailed descriptions of Oberammergau and its surroundings, and devotes a whole chapter to an account of the Passion Play.

So the question naturally arises as to whether she herself had been to Oberammergau. The descriptive passages in *The Chalet School and Jo* do suggest that the author had some personal experience, both of the place and of the Passion Play itself. And certainly it would have been possible for Elinor to have made the visit. Performances at Oberammergau normally take place in only one year out of ten, but 1930, when she was engaged in writing *The Chalet School and Jo*, was in fact a year when the play was given.

At this time, too, Elinor could have afforded the expedition quite easily. Living at home as she was, her day-to-day expenses were presumably minimal. And bearing in mind that a rail trip to Oberammergau, as advertised in a 1930 *Shields Gazette*, was available for a mere £4, the copyright payment on just one of her books (£40 at this stage for the Chalet School stories) could have paid the necessary travelling and other expenses several times over. The advertisement even mentioned special arrangements for travel direct from South Shields, and it would be hard to imagine that Elinor did not see this advertisement, since at this time she was writing regularly for the *Shields Gazette*.

Another piece of circumstantial evidence that Elinor had seen the Passion Play was provided by two of her younger acquaintances in South Shields, Olga Hargreaves and her sister, who recalled visiting her towards the end of 1930 and seeing her room filled with souvenirs of Oberammergau and the Passion Play. Both were convinced that Elinor had been there. However, in the end it has to be said that no definite proof exists — one way or the other. And the verdict, as so often with Elinor, must remain 'Not Proven'.

CHAPTER XVII

'MY NEW HOME IN THE WEST COUNTRY'

According to the British Library's catalogue, *The Chalet School and Jo* was the only book by Elinor to be published in 1931. But a school story entitled *The Feud in the Fifth Remove* did almost certainly appear that year; and this otherwise unremarkable book thus has the distinction of being one of the few that have ever escaped the British Library's net.

In the following year there were additions to both the La Rochelle and Chalet series (*Janie of La Rochelle*; *The Chalet Girls in Camp*); and also a children's historical novel, *The Little Marie-José*.

The latter represented a new departure for Elinor. For although *My Lady Caprice*, the first of the two plays she wrote for the Bainbridges, had been a costume drama, and she had also written at least one short story with a period setting (*The Yellow Gown* published in a 1925 children's annual), *The Little Marie-José* falls into quite a different category from any of these earlier efforts.

By the standards of the day it was not a long book — only 170 pages, whereas five of the Chalet series to date had contained over 300. But it was of sufficient size and also sufficiently well researched and serious in approach to merit consideration as an historical novel, if a slight one, not just as a children's story in costume setting. And yet Elinor herself (in a letter written in the 1960s to one of her editors at William Collins) described *The Little Marie-José* only as 'an historical tale', bracketing it with *The Little Missus* (1942), which, though quite charming in its way, is a much lesser book in both size and content. On the other hand, she did apply the term 'historical novel' to her *Elizabeth the Gallant*, published by Thornton Butterworth in 1935.

Today it is not easy to see why Elinor thought this romantic adventure story, set in the times of Cavaliers and Roundheads, a more significant work than *The Little Marie-José*. Still less easy to understand why both Elinor and the publishers apparently considered *Elizabeth the Gallant* to be an adult book. True the story does take its heroine right past the altar to her wedding-night, and beyond . . . even though in a heavily discreet and inexplicit way ('Lionel led his bride to the great room . . . Suddenly he caught her in his arms. "My beloved!" he whispered. She lay against him like a nested bird, and there was silence, deep and sweet, in the bridal chamber.'). So perhaps that was enough in the 1930s to render *Elizabeth the Gallant* unsuitable for children. Certainly, when the story was later adapted for publication in a schoolgirls' annual, all passages like the above were expunged.

By the time that *Elizabeth the Gallant* was published in 1935 a major change had taken place in Elinor's circumstances, which is indicated in the book's dedication. But, before coming to this, another matter should first be mentioned in order to keep Elinor's story more or less in chronological order.

It appears that during the year 1931 Elinor fell violently and hopelessly in love. Or perhaps it would be more exact, if less kind, to describe her state as infatuation, since there is no evidence that any close relationship existed between her and the man in question. But at least there is no doubt in this case (unlike that of 'Hugh' in the First World War) that Donald Edwards really did exist: he was an actor and belonged to a repertory company that was resident at the time in South Shields.

This apart, little enough is known about the episode, for apparently the only friend in whom Elinor confided anything was Hazel Bainbridge. And even she was not told very much.

Hazel, by 1931, had left school to become a full-time actress. And that summer a production in which she was playing the lead went on an extensive provincial tour. One of the places they visited was Newcastle upon Tyne; and, this being within easy reach of South Shields, Hazel accepted an invitation to stay with Elinor and the Ainsleys at 5 Belgrave Terrace.

On a superficial level Hazel remembers two things about that visit: one, the quite remarkable amount of tea that was drunk in the household, with cups of tea not only accompanying every meal but appearing at frequent intervals in between times; the other, that even more cats seemed to be around than there had been during her childhood.

But her main and important memory is of the way that, at intervals throughout the week, 'Len would pour forth about this man, this actor of hers that she was so taken up with'. Whenever Hazel and Elinor were alone together the subject would come up, sooner or later. And yet, despite all the outpourings, Hazel never managed to gather if Elinor and this man really knew each other well. Donald Edwards was clearly some years younger than Elinor, who was then thirty-seven; and judging from the signed photograph that was kept in Len's bed-sitter, he was extremely good-looking. Moreover, the fact that he was already happily married was apparently known, though possibly not to Elinor.

One way and another, Hazel, even at the time, got an impression that 'the whole thing was probably far more on Len's side'.

Probably she was right. After all the photograph, as Hazel points out, could have been obtained quite easily from the theatre. And the fact that Elinor 'spent a lot of time that week in crotcheting a white silk evening scarf' destined for Donald Edwards, does not provide evidence of anything but her own feelings and state of mind.

In any case it seems quite clear that nothing came of the affair — if it can be so called. Except that Elinor did work harder than ever at her writing, producing three full-length books in 1932 — the first year with three since 1928. And in one of the three, *Janie of La Rochelle*, it is possible with hindsight to see compensation at work.

With the best will in the world, *Janie of La Rochelle* could not be considered a very good book, even when every allowance is made for its type and period. Described in one review as 'a love idyll', it is not a genuine adult book nor yet a children's story, but hovers uneasily between the two — being possibly intended at the time for the 'older teenager'. But today a sympathetic reader who knows the background may perhaps find a touch of poignancy in Elinor's descriptions of the newly wedded couple and their happiness, and even in the rather stilted little fragments of dialogue which they exchange. (To be fair, lovers' dialogue is not often distinguished in real life for its originality.)

> 'Oh, Julian . . . I am so happy that I want to burst with happiness!'
>
> 'So am I, Janie — very happy, darling. This is the best day of my life.'

And at least Elinor does allow the happy pair to be 'most unromantically hungry', even if 'there was no lack of sentiment in the looks they exchanged over the tea-table . . . '

Janie of La Rochelle was the sixth book in a series which had begun ten years previously with Elinor's first story, *Gerry Goes to School*. And for almost twenty-one years it was not to have a successor — Elinor having in the mean time absorbed many of the characters into her Chalet series. Then in 1953, *Janie Steps In* appeared, and Elinor wrote to her friend, Mrs Phyllis Matthewman:

> Dearest Phyllis,
>
> *Janie of La Rochelle* was dedicated to the memory of Auntie Annie, who used to encourage both of us in our early writing days — I might say our earliest writing days. [Auntie Annie was Miss Annie M. Barton, and she was really Phyllis's aunt, not Elinor's. It was she who had first introduced Phyllis and Elinor — as described in Chapter III.]
>
> She never lived to see what we both accomplished [Phyllis Matthewman had also become a successful writer], but I think she would like to know that . . . I am dedicating this latest of the La Rochelle series to you.

Elinor was keen on dedications and a majority of her books are provided with them. Some are quite elaborate, and many contain autobiographical touches. The dedication of *Elizabeth the Gallant*, referred to above, is one of these: ' . . . TO ALL THOSE FRIENDS IN THE WEST COUNTRY WHO HAVE GIVEN ME WELCOME TO MY NEW HOME AND HAVE HELPED TO MAKE IT

PLEASANT TO ME'.

In fact, at the time *Elizabeth the Gallant* appeared Elinor must have been living in her 'new home' for nearly two years; for it seems likely that her move from South Shields to Hereford took place some time during 1933. That, at any rate, would fit in with the recollections of a Hereford lady, who went away to study at college early in 1934 and is clear that Elinor had arrived well before that.

The reasons for the move are not obvious. For Elinor it may have been a case of 'needs must': if her mother and stepfather were going to settle in Hereford, and she wanted to accompany them, that was that. But why Nelly and Septimus Ainsley, at the ages of sixty-four and rising sixty-eight, should have decided to give up their home in South Shields and go to live elsewhere is obscure. The most convincing reason to be suggested is that the climate in South Shields was considered too harsh for Mr Ainsley; and undoubtedly that exposed corner of the north-east could be trying for anyone in poor health, as Mr Ainsley appears always to have been. But there is no way of being sure about this. Nor as to whether the particular choice of Hereford was made purely for health reasons. Septimus Ainsley could have had relatives living in or near Herefordshire, since his family in the past had certainly had business connections in the district just over the Welsh border.

On one point there can be no doubt: the move must have represented quite an upheaval, and especially for Nelly Ainsley after a lifetime of sixty-four years spent entirely in South Shields. But her new home, Stoneleigh in St James's Road, did at least stand comparison with 5 Belgrave Terrace: it was a large, grey, semi-detached house with a pleasant garden. Moreover, in those pre-war days,

St James's was considered 'a very select road'.

It was also quite near the Cathedral and the Castle Green, where a footpath leads across the ancient ramparts, commanding a splendid view of the River Wye. Here, from the early days onwards, Elinor was often to be seen walking along abstractedly, 'her very pronounced nose held high in the air' and obviously (as described by an acquaintance, Mr Edward West, who was then a schoolboy) 'deep in the plot of some book or other'.

On these occasions Elinor would never notice Mr West, although he did eventually get to know her well — or, at least, as well as a schoolboy does know a woman of forty-odd. His mother attended the same church as Mrs Ainsley (St James's Church of England, for Nelly always remained C. of E.), and when Elinor heard that the young Edward West was going to university to read English she immediately took a great interest. She would often invite him to come to tea and discuss literature — the metaphysical poets and the Elizabethans in particular, since these were his special subjects; but the conversation would range over all manner of books as well.

Elinor's study, where they always had tea, was 'crammed with books', just as her bedsitter at Belgrave Terrace had been. And it was filled with 'Roman Catholic things, like crucifixes, and little statues, and pictures, especially pictures of Sir Thomas More'.

(There would of course have been a great many pictures of Thomas More around at this time, in Roman Catholic circles anyway, for 1935 was the year when he and John Fisher were canonised. But Elinor did in any case take a particular interest in Thomas More, and this will be considered in the chapter which follows.)

Edward West was among those who look back at

Elinor with mixed feelings. That she was undeniably kind, is something that struck him far more forcibly as an adult than it did at the time. Then he, like others before him, tended to find Elinor's manner just a bit overwhelming. She was positive to the point of being 'assertive' in her way of talking; her voice, too, was on the loud side. And there had been a rather embarrassing episode early in their acquaintance, when he was invited to take part in a Nativity play that Elinor had written. Edward West, still in his teens, was cast as Saint Joseph; Elinor, then rising forty, as the Virgin Mary. The play was given in the Percival Hall in Hereford, probably in aid of some charity; and the music was provided by the choir from St James's Church — Nelly Ainsley's parish church.

The trouble arose because Elinor, in her boundless enthusiasm, over-acted violently. Her every sentence was invested with such depth of feeling and accompanied with such a wealth of gesture that the listening choirboys would giggle hysterically. And although, forty years on, Mr West could find the memory amusing, being at the time little more than a schoolboy, he had then found it all acutely painful.

There is no doubt that Elinor did always tend to push things to extremes. Another of Mr West's memories is of her singing in the Festival Choir, which she had joined soon after arriving in Hereford, at one of the Three Choirs Festivals. It was the regulation that women members of the choir should wear black, and Elinor interpreted this rule so wholeheartedly that on the platform she was hardly visible for her all-enveloping black garments, which even included a vast black mantilla — with the result that she looked, truth to say, 'rather like a witch'.

In the ordinary way there were two things about Elinor's appearance that greatly struck the young Edward West. The first was the size of her nose: 'it was really huge' and apparently of an almost Cyrano de Bergerac type of prominence. The other was the extraordinarily riveting power of her eyes. The latter on the whole appears to have impressed him more.

All in all — although in later life Mr West always returned to Elinor's genuine kindness, it can be guessed that in his youth he found her rather too overpowering to be lovable.

On the other hand, someone else, who first got to know Elinor at about the same time as Mr West did, remembers her not only with affection but without any reservations. 'I liked everything about her,' recalls an ex-pupil, Mrs Helen Colam — who in those days was Helen Griffiths. And this affection shines through everything Mrs Colam writes or tells of Elinor. But then Mrs Colam was only nine years old when Elinor first came into her life; and a happy relationship was to grow between them, akin to that enjoyed by Elinor and the ten-year-old Hazel Bainbridge.

Elinor's introduction to the Griffiths family had come about shortly after her arrival in Hereford. One of her new acquaintances, Miss Mary Middleton, who later became a great friend, had heard that Mrs Griffiths wanted a daily governess to teach her two daughters, aged nine and twelve. Miss Middleton recommended Elinor as being a qualified experienced teacher; and after an interview — at which both Elinor and Mrs Griffiths appear to have taken each other's measure with some shrewdness — Elinor agreed to accept the post.

The Griffiths family lived then at Albion House in

Peterchurch, a village about fourteen miles from Hereford in the attractively named Golden Valley. In other words, in that same district towards the Black Mountains and 'on the English side of the Welsh Border' where Elinor would place her Chalet School during the war years.

Their home, now demolished following a fire in the 1960s, was a large rambling house, in part very old, which stood near one end of the village. 'It wasn't really beautiful from outside,' according to its former owner, 'but a lovely house inside. And it had a very beautiful old oak staircase.'

Perhaps Elinor had that staircase in mind when she wrote, many years later, in *Three Go to the Chalet School*: 'The morning sun streamed through the . . . window on the landing above [the entrance hall] . . . A beautiful oak staircase ran up to it, and then turned and went on to an upper corridor.' At any rate, Elinor must have gone up and down the Albion House staircase literally hundreds of times, since she was to spend more than four years acting as governess to Sybil and Helen, the Griffiths children, and their schoolroom was on the top floor of the house.

Another thing that became part of her life between 1933 and 1938 was the journey to and from Peterchurch: 'Miss Brent-Dyer came daily to us by bus . . . from Hereford. She arrived about 9.15 and went back at 3.30.' And later this journey would turn up regularly in the Chalet stories of the early 1940s. A few names of places and streets were to be altered, just as happened in the Tyrolean books. Hereford, for instance, becomes Armiford (a name that could have been chosen because, according to some authorities, the word Hereford originally signified 'Army Ford'). But the disguises are flimsy, and anyone who has visited Hereford and the district will not fail to identify them in passages such as the two quoted below (both from *The Highland Twins at the Chalet School*, 1942).

In the first Joey Maynard has left Plas Gwyn (*her* home in the Golden Valley) at a very early hour and is driving in to Armiford Station.

> It was just twenty-past six when she entered the built-up area of Armiford . . . [and drove] down the long road with its houses on either side which began below the railway bridge [still there, although this line is no longer in use]. She made the sharp turn where the Sors [anagram of Ross, i.e. Ross-on-Wye] road runs into what is known as Fairmount [Belmont] Road, crossed the old stone bridge which has seen eight centuries, and turned into King Street, and thence through Broad Street, past the cathedral — largely spoilt by 'restoration' at the beginning of the present century [but a lot of people might not agree with Elinor that Hereford Cathedral *is* spoilt] — and then through the bottle-neck of High Street, and across the fine quadrangle of High Town where most of the best shops in Armiford stand. Past the Old House — a Jacobean house once kept as a museum of Jacobean relics and now used for the Citizens' Bureau — and so down narrow St Stephen's Gate [St Peter's Street] into the magnificent sweep of Broome Road [Commercial Road] with the big chapel and bus-station at one side [both still there, exactly as describedl, and then up the station approach, till she drew up at one side of the station square.

Probably the most striking feature of that passage is the almost obsessive accuracy it shows. And when, only a few pages later, Joey has collected her visitors from the station and the homeward journey begins, Elinor is ready to oblige with further details. First the party drive 'through the now busy streets of Armiford. Then they flashed under a railway bridge with a train on it and into a country road with fields and hedges on both sides, and, in the distance, the long gentle slopes of the Black Mountains. Jo . . . swung the car round a sharp corner, past the aerodrome, and so up the slope of a steep hill. . . . [From the top] . . . they coasted down another slope, with the land rising on either side.'

And accounts similar to the above are given in several other books. Some of the descriptions are more detailed than others; but nearly all mention certain features of the journey which do exist in real life. That railway bridge, for one (it appears in both the passages quoted above); also the 'sharp corner' near the aerodrome (the latter still there, although oddly enough it is not shown on ordinary maps); and the 'steep hill', which is probably that known locally as the 'Batcho Hill'.

So many identifiable places are mentioned in the stories that this has led to much speculation among readers about the locations Elinor may have had in mind for 'Plas Howell', 'Plas Gwyn' and 'The Round House' — the houses which accommodate, respectively, the Chalet School, the Maynard family and the Russells during the seven books that are set in Herefordshire/'Armishire'. Various ideas have been put forward; and two ardent Chalet School fans, Beth and David Varcoe, have gone beyond mere speculation.

They have devoted much time and ingenuity to research in the Golden Valley area; and have painstakingly co-ordinated their theories, both with the books themselves and with the Ordnance Survey maps of the district. In their opinion, the fictional site of 'Plas Howell', where the Chalet School was housed from the early chapters of *The Chalet School Goes to It* (1941) up to and including *Three Go to the Chalet School* (1949), corresponds exactly with the real-life site of Michaelchurch Court at Michaelchurch Escley; the 'White House' at Vowchurch occupies the situation of Joey's beloved 'Plas Gwyn' (which of course means 'White House'); and the original of the 'Round House', home of the Russell family, is 'Poston House' on the other side of Vowchurch.

The Varcoes have made a good case to back their conclusions — in so far, at least, as concerns the actual sites. However, just as with the Alpenhof Hotel in Pertisau, the real-life buildings on at least two of these sites have little in common with the houses Elinor describes; the one possible exception, 'Poston House', with its famous Round Room, does fit the descriptions reasonably well. All the same, it is important to remember that Elinor was writing not a travel guide but a story. And plainly she enjoyed the fiction-writer's prerogative of letting her imagination embellish, or even alter, the real-life landscape; and perhaps allowing it to combine in one house the features of several she had known at various times. At no point did Elinor herself reveal whether she had exact places in mind for 'Plas Howell' and the other houses; or, for that matter, for the house, 'Sarres', near Jerbourg in Guernsey, which provides a temporary home for the school during parts of *The Chalet School in Exile* (1940) and *The Chalet School Goes to It* (1941).

Nevertheless it does seem indicated that Elinor drew some deep satisfaction from bringing real-life places and landscapes into her stories. Perhaps it gave her a feeling of 'belonging' in her own fantasy world. Whatever the reasons, she was also — and

Elinor's first home in Hereford, 'Stoneleigh' in St James' Road (left), and Lichfield House (right) premises of the Margaret Roper School between 1938 and 1948 and Elinor's home until 1964.

increasingly as time went on — to share personal experiences with her characters. For instance, it can hardly be a coincidence that when Elinor, for the first time in her life, is working as a private governess, Joey Bettany (in *Jo Returns to the Chalet School*, 1936) should soon be having a similar experience: ' . . . Jo could certainly coach Polly in history . . . [remarks Miss Annersley, then Senior Mistress at the Chalet School], geography . . . and essay writing.' And thus Jo, barely eighteen, and just out of school, is launched into teaching.

'It was not without some qualms that Joey . . . the next morning . . . made her way downstairs to a small class-room that was generally used for private coaching.'

So far, so good: every reader will appreciate how Jo was feeling. But from the next sentence onwards a curious shift of emphasis can be noted: '[Jo] would not have turned a hair if she had been asked to take on an entire form; but to face one girl, and have her all to herself for an hour and a half, required some doing.'

And this is odd. No doubt Elinor herself, with around twenty years' experience of class teaching, might have been more at home facing 'an entire form' than she was at first with an individual pupil. But it is straining credulity to suggest that Joey would have felt that way. She, after all, had never taught in her life; and most students at teacher-training colleges will testify how apprehensive they felt before first standing up in front of a class. Altogether there can be no question that much of this chapter, which is fascinating reading in itself, tends to demonstrate not Joey's complete inexperience — as by rights it should — but the wide experience and undeniable teaching gifts that Elinor herself possessed. This impression is strengthened by the lesson that Joey proceeds to give her pupil on the Cluniac Reformation — 'a model in miniature of how it should be done' is the way one reader, a teacher of many years' standing, describes it.

And the same comment could justifiably be made about the way in which Joey explains in Chapter VII of *Jo Returns to the Chalet School* how to make a history-chart: here the instructions are so precise that, in the old cliché, 'a child could follow them'.

Two children who did follow them in real life were Helen Griffiths and her sister, Sybil. Only their history-chart, made under Elinor's directions, was a rather special affair: 'The river of time, it was called; done on a large piece of drawing-paper, with the river winding backwards and forwards, and bridges drawn in to mark the dates' (and 'they *had* to be remembered too!').

The latter remark suggests that Elinor could in some respects be quite firm with her two pupils. And Mrs Colam also writes, in the same letter where she describes the history-chart: 'My sister has been reminding me what a demon Miss Brent-Dyer was over good manners. I had forgotten the speed with which we always leapt to our feet or opened doors!'

But Helen Colam's memories of her governess are above all coloured by 'much affection'. And admiration, too: 'Miss Brent-Dyer was such a wonderful teacher. She must have had a very great skill in keeping a child's interest. I never, ever, remember being bored.'

On the other hand, it must also be mentioned that Elinor was far less successful with Helen's elder sister. Sybil Griffiths did not actively dislike Elinor, but she often felt left out of things, for Helen, in her own words, 'was always teacher's pet'.

To say the least, Elinor was perhaps not sufficiently aware of the different temperaments and needs of her two charges. And the schoolroom regime at Albion House was far better suited to one child than to the other. For instance, every day Elinor insisted that her pupils must read the leading article in the *Daily Telegraph* and then take part in fifteen minutes' discussion of current affairs. This Helen always enjoyed; Sybil, according at least to her mother, 'was put off reading for life'.

But then Elinor always had a capacity for arousing at one and the same time quite different reactions in different people. The attitudes of the Griffiths' family provide a good example. As put by Mrs Colam: 'My father and I liked and got on with her so very well; my sister not so well; and my mother not at all!'

Not that Helen herself was totally blind to the eccentric side of her governess, particularly as regards her appearance: 'I shall always remember her wearing one of her stepfather's old hats, and a suit she had knitted herself, without a pattern, and which even I as a child thought was a rather odd shape'.

Apparently Elinor 'always was knitting, and her lap was always full of wool; knitting needles too — pencils — rubbers — cigarettes and matches — all sorts of weird things'. Undoubtedly there would have been cigarettes, for Elinor was quite a heavy smoker. And Helen Griffiths, at nine years old, was fascinated by one thing: 'When Miss Brent-Dyer first came to us she had her own teeth, and quite a gap between the front ones, and she used to funnel the smoke out through it. I was quite upset when she had her teeth out, and replaced by rather pearly ones.'

Elinor herself appears to have made surprisingly

little of losing her teeth. Perhaps, at forty plus, she accepted it as inevitable. Perhaps she actually preferred those pearly ones. At any rate she continued, minus her gappy teeth, to smoke right to the end of her life. Not only that: she was to portray many of the Chalet School staff and other adults, not excluding the exemplary Jo Maynard, as regular smokers. Indeed the number of cigarettes mentioned in the pages of the Chalet series might perhaps excite disapproval in some quarters today, in view of changed attitudes to the whole question.

Elinor, according to a Hereford friend, even smoked when she was writing; or rather typing, to be more exact, for all her books went straight on to the typewriter. It seems that she always worked with enormous energy and at high speed. And the speed could well explain two things. One, the many careless mistakes and inconsistencies that crept into her Chalet series, right from the beginning. Examples must occur even to her most devoted admirer. The other — and this to her credit — the fact that during the 1930s her output was seventeen books, although for several years she was doing what many would consider a full-time job.

For that matter, during these early years in Hereford Elinor was busy not only with teaching and writing; she had also launched into a new activity, that of giving historical lectures at Mothers' Union or WI gatherings, or the like. The subjects included Queen Victoria, King Charles the First and, inevitably, St Thomas More.

Even nominally spare time was always crammed full. There was reading, of course. And she had become an active parishioner of St Francis Xavier's Catholic Church in Broad Street. She was singing regularly in the Festival Choir; getting to know Hereford and the surrounding district; visiting her considerable number of new friends.

Altogether it would seem to have been a full and happy time in her life. But simply in the natural course of events it could not have continued unchanged. The Griffiths children were growing up; and even had the war not come, bringing with it a gradual end to many such institutions as private governesses, it is unlikely that Elinor's services would have been required at Albion House after the early 1940s. As things turned out, her days as governess were to end much sooner than that. For in the autumn of 1937, almost two years before the war, Septimus Ainsley, whose health had been deteriorating for some time, became seriously ill. And on 16 November 1937 he died.

CHAPTER XVIII

CHALET SCHOOL — MARK II

It is unlikely that Elinor was deeply affected on a personal level by Mr Ainsley's death. True, her feelings do appear to have mellowed since the early days when she had gone around chanting 'I hate my stepfather'; for, according to Mrs Griffiths, who knew her well at this period, she 'always spoke quite nicely of Steppy, even if she poked fun at him a bit sometimes'. But the general impression seems to be that Elinor's attitude was one of tolerance, not affection.

However, in practical terms, Septimus Ainsley's death was to bring many changes for Elinor as well as for her mother. First of all, there was plainly some alteration in their financial circumstances. This cannot easily be assessed, but one rather odd thing emerges: Mr Ainsley's estate, leaving out of account the house in St James's Road, was valued at less than £900. And that, even in 1937 and making every allowance for inflation, was not a great deal of money. Moreover it is far less than could have been expected, not only in view of Septimus's original handsome inheritance, but from the standard of living maintained by the Ainsleys, who struck more than one visitor as 'comfortably off'.

Perhaps the family had been living on their capital. But since Mr Ainsley appears to have had a good business head it is more likely that he had already made over part of his money to his wife and/or his stepdaughter. And, in possible confirmation of this, Elinor did mention to Mrs Griffiths at this time ‘something about a trust’. However it is impossible to do more than speculate about this.

Of course there was Stoneleigh, the house in St James’s Road. A solid, respectable property, it was undoubtedly worth, in house agents’ parlance, ‘a substantial price’; and Nelly Ainsley still had her own money — the far-sighted Isaac Rutherford had assured that. But Elinor was now placed in a difficult position, for although her combined earnings as governess and author had no doubt provided a reasonable income, it is unlikely that her writings on their own could have done so. On the other hand, had she continued her job at Peterchurch, this would have meant leaving her widowed mother alone all day on five days of the week.

In the end an obvious solution was found to this particular problem and it was arranged that the Griffiths girls, who were now thirteen and sixteen, would travel daily into Hereford in order to have their lessons. And once that had been decided it was only another step in the same direction for Elinor to consider setting up a school of her own. This was something that Madge Bettany, and numerous others in fiction, had done with resounding success. In real life people had done it and got by. Why shouldn’t *she*?

Whether the idea originated in her own mind, or with her mother, or perhaps with someone quite outside, the scheme appears to have fired Elinor’s imagination, And full of enthusiasm, as always in the initial stages of any enterprise, she launched into a search for accommodation. The house at St James’s Road did not offer anything suitable for a school — or so it seems. But a friend had a large hut, of the ‘summer-house’ variety, standing empty in her garden, and arrangements were quickly made for the school to begin its life there.

In practical terms this was just about feasible. The shed contained two 'rooms', and it was easy enough to acquire a few desks and chairs. But with winter still in full swing it looked as though conditions would be, to say the least, primitive. Elinor characteristically remained undaunted. After all, the shed had a stove: that took care of the present. Then, as soon as the warmer weather began, the children would be able to have their lessons in the garden. So she turned her attention to the enjoyable, if not strictly essential, task of designing a school uniform — in fact, two uniforms, one winter, one summer. And in happy disregard of the fact that the school as yet numbered only Sybil and Helen Griffiths on its roll, she placed a notice in the *Hereford Times* of 5 February 1938 announcing: 'The Margaret Roper School . . . for Girls . . . To be opened after Easter. Terms on application to the Principal, Miss Brent-Dyer (Inter. Arts. N.U.T.C.)'.

The naming of her school would have given Elinor no difficulty. Perhaps her beloved Thomas More would really have been her first choice. But in 1938 the name 'St Thomas More's' would immediately have marked out the school as Roman Catholic, and Elinor wanted it, like her Chalet School, to be open to all denominations. In any case, More's eldest daughter, Margaret (who married Will Roper) provided an ideal model for schoolgirls to emulate. To quote Elinor herself (in *Bride Leads the Chalet School*, 1953), 'as early as the days of Henry VIII *one* family of girls [that of Sir Thomas More] had been encouraged to become learned ladies'.

And Thomas More did indeed hold the opinion, most unusual then for anyone outside royal or noble families, that girls should receive the same academic education as boys. His daughter Margaret had profited from her opportunities and had grown up an accomplished young woman, well able to hold her own in scholarly conversation. (Those who saw Robert Bolt's *A Man for All Seasons* may recall the scene where King Henry, on a visit to the Mores' Chelsea home, is astonished and perhaps not altogether delighted to find the youthful Margaret as fluent in Latin as he is himself.) The name 'Margaret Roper School' also had the great advantage that, while it might strike a special chord among Roman Catholics, nothing about it was likely to put off others.

With the school's name and uniform now settled, there was still the matter of finding proper buildings, not to mention attracting a few more pupils. And, astonishingly, as regards the former requirement, Elinor was to have an almost Chalet School type of good luck. For it turned out that a school in Hereford, known as the 'Grey School', was just on the point of closing down; their premises at Lichfield House, Bodenham Road, were soon to be for sale; and in a short time Elinor had made arrangements to buy the house (doubtless with some financial assistance from her mother and perhaps also from the trust she had mentioned to Mrs Griffiths).

Apparently there was no question of her taking over the Grey School as a going concern, since the remaining pupils and staff moved in a block to 'The Elms', one of Hereford's long-established private schools. So Elinor obtained possession only of Lichfield House itself and the large garden in which it stood (perhaps also of some school furniture and effects). But this did not prevent her from inserting an optimistic notice in the *Hereford Times* to the effect that the Margaret Roper School would be opening on 5 May 1938.

The house she now owned was a Victorian villa of imposing size. Built originally to accommodate large Victorian families with tribes of servants, it was by this time about eighty years old and most likely a bit shabby following its years of occupation by a school. Or, to describe it in the words of the local newspaper: Lichfield House was 'a spacious private residence . . . in Bodenham Road'; the latter being, then and today, a pleasant residential road about three-quarters of a mile from the centre of Hereford.

There could be no doubt that the house offered scope for running a school of considerable size. Now it only remained for Elinor to find the pupils. And it was here that things ceased to run as easily as they had in the Chalet stories. Certainly Madge Bettany had started off with only two pupils: her sister Joey and Grizel Cochrane. But almost immediateiy Madge had gained another in Simone Lecoutier, her partner's young cousin. Moreover in no time at all there had been also six Tyrolean girls.

Elinor had got her 'foundation stones' in Sybil and Helen Griffiths; and she, too, had the promise of a third pupil, who was to have joined the others at the beginning of the summer term. But at the last moment this girl developed appendicitis (a far lengthier and more serious matter in 1938 than it is today) and she did not turn up at the school until many months later.

For a while it looked as though the Margaret Roper School was condemned to exist as an eternal duet. The only thing was to soldier on and hope that by September more girls would have enrolled. But in the mean time Elinor, sanguine as she was, must sometimes have had an uncomfortable feeling that she had been unwise to purchase such an enormous house. (Since those days Lichfield House has become, first an hotel — with about twelve bedrooms, in addition to lounges, dining-room and offices — and more recently an old people's home.) So it was almost certainly at this stage that she and her mother decided to assist matters financially — and justify the existence of all those rooms — by taking in a few discreet lodgers. This was the beginning of what has been called 'Elinor's old ladies', for most of those who came at various times to live in Lichfield House were elderly women. Some were to remain for years and to become an integral part of the household. And Elinor, according to a friend, was always very good to her old ladies: 'she seemed to have a kind of bond with older people, just as she often did with much younger ones'.

One, at least, among the lodgers became a close friend. Her name was Elizabeth Pearce, but she was known by everyone as Aunt Elizabeth, although no relation. She is remembered by Chloe Rutherford, who was a schoolgirl at the time, as 'a really beautiful old lady; a rare soul'. Elinor was particularly devoted to 'Dearest Aunt Elizabeth' (the dedication of *The Highland Twins at the Chalet School*, 1942) who was to continue living at Lichfield House until her death. That, however, did not take place until many years later, and by that time the Margaret Roper School had come and gone.

In the end it had seen ten years of life. So, looking back, it is odd to think how nearly the school had come to a dramatic ending in 1938 — even before it was properly started. There is no difficulty in seeing how it happened; nor in understanding that Elinor was under considerable pressure throughout the spring and summer of 1938. There were all the complicated arrangements, practical, legal, domestic and scholastic, that had to be made for the school's opening. There were letters to be written and people to be interviewed. There was work connected with her books: two appeared in 1938 — *The New Chalet School* in April; *They Both Liked Dogs* later in the summer — and that involved much proof-reading, a task that Elinor seems to have disliked as much as Joey does in the stories. Above all, there was the constant battle to find time for writing, and the inevitable sense of frustration when every moment was filled in meeting other demands.

It was the conflict between teaching and writing that almost wrecked the Margaret Roper School. The struggle was unequal, for Elinor seems to have been oddly uninvolved with her teaching at this time; with the result that her two pupils at the temporary school began to find everything increasingly disorganised. On most mornings Elinor would be late, whereas Sybil and Helen, who always travelled by the 8.15 bus from Peterchurch, would naturally enough arrive each day at about the same time. This meant they often had to spend quite long periods waiting outside the hut. One day they both — Sybil in particular — became 'so fed up with hanging around' that they left and went back home to Peterchurch. 'I remember that on the way my sister dragged me through a churchyard — that somehow made it all seem worse!'

The whole episode can hardly have been popular with Mrs Griffiths. And afterwards Elinor did presumably pull herself together up to a point, for the arrangement with the Griffiths was to continue into the next term. However, 5 May — the day that Elinor had planned for the Margaret Roper School's official opening — went past unobserved.

No one remembers exactly when disaster struck, but it came towards the end of the summer term. Sybil Griffiths was then about sixteen and she was supposed to be preparing intensively to take an examination the following year — most probably the School Certificate, forerunner of today's GCSE. And then one day (history does not relate exactly how) Mrs Griffiths discovered that Sybil was frequently being taught, not by the qualified and experienced Miss Brent-Dyer, but by her quite unqualified mother. That was too much. Understandably Mrs Griffiths was outraged. And despite the fact that both summer and winter uniforms had been bought for Sybil and Helen, their days at the 'school' were brought to an abrupt end.

For Sybil this caused no great pangs. She had never got on particularly well with Elinor; and, in any case, at sixteen she was able to enrol as a student at Hereford's Art School, where the work was far more congenial to her than academic lessons had been. But her younger sister was heartbroken. 'I only found out from my mother . . . years and years later, as to why we left', Helen Colam recalls; 'I shed many tears at the time.' And since Elinor was genuinely devoted to Helen ('my little pet') it is clear that she, too, must have been most unhappy, especially that things had ended in the way they did. It is not easy though to find excuses for her, since the reason given for her many absences from the schoolroom does seem inadequate: 'It was because Miss Brent-Dyer was working on a historical novel.'

Probably Elinor was in fact doing just that. Although a question does arise on this point: for what became of that historical novel? None by Elinor was published in the years that followed. *The Little Missus*, as already mentioned, is too short and slight to qualify as a novel, and in any case did not appear until 1942. So what book was absorbing all Elinor's time and attention in 1938? That she was indeed busy over something is clear; and that it was unsuccessful can be deduced, for in the following year not only did no historical novel appear but, for the first time since 1922, no book of any kind by Elinor was published.

A possible solution to this puzzle was provided by Mr Edward West (some of whose memories of Elinor appear in the previous chapter). Mr West recalled that on one occasion, when he was having tea in the study at St James's Road, he was somewhat taken aback to be given and asked to read the manuscript of an historical novel: it had the not very prepossessing title *Ripe Corn* (based on a verse in St Mark's Gospel, Chapter 4) and concerned Elinor's favourite St Thomas More. Apparently the novel had recently been rejected by a publisher — no doubt with reason, for it does seem to have been, in Mr West's words, 'pretty poor stuff' (an opinion supported by the only part of the manuscript to have survived). But nevertheless it is probable that Elinor made an attempt to revise the book; and it might well have been this revision that kept her so busy during the summer of 1938.

There could of course have been other reasons for that curious gap in 1939. At this point Elinor's Chalet series, which then numbered only thirteen books, had reached what might easily have been the end of the road — incredible as this may appear today when those fifty-nine stories are known to exist. The fact remains that things looked different in the 1930s, when for a time sales were falling and Elinor's publishers were even writing to announce that the series must be discontinued, both on financial grounds and (a statement that hindsight makes wryly amusing) because 'there are now twelve [of the books] and that is enough'.

Besides there were difficulties inherent in the stories themselves. For with Joey Bettany now irrevocably grown-up Elinor had yet to find her a new role. And it may well have been at this point that Elinor wrote about a visit to India by the grown-up Joey and the Robin, in a book entitled *Two Chalet Girls in India*. Unfortunately, the manuscript of this story, which was known still to exist in the late 1950s, has now disappeared. And although reference is made to Joey's Indian trip in several of the later Chalet School books, no mention of it is made in any of those earlier than *Lavender Laughs in the Chalet School* (1943). In any case Elinor had a graver problem to face in 1938. For by this point it was becoming clear that even a fictional school could hardly remain in the Tyrol. That March the Nazis had over-run Austria; and then, in September 1938, the Munich crisis was to bring home to many people that war with Gemany, which now included Austria, was not far away.

Elinor must be credited with having more real awareness of the Nazi menace, and at an earlier stage, than certain of her critics might imagine. There cannot, for instance, have been many children's books written as early as 1933 where reference is made to 'the spirit of young Germany' — as it is in Chapter IV of *The Exploits of the Chalet Girls* — and in a manner that makes it quite clear this was something to be deplored. Nor was it usual for any school story to contain a scene of street violence, such as that in Chapter IX of *The Chalet School in Exile* ('A Nazi "Sport" '), which depicts with some realism the baiting of an elderly Jewish man by Nazi-incited crowds (Elinor is always most careful to distinguish between those who follow the evil creed of Nazism and the Germans or Austrians as such).

Plainly Elinor would have felt unable just to ignore world affairs as a number of other children's writers did. Some, including Elsie Oxenham and Arthur Ransome, simply disregarded the Second World War and continued to write in a timeless Never-Never Land. Elinor, on the contrary, managed eventually to turn the international turmoil to good account. Her *Chalet School in Exile* (1940) tells of an exciting escape from Austria (which may appear to have affinities with that in the famous *Sound of Music*, but of course Elinor's book was written almost twenty years before the Von Trapp family's adventures were generally known); and this book was to become one of the most popular in the whole series. Not only that: it was to ensure, and to prove along with the other wartime Chalet books, that the Chalet School as an institution could survive even being transplanted from its first exotic Tyrolean location.

Oddly enough, it was also the international situation in 1938 that saved the Margaret Roper School. For the threat of air-raids, at the time of Munich and onwards, was to drive numbers of middle-class families from the cities to places like Herefordshire which were considered 'safe areas'. Naturally, many of the newcomers needed schools for their children. And since few of the established schools in Hereford had vacancies, there were plenty of applications to the Margaret Roper School. Other new pupils came from local families who might in the ordinary way have sent their daughters to boarding-schools, but who now preferred a school that was, so to speak, on the doorstep.

One way and another, by the end of September 1938 when the autumn term began, Elinor's school — now advertised as a boarding and day school — had gathered enough children, even without the two Griffiths girls, and of sufficiently varying ages,

The Margaret Roper School, Hereford, taken in the summer of 1941. Elinor is in the centre of the second row, with her mother on her right.

really to be considered a *school* at last. From this point until after the war had ended there was to be no further problem over numbers. September 1939 saw more new arrivals, and the school began to accept small boys as well as girls. It also, according to the *Hereford Times*, had acquired 'A GAS-PROOF ROOM'. Yet more pupils came in 1940, when the headmistress's December report mentions the 'air-raids on defenceless people [which] have brought an influx to our beautiful Hereford'. And by the summer of 1941 there were about forty-five children attending the Margaret Roper School, as can be seen in the school photograph (see previous page).

This photograph also reveals something significant about the two schools in Elinor's life, especially when it is considered alongside certain passages in her writings. For example: The 'brown-and-white checked ginghams, which were the summer uniform of the school . . . looked very fresh and crisp with their white collars and cuffs and their short sleeves. The girls wore the flame-coloured school ties with them, and belts of brown leather.'

Here, as a glance will show, Elinor has provided an almost exact description of the uniform being worn at the Margaret Roper School in the summer of 1941, when that group photograph was taken. And that the Margaret Roper colours were indeed brown and flame has been verified by several ex-pupils. The only item to differ is the belt — those worn in the photograph do not appear to be made of leather. And yet the school described in the above passage is, of course, the Chalet School — not the Margaret Roper.

This similarity of uniform is only one of many resemblances which existed between Elinor's real and fictional schools. Often these parallels were deliberately contrived, as in the case of the uniforms. Some happened by coincidence. And one in particular: for it so happened that the Princess Elisaveta of Belsornia, who spent two terms at the Chalet School, was to be matched in real life, when two granddaughters of Haile Selassie, Emperor of Abyssinia, became pupils for a time at the Margaret Roper School.

The identity of these little Abyssinian princesses was meant to remain a secret (as was that of *The Princess of the Chalet School*), but in practice most people at the Margaret Roper School knew who the children were. One of their schoolfellows remembered them with affection but also with a touch of sadness; partly because of the fate that may well have overtaken these two during the troubled conditions prevailing in Ethiopia for many years past; partly because she cannot forget how one of them would sometimes be heard 'praying aloud to be made white'.

Not that there appears to have been any colour prejudice shown at the Margaret Roper School. Elinor, it seems, really did attempt to foster in practice the ideas of international co-operation and religious tolerance that had become familiar in the pages of the Chalet School. And it is no surprise to find that the basic aims and aspirations of the two schools had much in common. ' "We are trying to train our girls — and our boys — to become practising Christians and good citizens, two things which are going to be most vital to our land and indeed to the whole Empire," said Miss Brent-Dyer, Principal of the Margaret Roper School, at the school's ninth Speech Day.' (*Hereford Times*, 6 July 1946). And, minus only the passing reference to boys, Elinor could have handed over her speech unchanged for Miss Annersley to deliver at a first-night assembly in the Chalet School. It is clear, too, that Elinor wanted her real-life school, wherever possible, to do the same things the Chalet School did. That at least is the impression to be gleaned from reports in the local papers, where the Margaret Roper School's activities always had exceptionally good coverage — perhaps because of the headmistress's reputation as a children's author. Thus many traditional features of life at the Chalet School became familiar at Lichfield House, among them concerts, folk dancing, pageants in the garden, exhibitions and sales of work, collections for charity, Girl Guides, expeditions to places of historical interest, school songs and plays (these latter often being specially written by the headmistress).

Of course it would be foolish to press the matter of resemblance too far. After all, the majority of schools do take part in some, perhaps all, of the activities listed above. Most schools have — or had in those days — prefects and headgirls. Schools other than the Margaret Roper and Chalet schools have magazines, accept pupils of different nationalities and religions, and may choose brown and flame for their school colours. Nevertheless the likeness between the summer uniforms — and the same was true of those worn in winter — could not by any stretch of the imagination have been a coincidence. And there were other parallels, equally unmistakeable — as in the following two descriptions of a Nativity Play.

The first states that the play, *The Youngest Shepherd*, is 'a cleverly written piece which, with effective simplicity, not only tells the moving story of the Nativity but brings out the significance of the various pilgrimages to the stable'; and it comments on the accompaniment of carols, and on the 'striking finale in which the children of many lands join in the adoration of the Holy Child'.

The second, after explaining that the play 'is called *The Youngest Shepherd*, continues, 'As you all know, it was to the "shepherds abiding in the field, keeping watch over their flocks by night" that the angel of the Nativity told the good news of Christ's birth. Our little play is based on that story.' Here, too, there are references to the accompanying carols; and to the finale where 'one by one, the worshippers stole in to kneel before the Manger . . . The Shepherds . . . the Wise Men . . . the children eagerly laying their treasured possessions before the Holy child . . . The poor Man . . . the [great] Lady . . . the Youngest Shepherd . . . '

The first of those two passages comes from the *Hereford Times* of 23 December 1944, and it describes a real-life performance by the Margaret Roper School of a Christmas play written by their head-mistress, Miss Elinor Brent-Dyer. The second, which dates from 1926, eighteen years earlier, relates to a performance at the Chalet School of what is quite obviously the same Christmas play, but written, theoretically, by *their* headmistress, Miss Madge Bettany.

And this trading of ideas between reality and fiction was to work both ways. Thus, when girls from the Margaret Roper School went hop-picking in the fields of Herefordshire, it was not long before the Chalet girls in 'Armishire' were doing the same. And when Elinor went with a friend to visit Bournville, there sure enough in the next Chalet book is a description of the chocolate factory, given in exhaustive and, it must be confessed, rather boring detail.

All that was fair enough. The practice of basing fiction on reality is common and legitimate. But there is surely danger awaiting anyone who tries to do the same thing in reverse, as Elinor undoubtedly did with her Margaret Roper School. And this must inevitably have led to disappointments when the real school failed to match its fictional equivalent. For there can be no question: despite all those plays and other activities mentioned above, and the fact that numbers remained satisfactory during the war (seventy pupils in 1945), the Margaret Roper School was quite simply not in, or even near, the Chalet School's league.

For one thing, Elinor herself was totally unsuited to being a headmistress. As a teacher she had undeniable talents; and that she had a compulsion to teach is clear from the amount of instruction that she tries to cram into her books. She also had a gift, when she chose to exercise it, for getting on outstandingly well with individual children, and for building genuine friendships with them. Hazel Bainbridge and Helen Colam would testify to that; as would many others, including a former pupil of the Margaret Roper School, Luella Hamilton, who remembers her headmistress with much affection. But plainly Elinor was out of her element when it came to dealing with numbers. Not for her the fictional Miss Annersley's capacity to quell with one glance a host of insubordinate girls. 'Poor old B.D.! — we ran rings round her,' recalls one ex-pupil. And another, now Mrs Margaret Mann, remembers the high jinks that went on when Elinor was late, as she nearly always was, in coming to take their Latin class; and that sometimes she completely failed to turn up: 'We knew then that she'd got buried in something or other she was writing. And we used to dare each other to go up to the study and get her out.'

It is more than likely, too, that Elinor became thoroughly bored with all the day-to-day routine of a headmistress's life. She could, moreover, have been aware that she lacked certain essential qualities; for when Joey, with whom Elinor certainly identified, makes a suggestion (in *Gay from China at the Chalet School*) that she might act temporarily as head of the Chalet School's English department, the idea is 'instantly squashed' by her sister (an experienced headmistress): 'do you mind explaining how you imagine that you, of all people, could see to the organisation? It needs a tidy mind for that sort of thing, my child.'

Whether or not that passage was autobiographical, Elinor was assuredly no organiser; and she was just as certainly not tidy, either in appearance or with her possessions. Nor was she a methodical person. Her friends agree unreservedly about that; and the number of inconsistencies in her Chalet books provide supporting evidence.

One way and another, it is no wonder that things happened at the school in Hereford that could never, never, have happened at the Chalet School. There were, for instance, endless grumbles about the food. Now, in the stories, the cooking and household affairs were always in the hands of some matchless paragon — Marie Pfeiffen, or Rosa, or Karen; and generations of schoolgirls and other readers must have envied the menus that are lovingly described — particularly the Tyrolean specialities: those delicious spicy soups and the various concoctions made from recipes of which 'Marie alone knew the secret'.

At the Margaret Roper School it was Nelly Ainsley who took charge of domestic matters, which included the cooking; and in the recollections of many people 'the school meals were awful'. Of course Mrs Ainsley was far from young: she had been seventy in the March before the war began, and probably she had no previous experience of cooking for large numbers; In addition she had to contend, during all but the first year of the school's life, with the many problems caused by food rationing. All the same it has to be faced that the general running of the house left much to be desired. 'The kitchens were filthy,' as one ex-pupil bluntly puts it. And much trouble was caused by Mrs Ainsley's beloved cats; there were apparently five of them, and they were allowed to wander everywhere unchecked; moreover 'they did what they should not all over the place, and would jump onto the tables and lick the milk out of the jugs,' as one scandalised person relates. It has even been suggested that complaints were lodged with the health authorities; and further that it was rumoured the sanitary inspector was coming to close down the school.

Presumably that particular rumour was unfounded, for the upheaval did eventually subside, and Elinor's school was in fact to continue for several more years — with, it is to be hoped, different conditions prevailing below stairs. But the storm had not left the school undamaged. The assistant mistress, Miss A. N. Ovens, resigned; and was later to set up her own school in Hereford, which then ran in opposition to the Margaret Roper School, and even outlived it. And this must have been extremely hurtful to Elinor, not only professionally but personally, for Miss Ovens had been among her closest friends.

An old acquaintance who knew the situation well at the time was inclined to blame much of the trouble at the school on Mrs Ainsley, who 'simply ruled the roost'. And the impression does begin to emerge that the real Nelly Ainsley was by no means just a sweet, gentle and helpless old lady. On the contrary, many of Elinor's friends have suggested that her mother was one of those people who can hide inflexible determination beneath a quiet manner; and that it was she who dominated her far more forcible-seeming daughter. 'She had Elinor right under her thumb' was the comment of one friend, Mrs Phyllis Matthewman — who nevertheless liked Mrs Ainsley a great deal.

On one point, though, there seems to be no disagreement: Nelly Ainsley was devoted to her daughter and immensely proud of her achievements as a writer. So it does seem possible that when Nelly undertook such tasks as the catering in the school — perhaps also the teaching of Sybil Griffiths — she had the very best of intentions. It might well have seemed wrong in Nelly's eyes that her gifted Elinor should have to spend time in anything other than writing.

But this cannot exonerate Elinor. It was her school. Sybil Griffiths had been her pupil. Elinor did at the very least show a lack of responsibility in letting control pass from her hands (if this was, in fact, the way things happened). She had, of course, always tended to get bored with things once they were no longer new. Hence it appears only too likely that, as time passed, Elinor became less and less interested in the Margaret Roper School. Especially when the numbers began to fall, as they did dramatically during the years immediately after the war.

Nor was the decline in numbers the only trouble. At this time there was also (in the words of Mrs Margaret Mann, an ex-pupil, who first apologised for sounding snobbish) 'a marked change in the social class of girls coming to the school'. And in the mid-1940s that mattered; enough at any rate to put off any parents who were looking for an 'exclusive' school. Elinor had often written against snobbery, and at times with a fervour that suggests she may have known how it felt to be at the receiving end. There is, for instance, a scene in *Exploits of the Chalet Girls* where the aristocratic Thekla von Stift is rebuked for her attitude to girls who belong, as she considers, to 'the trading classes'. That book appeared in 1933, a couple of years after *The Feud in the Fifth Remove*, where there had been an outpouring against snobbish attitudes; one which can be matched almost exactly in *A Problem for the Chalet School*, written twenty-five years later, where Joey Maynard speaks forcibly and at some length on the subject, concluding:

> 'It's a pleasant thing to know that one comes from a long line of gentle folk,' Joey used the words separately, 'but it only means you've a lot to live up to . . . when you come to the root of matters, it's you — *you* — *YOU* that matters all the time — what *you* are!'

In that discourse Joey, who 'had never had the slightest use for snobs', is undoubtedly stating her author's own sincerely held convictions. Nevertheless there are signs that in real life Elinor's attitude to social class was less broadminded than she perhaps imagined. One of her least critical friends thought of her as 'not without a touch of snobbery'. Another remembers Elinor remarking that one of their acquaintances had let herself down by marrying outside 'her class'. And there is a revealing moment in *Three Go to the Chalet School* (1949), where Mary-Lou is told by one of Joey Maynard's children: 'There isn't any other [school] near, 'cept the village school; and you [with the accent on you] won't go *there*.'

One way and another, it is unlikely that Elinor would have favoured her own school's becoming more mixed socially. Of course the change was almost inevitable in the post-war period; and to a certain extent so was the fall in numbers. Once the bombing had ended there was a general drift of city-dwellers back to their homes; and a general tendency for people to try and resume old habits, which among the better-off would frequently include sending their daughters to boarding-schools.

It is only fair to record that by general agreement Elinor's school did some good work during the ten years of its existence, and that, in the words of one Hereford lady, 'it filled a local need'. This does not alter the fact that Elinor was simply not cut out be a headmistress. And it is plain that she cannot have found the life congenial. All in all she was perhaps not really sorry in 1948 when the Margaret Roper School finally closed its doors.

Now at last she could give her undivided attention to the Chalet School.

CHAPTER XIX

MOTHER — DAUGHTER — AND MARRIAGE

During the ten-year life of the Margaret Roper School, Elinor had managed, despite all her commitments (variously discharged) to write and publish fourteen books. In the decade that followed, her output rose to the remarkable total of thirty-eight — sixteen of the books being completed within two years.

That speaks for itself about the change in her circumstances. And yet it would be wrong to assume that Elinor found endless time available once the school had closed down. Apart from anything, since she and her mother had for some reason decided against moving to a new home, Elinor's daily life continued to include all the problems of running an enormous house with, almost certainly, inadequate help.

In a way it is difficult to see why she and Mrs Ainsley did not at this point look for a smaller and more practical house, even bearing in mind that they still needed rooms for a number, unknown, of 'Elinor's old ladies'. But possibly Elinor was reluctant to subject her mother to the upheavals of a house removal. Nelly, after all, had been nearing eighty at the time of the Margaret Roper's demise. And undoubtedly she was beginning to grow frail, for there are signs that her health quite often gave cause for anxiety. One indication of this can be found in a letter Elinor wrote on 24 September 1950 to the elder of Hazel Bainbridge's two children — now the well-known actress Kate O'Mara of

Dynasty and *Triangle* fame; and this letter is worth quoting also for the picture it gives of Elinor, and her own life at the time:

> . . . so delighted to hear from you, as my last letter (written in May or thereabouts — but it might have been June!) was returned, and I hadn't the foggiest idea where to get hold of you . . .
>
> Tell Mummy that Auntie Nelly [Mrs Ainsley] has been very ill this year with heart trouble. She was in bed for 9 weeks in the spring, and then only up in her room for the next month, so I had my hands full — especially as I was trying to finish my geographical readers. She is better now; but it was rather a hair-raising time. The readers were done, too, and the first two may come out any time now — *Verena Visits New Zealand*, and *Sharlie's Kenya Diary*. The other two are *Bess-on-her-own*, about fruit-farming in British Columbia; and *A Quintette in Queensland*, which describes life on a sugar plantation.
>
> What lovely presents you had for your birthday! I am sending another Chalet book as my offering . . .
>
> Poor Mummy! What a fright she must have had when Binny [Hazel's younger daughter] fell into the river! I should have wanted to tie her up after that!
>
> I like your picture of Bessie. She must be a very sweet-tempered little dog . . .
>
> How are you getting on at school? . . .

The letter, which is signed 'Auntie Len', finishes: 'I am quite well and working very hard on a new book'. And the second part of that sentence more or less sums up Elinor's life during the fifties and sixties. No one could deny that her writing achievements were impressive in terms of quantity. And those thirty-eight books she produced in the 1950s show also a considerable variety of styles. Twenty-three of them were, of course, additions to the Chalet series (among them *Tom Tackles the Chalet School*, which will be the subject of a special note in Appendix II, since there has been much confusion about the proper place in the series of this title). But the others included a number of adventure stories (some unisex; a couple definitely *Boys' Own Paper* tradition); a recipe book, with Chalet School trimmings; a final addition to the La Rochelle series; a 'doggy' story (*Kennelmaid Nan*); three school stories (not Chalet School), all with a specifically religious slant; and four educational books, the geographical readers (mentioned in Elinor's letter).

The latter books represent an entirely new departure for Elinor. And it is not suggested that she had personal knowledge of the countries in question — Kenya, New Zealand, Canada and Australia — although she did apparently have relatives in the two latter, and by this time was getting fan mail from all four. But it had struck Mr Thomas Collocott, one of her editors at W. & R. Chambers — her main publishers throughout her life — that, since Elinor was both an experienced teacher and a popular children's author, she was particularly well qualified to undertake this kind of work. The background research could easily be done in libraries; the illustrations would be provided by Chambers — and each of the four little books contains a generous number of photographs. Altogether there seemed no question that 'Miss Brent-Dyer [who] had been able to produce all those Tyrolean Chalet books after only one visit to Austria' would cope with any difficulties presented by this assignment. The readers were in fact to be quite popular, at least at the time, when there was a certain vogue for this type of educational story. Nowadays none of them could be classed as thrilling reading; but all are instructive in a quiet way, and, at 2s. 6d. each (12½p) in 1951, they undoubtedly represented good value for money.

So far, then, as concerns quantity and variety, it would be hard to fault the work Elinor did during the years after she gave up her school. But from the point of view of quality things look different. To take only those twenty-three books which were added to the Chalet series, it is no doubt possible for Chalet School addicts to find good things in all these stories, but in themselves they are undoubtedly inferior, not only to the early Tyrolean books (which might be expected), but to those written during the 1940s when Elinor's life was apparently far more difficult. So it does appear that Elinor's imagination had thrived the more when time to express herself was in short supply. In *Three Go to the Chalet School*, for instance, which was published in 1949 (and is dedicated 'To the Staff and Girls of the Margaret Roper School. A Farewell Gift from their Head Mistress'), Elinor's creative faculties were still very much alive; enabling her to produce a new character in ten-year-old Mary-Lou Trelawney with enough stamina to last out the series; and enough personality, like it or not, to take a leading part as she grows older, thus allowing Joey Maynard to get off the stage from time to time. But later on, although Elinor writes a multitude of new people into the series, few have any real interest. Perhaps it can be allowed that the Maynard triplets show signs of life, as does one newly introduced grown-up, Kathie Ferrars, who is *The New Mistress at the Chalet School* (1957), but these are exceptions. And a question naturally arises: was the change for the worse due in any way to Elinor's having withdrawn from active day-to-day school life? The famous Angela Brazil would not have thought so. Or, at least, she had written of herself in *My Own Schooldays* — and with some fervour: 'I have always had the strong feeling that had I . . . forced myself into a scholastic mould, and become a headmistress, I should never, never, *never* have written stories about schoolgirls, at any rate not from the schoolgirl's point of view.'

That theory was not put to the test in her own case for at no time did Miss Brazil teach in a school. And with Elinor it seems more likely that the opposite was true and that something actually vanished from her writing after she gave up her school. But then no one can be surprised that these two writers show different reactions. for their ideas and attitudes were in so many ways unalike. There is, too, a fair presumption that Elinor did not greatly admire her best-known rival. For one thing, it is noticeable that when Elinor's characters talk of school stories, as they do in various books, there is never a word about Angela Brazil. Not a single Brazil appears in the bedroom of thirteen-year-old Gwensi Howell, described in some detail in *The Chalet School Goes to It* (1941): and yet Gwensi's bookcase contains 'a whole shelf of Elsie Oxenham, and another of Dorita Fairlie Bruce and Winifred Darch'. Not to mention all the works to date of Josephine M. Bettany — that being about as near as Elinor could get to putting herself on Gwensi's bookshelves.

The three authors favoured by Gwensi are often mentioned appreciatively, as are various other school-story writers, including Elinor's friend Phyllis Matthewman, whose Daneswood series gets more than one nice little 'puff' from the Chalet girls.

But none of them ever breathes the name of Angela Brazil.

And it can hardly have been jealousy that caused Elinor to make this exclusion, for both Elsie Oxenham and Dorita Fairlie Bruce were among her most successful competitors. A possible explanation would seem that Elinor found something off-putting in the type of extravagantly sentimental utterance to which Miss Brazil and her schoolgirls are frequently prone. Examples can easily be found. First, from *A Fourth Form Friendship* (in its way an absolutely splendid school story): ' "I'd have given my life for you gladly!" gulped Aldred. "I know, and I feel almost unworthy of such love." "Will you kiss me to show you can forget what's past?" Mabel bent her head. It was a kiss of complete reconciliation and forgiveness.' Then, in *The Fortunes of Phillipa*, the heroine has 'simply fallen in love with Catherine Winstanley'. In *Bosom Friends*, Isobel 'was ready . . . to offer her utmost in way of friendship' and to find her idol's 'pretty thanks and kisses a sufficient reward'. And in *The Third Class at Miss Kaye's*, a younger child protests to the heroine (albeit falsely) ' "I'll love you always . . . I don't want anybody but you". . . she clasped her arms round Sylvia's neck, and kissed her again and again.'

It all contrasts sharply with the twelve-year-old Joey Bettany's horrified reaction when one of her contemporaries, a French girl, treats her to a sentimental outburst: 'I don't kiss anyone very much. You mustn't go feeling hurt 'cos I don't kiss you every day. We don't in England.' That comes from *The School at the Chalet*. And it would not seem impossible, although this is only guessing, that Elinor had some of Miss Brazil's more flowery paragraphs in mind when, later in the same book, she contrived that imaginary school story *Denise of the Fourth* by

Muriel Bernardine Browne, a book that Joey is shown one day by Gisela Marani, then Head Girl of the Chalet School.

> Joey . . . skimmed through the chapter with a widening grin on her face.
>
> 'It is amusing?' queried the Head Girl [a Tyrolean, with a fair knowledge of English but very little of schoolgirl fiction]. 'You find it funny?'
>
> 'It's a shriek . . . just listen to this!' And Joey read aloud: "The glory of the sun lingered long o'er tree and flower; his molten rays kissed the silvery river as it slid silently past, crooning a tender lullaby to the fragile flowers which bent to kiss their reflections on . . . " [she broke off]. Is there a lot of kissing in the book?'
>
> 'They do kiss each other very often,' returned Gisela.
>
> 'I thought so!'

And, although this proves nothing, there is unquestionably a deal of kissing in Angela Brazil's books; even the short extracts quoted above furnish some evidence.

Nevertheless, however little Elinor may have liked this, and possibly other things, in Miss Brazil's writings, there is one point on which she and that other giant of the school story were in full accord. Both had an absolute belief in the reality, not to say the almost independent existence, of their fictional characters. 'All the characters in my books became as absolutely real as were my friends in actual life,' Angela Brazil explains in her autobiography; (although, characteristically, she had expressed regret at an earlier point in the book that 'The dream children are not solid and I can't *kiss* them').

Elinor is yet more emphatic: 'Make no mistake!

[she wrote in the first Chalet Club newsletter] So far as I am concerned, the people [in the books] are *there*, just out of sight, but otherwise alive and panting to tell their stories. I am merely the loudspeaker through whom they broadcast to the world of girls who have made friends with them and wish to know what happens next. It is *they* who tell the stories. I am merely the instrument.'

That paragraph tells much about Elinor. And in particular her choice of words is revealing: for she had already used many of the same phrases and images in a book she wrote more than five years earlier — only in the book, *Joey Goes to the Oberland* (1954), Elinor was not, at least not avowedly, writing about herself:

> 'Oh, I suppose a day will come . . . [Joey Maynard explains to her adopted sister Robin Humphries] when . . . I'll have to sit down at my typewriter and be a loud-speaker again.'
>
> 'That's what you always say,' Robin returned thoughtfully. 'Do you really and truly feel that way about it, Jo?'
>
> Jo nodded. 'Exactly that. The people in my stories are there, alive and kicking, and longing to make friends in *this* world. They tell their own story. I'm just the — the instrument used for broadcasting it.'

The two passages are substantially the same. And there can be no possible question that Elinor had by this time become inextricably mixed with Joey. Yet, interestingly, she herself always denied that a close connection existed; more than that, she appeared even to resent any suggestion that it did.

'Jo is not based on myself nor anyone in particular,' she states firmly in a Chalet Club newsletter

(July 1964); in another, 'Jo is based on no one in particular, and certainly not on Jo March' (June 1965); the following year, 'Joey isn't me any more than half-a-dozen other characters' (September 1966; a slightly involved statement, but the intended denial is plain). And much earlier Elinor had discussed the matter at some length, in the Chalet Club's second newsletter (November 1959). 'People have accused me [she begins, with a choice of phrase that could be significant] of writing myself into Joey. I haven't done so consciously. It's true I always loathed maths [as Joey does] . . . I also dislike needlework, though I am very keen on knitting. And, of course, Joey and I both write. Apart from that I don't think there is much likeness. Oh, yes; we are both musical. I used to play the piano and 'cello, and sang too.'

Here the sentence 'Apart from that I don't think there is much likeness' may contain a clue, for it indicates that Elinor was concerned only with obvious superficial differences and resemblances. And there is no denying that her own circumstances were quite unlike Joey's. For one thing, there was the wide gap between their ages and this continued to increase, for although in real life it took forty-five years to write the Chalet series, Joey, who began at twelve, has still not quite reached forty in the last book. Joey, then, was younger by far. And, as Elinor might also have pointed out, she was married with a large family of children. She had been educated mainly at boarding-school. She had spent much of her early life abroad; and as an adult was able to travel extensively not just in Europe, but as far afield as Canada. She had black hair, cut with a fringe, 'eyes like pools of ink' and a delicately pointed face. She was tall and slim — originally even thin. In short, she looked nothing like Elinor.

And that, no doubt, was that — at least in Elinor's mind. So perhaps she was genuinely unaware of the extent to which she had been absorbed into her creature. Apart from anything else it had happened so gradually, for there are clear indications in the early books that Elinor then identified with the grown-up Madge Bettany, and not with her younger sister who was still only a child.

In any case, it would be over-simplifying things just to state that Elinor identified with Joey and leave it at that. There is no doubt that she also lived moments of wishfulfilment in other characters, most of all in Miss Annersley, that very model of a successful and popular headmistress. And bearing in mind the difficulties Elinor had in her own school, her feelings about Miss Annersley can be understood. On the other hand, her attitude to another of her long-standing Chalet School characters, Grizel Cochrane, is less easy to fathom. Grizel is important in all the early Chalet books; but there are signs that she is not Elinor's darling, for she is seldom allowed to appear in a wholly favourable light. Then, all of a sudden, in the fourth book, Grizel is given a star role as *The Head Girl of the Chalet School*, and is apparently admitted to high favour.

The change of angle is not altogether convincing. It also represents something quite unusual in the Chalet series; for although Elinor can be monstrously careless over details, she usually manages to keep her characters behaving with remarkable consistency. But plainly Elinor's heart was not really in that transformation of Grizel, who only a few books later is showing once more the 'certain hardness in her character' that had been spotlighted in all the early stories. Moreover Grizel was to be among the unfavoured few on whom Elinor did not lavish an early marriage and flocks of children — which must be significant, in view of the fact that Elinor, like many other writers in the genre, clearly considered marriage a kind of good conduct prize.

In the end, even Grizel does make it to the altar, and at least one baby, but not until the fiftieth book of the series, where at rising forty she is at last allowed to find happiness with a doctor. And perhaps it was, at least in part, because the coveted matrimonial prize had never come Elinor's own way that she so conspicuously grudged it to her unfavourite Grizel. For there seems little doubt that Elinor herself was never fully resigned to remaining unmarried. Her books do make it almost painfully clear that she thought of spinsterhood as second-best. It would be hard, for instance, not to hear a personal note beneath the following comment in *The Chalet School Goes to It*.

' "So the last of our old quartette is married" . . . [Frieda] said softly. "I am so glad. Simone is too dear and sweet to spend all her life teaching." '

And Simone, it must be pointed out, cannot be more than twenty-three at this time. Elinor, when she wrote the lines, was forty-seven and had been teaching on and off for nearly thirty years.

Nor was it only in fiction that Elinor revealed herself. One friend who, perhaps unexpectedly, got married when already into her forties, recalls the vehemence with which Elinor exclaimed: 'Oh, you are so lucky'. Another, Mrs Vivien Pass, who knew Elinor well for many years, is certain that 'she longed to marry . . . [but that] men in general found her exuberance embarrassing'. This friend pointed out, too, that 'the Great War left so many unfulfilled people'; adding, a little sadly, 'If she could have married, maybe there might not have been so many Chalet books, but there would have been a contented Elinor'.

That, however, seems an over-simplification. It is at least questionable whether Elinor would have been contented in marriage either. For one thing her books suggest that she had impossibly rosy and unrealistic views on the subject. And her true feelings towards the opposite sex remain obscure (as already discussed in Chapter IX). The idea has also been put forward — and inevitably — that Elinor might have had a latent tendency to lesbianism. Mrs Phyllis Matthewman once said she 'would not be surprised'. Nevertheless, it is plain that nothing definite has been alleged at any time, from any quarter. Moreover that it was particularly noted during Elinor's college days that her most extravagant gestures of affection were (as described) 'perfectly harmless'. And it is virtually certain that, if any such latent tendency did exist, Elinor herself was not consciously aware of it.

One other point on her attitude to marriage: since Elinor had undoubtedly convinced herself that she would have preferred to be married, it hardly matters whether she was right or wrong in supposing so.

It seems probable, too, that any resentment she may have felt at being condemned to spinsterhood must to some extent have coloured her relationship with her mother. Eleanor Ainsley — or Dyer, or Rutherford — is something of an enigma. Reactions to her vary from great affection to frank dislike. But there can be no doubt that she did in some ways outshine her daughter, at least in the social sphere. She was generally considered to possess both good looks and feminine charm — the first of which Elinor could never have claimed, although she could in her own way show a certain kind of charm. And reading between the lines it appears that Nelly could always contrive to get her own way and to 'rule the roost' without stepping outside the character of gentle old lady.

Quite possibly Mrs Ainsley was less clever than her daughter, and certainly she was less well educated: her handwriting alone would confirm that. But for Elinor there was no escaping the fact that her mother had achieved two marriages (no matter that the first was unsuccessful), whereas she herself had not been so much as engaged; and that did carry some weight in those days, when the wedding ring was still widely regarded as a woman's most desirable status symbol. One way and another it is not surprising to find that some friction existed between Nelly and Elinor. Theirs indeed appears to have been the classic love-hate relationship: 'Miss Brent-Dyer was always having terrible arguments with her mother,' according to one ex-pupil of the Margaret Roper School; whereas another acquaintance from this same period remembers 'how extremely and openly affectionate Miss Brent-Dyer always was with her mother . . . she would often throw her arms round her and embrace her.'

That, of course, might just have been Elinor's theatrical manner. But in fact no one seems to question that she and Mrs Ainsley really were devoted to each other; nor that Elinor looked after her mother most faithfully during the last period of her life. Nelly must have had a tough constitution, for she was to live for seven years after that illness in 1950 (described in the letter to Hazel Bainbridge's daughter); and, despite other heart attacks, to reach eventually the age of eighty-eight.

In the mean time Elinor continued to pour out book after book, although she was almost as tied during the 1950s as she had been in the days of the Margaret Roper School. There was not only her mother to be cared for: 'Aunt Elizabeth' apparently lived for many years, and she also became very frail towards the end. It seems, too, that there may also have been other elderly residents in the household. All of which makes the production of those thirty-eight books within a single decade the more remarkable.

Nelly Ainsley's death, when it came on 22 August 1957, was possibly a release both for her and for her daughter. And yet Elinor would almost certainly have been stricken at the time. At sixty-three years old she was left without any close relatives. She was herself coming within sight of old age. It was unlikely now that new doors would open.

CHAPTER XX

LIVING IN CHALET LANDS

In theory it might have been possible at this point for Elinor to build herself a new life. And perhaps another person in her situation would have done so, even at sixty-three years old. For that matter, there are women who, even at eighty-three, would have dropped everything, chucked the Chalet School out of the window and gone off to do some of the things that had been impossible during earlier life.

Elinor could for instance have considered taking another continental holiday — something that for many years had been ruled out for her, first by World War II, and later by the demands made on her as a 'carer' for Nelly Ainsley and others. Clearly her thoughts had already been turning towards Europe in the early part of the 1950s; for it was at this point that Elinor decided to send her Chalet School off to Switzerland, which then becomes the setting for the twenty-sixth book, *The Chalet School in the Oberland* (1952) and for most of the remaining books in the series from No. 29, *Joey Goes to the Oberland* (1954) and onwards.

For this part of the Chalet School saga Elinor devised a fictional location, the 'Görnetz Platz'. This, though imaginary, is recognisably placed in the real-world landscape of the Lauterbrunnen valley (Elinor changes the name to 'Lauterbach') and is descrbed as being near the well-known resort of Interlaken. The 'Görnetz Platz' also appears to have considerable affinities with the two real-life villages of Wengen and Mürren — its situation resembling that of Wengen, while its size and general layout are more akin to Mürren. And the question naturally arises as to how much Elinor's personal experience went into the drawing of the scenic background. Descriptions abound in the Swiss books, and many real places are mentioned, for the Chalet School girls make the customary regular expeditions, both in the vicinity of the Görnetz Platz and further afield. But the local colour in this part of the series lacks that personal touch that lends so much charm to the early books — including some of those set in 'Armishire'/Herefordshire.

The matter of whether Elinor herself had ever visited Switzerland has been much discussed by Chalet fans. And here, as so often in Elinor's life story, the question can have no definite answer. But one thing at least is certain. Any visit she made to Switzerland must have happened no later than 3 July 1932, for it was on that date that Elinor's one and only passport expired. It had been issued on 4 July 1922, and the Passport Office has confirmed that she never either renewed it or applied for another. Hence any visit to Switzerland could only have taken place during the decade between July 1922 and July 1932. Thus, in the midst of much uncertainty it can be stated with authority that, whatever moves towards independence Elinor may have made following her mother's death in 1957, a holiday abroad was not among them.

In any case, it seems plain that Elinor did not set great value on independence — as already noted on several occasions. What she in fact did at this point was to remain at Lichfield House, to continue pouring out books, and moreover to write them on exactly the same lines as before. Even the new location of the Chalet School brought no discernible changes to the character of the stories.

To some extent Elinor had now become the prisoner of her own success. Her Chalet books were being read not only throughout Britain but also in most parts of the English-speaking world, and in some European countries. Some were to be translated into Portugese; others, it seems, were adapted in cartoon form by a French publisher. Her fans were continually writing to demand yet more Chalet stories, and the earlier books were constantly being reprinted. By 1959 there were forty-two Chalet books, and many of them were selling well. Naturally her publishers were urging her on. And of course she did need the money. One way and another it would have been difficult for Elinor to have turned from the Chalet School to new paths.

Whether she ever wanted to do so is questionable. For one thing, it does seem that she lacked self-criticism. And there is little doubt that after her mother's death Elinor (in the words of her old friend Mrs Vivien Pass) 'began to live more and more in Chalet lands'. Possibly she found less and less to demand her attention in the real world. Besides, she had always shown a tendency to withdraw into fantasy. One of her closest friends in the Hereford days, the late Miss Rose Farr Smith, would have endorsed that. Miss Farr Smith (who at ninety was still active in the world of Girl Guides) wrote warmly that 'Elinor had a remarkable personality . . . She and I were good friends for many years. We understood each other'. But she noted, too, that Elinor was 'capable of being with you and giving you all her attention, then suddenly becoming completely aloof, wrapped up in a world of her own'.

Oddly enough, Elinor quite often describes this kind of thing happening to other people. At one point in *The Chalet School in Exile* (1940) Joey is 'far too busy with her new book to give more than a third of her mind' to anything she is being told. On another occasion (in *A Problem for the Chalet School*, 1956) it is Con Maynard (Joey's daughter, and a writer in the making) who is simply 'no use to man or beast when she's writing a story'; yet another time, Con is 'too busy with her imaginary people to worry much about outside affairs' (*Excitements at the Chalet School*, 1957). And yet it is quite unlikely that Elinor was aware how often she herself became abstracted in just this way.

Viven Pass, who fully agrees about the extent to which Elinor lived in a fantasy world, also commented — and quite without rancour — that 'Elinor really preferred all cats and dogs to any of her friends'. And although that may be an exaggeration, no one would deny that Elinor had a great love of animals. She was for many years an active supporter of the RSPCA, and throughout her life was seldom without at least one beloved dog or cat.

At Lichfield House there were always plenty of cats — even after that rumoured upset with the health authorities. Apart from Mrs Ainsley's tribe, Elinor had her own special 'amber-coloured' cat, her 'precious Bobby' — full name 'Bobby Shaftoe' — who first came to her in about 1941 as a six-week-old kitten, and was to be her constant companion until his death nearly twenty-one years later.

Then there was Bryn, an Alsatian bitch that Elinor owned during the latter part of her time in South Shields, and to which she was much devoted. Bryn is remembered by several friends as an extremely handsome animal, if rather fierce in appearance (Hazel Bainbridge confessed to having been frankly terrified of her). Bryn's ultimate fate is unknown; no one seems to recall how long she survived. Nor can anyone give the dates when

Elinor owned the 'dear cocker bitch called Sarah', which is mentioned in the *Chalet Club News Letter* for September 1966. But the last of Elinor's pets, described by her in a letter as 'a most intriguing dog called Simon', is still remembered by many people (including the author of this book), for he was to survive her and to become the much beloved and faithful companion of Mrs Phyllis Matthewman.

And quite apart from the testimony of her friends, Elinor's books provide ample evidence about her love of animals. Dogs in particular are important in many of her stories. There are Joey's two St Bernards in the Chalet series: Rufus first — his rescue as a tiny puppy is most effectively presented in *Jo of the Chalet Schoo*l; then Bruno; both these are described with unmistakable affection and understanding. Then there is Sanchia, Jesanne's Alsatian puppy in *The Lost Staircase*. And of course dogs are naturally the central theme in *Kennelmaid Nan* and *They Both Liked Dogs*.

Whether Elinor really preferred animals to people is unproven. But most certainly she did not lack friends during the thirty-odd years she spent in Hereford. Perhaps few of them were close to her, for beneath that flamboyant manner she was 'very reserved until you got to know her'. Possibly, even when you did. But at least two people managed to get past the reserve: Miss Mary Middleton (who died some years before research for the original edition of this book began) and Miss Rose Farr Smith (mentioned above). With these two Elinor made real and lasting friendships.

And there was a wide circle of others in whom she took a friendly if somewhat erratic interest. She would write to them occasionally, or perhaps to their children, as with Hazel Bainbridge's daughter. She would present them, either in person or by post, with copies of her books. She would chat to them in the street — if she happened to see them — or the library or the bank; and would hold forth on any subject that had lately caught her interest; at one time it was flying saucers. She would lend them books and invite them to lunch or tea or, in the case of those who lived far afield, to come and stay in Hereford.

Both she and her mother were hospitably inclined, and it seems that Lichfield House was often filled with visitors, especially during the war years. Some of the guests, according to Elinor's autograph book, were professional musicians who were giving concerts around Herefordshire. But naturally most of them were personal friends. They included at various times Hazel Bainbridge and Vivien Pass. And in 1944 a very old connection was resumed, when Phyllis Matthewman and her husband Sydney, whose home was in Surrey, came to find a temporary refuge from the flying bombs, which were then raining down on the south-east of Britain.

Phyllis and Elinor had of course known each other as children, almost forty years earlier. But on growing up the two had gone their separate ways and there had not been many meetings nor even much contact between them. And although Elinor's attitude to their early relationship is not known, Mrs Matthewman was clear about hers and ready to state with perfect frankness: 'As a child, I didn't like Elinor at all.' Moreover, despite Phyllis's anxiety in later life to stress that when they met again she had 'liked Elinor much better', it became fairly plain in talking to her that 'much better' did not really imply a great degree of liking. Into the bargain Mrs Matthewman's reactions were perhaps coloured also by some professional jealousy, unconscious no doubt but perceptibly underlying many of her comments.

Nevertheless a perfectly cordial relationship was established following the Matthewmans' first visit to Hereford. And after that Phyllis and Sydney were to be regular guests at Lichfield House, visiting Hereford at least once each year, and sometimes bringing with them their young niece, Chloe, who became much attached to Elinor. 'She was extremely kind to me and surprisingly understanding. I always remember that she gave me my very first lipstick as an Easter present. It was a very pale one, of course, but I was only thirteen or fourteen and no one else would have thought of anything like that, so I was thrilled.'

Sydney Matthewman was later, in about 1949, to set up a literary agency, Books for Today, and Elinor then became one of his first clients. That unquestionably was a piece of good luck for Sydney in his new venture, for at that time Elinor was both well established and successful as a children's writer. But there is no doubt that Elinor, too, was fortunate in that she now had someone reliable to advise her and to look after her career. Sydney had some experience of publishing and had worked on the editorial staff of a magazine. Most important, he also had a certain amount of ability for organisation, whereas Elinor herself was always hopelessly disorganised and unmethodical.

It seems, too, that she was incapable of any kind of order even where her beloved writings were concerned. 'The most peculiar things used to happen to Miss Brent-Dyer's manuscripts,' according to Mrs Phyllis Kerr (then Miss Peattie), who for many years worked at W. & R. Chambers. Once it was 'the puppy eating some of the pages for his dinner'. Once — far worse — publication of a book actually had to be delayed because Elinor's cat had chosen the current manuscript as a suitable place to have kittens and could not be disturbed. 'The then Managing Director was not amused on these occasions.'

However it is clear that on the whole Elinor had quite a friendly relationship with her publishers. And as recently as the 1980s the mention of Miss Brent-Dyer and her extraordinary manuscripts — 'typed from edge to edge of the page' — might well have brought smiles at Chambers, where those who remembered Elinor, clearly did so with not only amusement but affection.

As formally recorded in the final *Chalet Club News Letter* (November 1969), which announces 'the death of our authoress and very dear friend, Miss Brent-Dyer', the firm who had 'been publishing her books for over fifty years remember her indomitable spirit, often in face of great difficulties, her wonderful letters teeming with kindliness and interest; the tremendous fertility of her imagination that gave schoolgirl literature the most varied yet lovable assortment of characters it has ever known; and behind it all that deep sense of religious values that has meant so much to her thousands of reader.s.'

That, of course, was an official pronouncement by the firm. But their comments in letters and during informal conversations suggest that the sentiments expressed were genuine.

It is evident, too, that anyone at W. & R. Chambers whose work concerned Elinor and her books began, over the years, to feel a genuine involvement with the Chalet School. And this interest was not purely financial, but personal. Of course the series did undoubtedly hold money-spinning attractions for a publisher. There are not many figures available; but, for example, a letter from Sydney Matthewman's agency refers to sales of *Three Go to the Chalet School* (1949), which had reached almost 10,000 copies within a month or two of publication. And although sales probably did not remain at that level, there was obviously a continuing demand for Chalet books throughout the fifties and sixties, since Elinor had to produce the astonishing number of thirty-eight new stories in an effort to satisfy her fans.

This kind of success might not have appeared unusual during the heyday of the school-story genre. But for Elinor to have kept such a faithful following all through the post-war decades is remarkable. By this time ideas and fashions in children's literature had changed radically and there was no longer a ready market for the school story as such. Yet enough people went on reading — and buying — the Chalet books to make their production a paying proposition.

Still more extraordinary — there was the Chalet Club, which began in May 1959 and lasted until after Elinor's death more than ten years later. Fan clubs are of course familiar in the world of pop music, and among football supporters. In the literary field, too, there are societies, dedicated to such widely different figures as Sherlock Holmes and Rupert Bear. But the Chalet Club was then unique in the history of the girls' school story.

The club moreover enjoyed an astonishing growth rate, not unlike that of the Chalet School itself: in five years the numbers rose from an initial thirty-three to just under 4,000; and the members came from an impressive number of different countries. They were not all schoolgirls, either; but this point, and others connected with the Chalet cult, including the revival of Chalet School fan clubs in the 1980s and nineties, will be discussed in the next chapter.

Originally the idea of a Chalet Club had come from Elinor's publishers; and the club really owed not only its beginning but its entire existence to Mrs Phyllis Kerr (mentioned above) and Mr Thomas Collocott, a director of W. & R. Chambers, who was one of Elinor's principal editors for many years. These two were long-standing Chalet fans and together they worked out a scheme; at the beginning of 1959 this was put to Elinor, who gave her enthusiastic approval, and also her agreement in principle to write a couple of newsletters each year. (In practice it was often difficult to get these out of her on time.) A badge and a membership card were designed; and in May 1959 the club was launched.

Its avowed object was 'to form a closer link between Chalet enthusiasts the world over'. And the huge quantity of fan mail, that arrived from quite literally 'the world over', proves beyond doubt that the club was successful in doing this. There were times, in fact, when the correspondence threatened to get out of hand, for Elinor was not always very good about answering letters. And it is easy to understand something the former Miss Peattie wrote in a letter to another publisher who was considering whether to set up a similar club: 'For your sake I can only hope that all your authors do not have such a prolific fan mail as Miss Brent-Dyer!'

Unquestionably the running of the club entailed a tremendous amount of work. But of course there were sound business reasons behind the whole enterprise. Perhaps it may never have struck the members, but, as Mr Collocott was quite frank in stating, their Chalet Club gave splendid publicity to both Elinor and her publishers. It also provided a handy way of testing what might be called audience reaction. Here, the fan mail was obviously helpful as it gave direct information about readers' likes and dislikes. And the competitions (there were two every year, one in each newsletter) were often ingeniously slanted. Perhaps the readers might be asked to state which character they considered should take a leading role in the next story, giving their reasons. Or sometimes there would be a list of ten or more Chalet titles which had to be placed in order of preference. The latter type of competition proved doubly rewarding: the winner — that being the entrant whose list most nearly matched Miss Brent-Dyer's own — naturally got a prize; and Messrs Chambers got valuable material to help them in planning which Chalet book to reprint next.

The newsletters usually gave a list of all the Chalet titles that were currently available. And they always contained a snippet or two of information about the story that was to be published next — just enough to whet the appetite.

Regular features included a letter from the author, where Elinor would range over a variety of topics — usually but not always connected with the Chalet School. Advice for aspiring young writers was a favourite subject. And, as can be seen in the issue for June 1961, it was all good down-to-earth stuff with the emphasis on hard work and technical preparation:

> Remember this: you [cannot] . . . hope to sit down and reel off a book that some publisher will accept without long and severe training . . . you must learn your craft . . . pay attention to your English lessons . . . Learn to use words well and correctly . . . *Vary* the words you use . . . you can [also] prepare . . . by reading . . . the standard authors.
>
> . . . Write about people, places and things that you know. Otherwise you may make fearful

> mistakes . . .
>
> Avoid fairytales like the plague. It takes a genius to write a good [one] . . . another tip . . . [count] the number of words that go to a . . . [page] of print in a book . . . [multiply] that by the number of pages to a chapter . . . Think that [total] over and then you won't send out something that is, perhaps only 15,000 words in length and hopefully call it 'a book'.

Requests for still more advice on writing books would often appear in the correspondence columns. But most of the letters did of course concern the Chalet School. There might be just an occasional query about one of Elinor's other books; but these were already becoming scarce in the 1960s and they are now all out of print.

Certain questions were asked again and again. Was the Chalet School a real school? Some people simply took for granted that it was and wrote to ask for prospectuses . . . Were all, or any of the places described in the stories real? Were the characters modelled on real people? — and especially was Jo — or sometimes Madge — modelled on Elinor herself? (See previous chapter.)

Then there would be people who needed help to disentangle the complications of the Bettany or Maynard or Russell families. (From time to time these seemed to puzzle even Elinor herself.) And there were endless queries about what certain characters were doing *now* — the word 'now' being used apparently in the sense of 'right here and now in the present'. In fact the manner in which the questions were asked often suggested that the enquirer had real people in mind; and the answers would be given in the same spirit:

> The triplets are still at school. Elisaveta is living at Arosa in Switzerland. Robin is a member of the La Sagesse Order.
>
> Joey [Maynard] has eleven children now.
>
> Rosamund left at Christmas . . .
>
> The Maynards have succeeded in buying the place that was once St Scholastika's School, and spend summer holidays there.

It all becomes disconcertingly like the 'News of our Old Girls' page in some real-life school magazine.

Others among the multitude of correspondents wrote with enthusiasm about their holidays abroad, especially when they had visited Switzerland or the Tyrol. Even more fans expressed a desire for foreign travel. A grown-up reader, typical of the first group, wrote (issue no. 18, July 1968): 'It is now 12 years since I first visited Austria as the direct result of reading the Chalet books, and since then I have been six times. Strange to think that but for the books I might have missed these wonderful holidays'. And a fifteen-year-old from Newcastle upon Tyne probably spoke for many other schoolgirls, besides the two she mentions, when she wrote: 'Because of reading the Chalet books I have gained a longing to visit Austria, Switzerland and Oberammagau. I find you have also created such an idea in two of my friends'.

And in view of all this enthusiasm it seems odd that a plan for the Chalet Club to visit Austria in order 'to celebrate the Golden Jubilee of the Chalet School' (in other words, the appearance in 1963 of Chalet book no. 50) had to be abandoned for lack of support. The proposal had been that members would spend a short holiday in 'the Chalet School country in the Austrian Tyrol', and it had all been carefully thought out. The expedition was to have been 'organised by Cooks . . . led by Miss Brent-Dyer herself and accompanied by adult friends of the Chalet School Club'. The estimated cost was only 'in the neighbourhood of £33' to include 'travel . . . reserved seats and couchettes where available; food on the journeys; insurance . . . full board and accommodation at a good-class hotel or pension'.

Today, thirty-odd years later, that seems remarkably good value, even keeping an eye on inflation. But comparing prices can be tricky, and at the time it may have compared unfavourably with, say, a package tour to Majorca. Possibly it was also more than parents could afford, or wanted to spend, when the outing, being aimed mainly at schoolgirls, was not going to replace the family holiday.

At any rate, whatever the reasons, the plan for visiting the Tyrol was fated not to get off the ground. But 1963 did nevertheless see a number of celebrations to mark the Chalet School's 'Golden Jubilee'. And that fiftieth book, *The Chalet School Reunion*, was in itself a rather splendid production: it had a special binding in white and blue; and in addition to 'a coloured frontispiece and four illustrations in colour' there was a picture on the dust jacket, 'extending over the back and "spine" of the book as well as the front', which portrayed 'many of the "Old Girls" at the Reunion', not to mention staff, present pupils and Joey Maynard's St Bernard dog. (A key was supplied to help in identifying the characters.)

Then there was a jubilee edition of the *Chalet Club News Letter*, with six pages instead of the usual four; and in it were several most attractive colour pictures of Pertisau and the Achensee district — the original 'location' of the Chalet School. ('So my secret is out at last' — Elinor wrote, in characteristically dramatic fashion, about this final identification of the 'Tiernsee'.) An extra touch: on the back was reproduced a collage that had been made with stamps and envelopes from Elinor's overseas fan mail, and this too was in full colour.

However the most important event was undoubtedly the party at the National Book League in London, which was held in November 1963. Here Elinor met a large number of her fans (one came all the way from Denmark) and was given a presentation: 'A lovely bouquet and, more valuable because more lasting, the original of the jacket for *The Chalet School Reunion* . . . beautifully mounted and in a white frame' (July 1964). (The latter was presented to Elinor on behalf of the club by W.& R. Chambers.)

That day was probably the most memorable to date of Elinor's writing career. But something yet more important in terms of publicity was to follow. She herself gives a minutely detailed description of it in the Chalet Club newsletter for July 1964.

> On January 2nd [1964] I had a new experience — I was on Television in the programme "Tonight" . . . It was most interesting. First the official interviewer, Brian Redhead, met me and explained to me the sort of thing I should be expected to answer. The editress, Elizabeth Cowley, came along and joined in and then we were escorted to the studio . . . a great room filled with cameras moving about the floor and brilliant lighting. Cliff Michelmore was in charge of the programme as usual and when we sat down, we found he was about to interview someone with some most beautiful fowls. We were all warned to be prepared to leap to the rescue if the birds became restive and showed signs of scuttling. Far from it, they seemed dazed by their unusual surroundings

> and declined to show off in the least Then came a recorded interview with the Astronomer Royal, and finally myself. Everyone I know who saw me has informed me that I might have been accustomed to being interviewed daily. I seemed so calm. It wasn't like that, you know. It was simply that there was such a friendly atmosphere about the whole place I couldn't have felt nervy if I had tried.

To this day a few people still remember that interview. And apparently Elinor did not exaggerate in saying that she had 'seemed so calm'. By general agreement she really had spoken extremely well. 'Unexpectedly well' was the verdict of Mrs Phyllis Matthewman; but another friend was in no way surprised, having always considered her 'a larger than life, flamboyant sort of person'; and Miss Farr Smith commented that 'Elinor could make a most amusing speech, just like that — anytime'.

That 'gift of the gab' was something else that Elinor shared with Joey, who naturally was to follow her author on to television. And Joey too discovered that 'thanks to . . . [the interviewer's] experienced questioning and her own lack of real shyness, it was . . . easy enough' (*Chalet Club News Letter* 18, July 1968).

For Elinor, the thrill of being on 'Tonight' was followed the next day by an official tour of the Children's Book Exhibition at Olympia, which she visited at the invitiation of W.H. Smith and Son. This, not being a new experience, 'wasn't quite such an excitement as the Television'. Nevertheless, 'everyone was delightfully kind', and Elinor wrote that she had 'thoroughly enjoyed it'. No doubt, too, her TV appearance the previous night had given an extra boost to the Chalet School, for, as she herself puts it: 'Honestly, I signed autographs until my hand was aching!'

And throughout 1964 the Chalet School boom was to continue. That June Elinor 'paid a surprise visit to the magnificent World Book Fair at Earls Court [where] an . . . announcement over the loudspeaker brought dozens of . . . young readers', all clamouring for autographs.

In the mean time Elinor went on adding to her series; and although her rate of production fell noticeably in the sixties, she was to manage another eight Chalet stories after that Golden Jubilee number. She also published a couple of 'non-Chalet' school stories in 1962 and 1963 — but from 1964 onwards the Chalet School monopolised her entire attention.

The Chalet Club was also flourishing. Numbers kept up well and there were several new club activities, including: a penfriends' service, with sections for French and Swedish correspondents; a scheme whereby readers could buy sixpenny (2½p) savings stamps and put them towards the eventual purchase of a Chalet book; and even some 'Chalet Club groups' in various parts of Britain which met 'in one another's houses about once a month' to discuss 'Chalet and other matters'. One newsletter contains an advertisement asking for club members in India to form a group of this kind, although it seems that at the time this particular venture did not succeed.

A further milestone was reached in 1967 ('Another Historic Day for the Chalet School', as the newsletter puts it) when the firm William Collins (now HarperCollins) purchased the rights to publish a number of Chalet books in their 'Armada' paperback series. The first batch, consisting of four stories (nos. 1, 2, 14 and 30), appeared in May 1967, two more books were added that autumn, and from then onwards new titles were added each year. The rate of production has varied, but by the spring of 1995 'Armada's' republishing programme had covered the entire series. (It should be mentioned, in order to avoid possible confusion that a number of the original stories were divided into two parts for publication in paperback, the second part being then renamed, and hence the number of titles in the 'Armada' series exceeds the original fifty-nine.) Not all the titles are available at any one time, but it must be a tribute to the Chalet School's remarkable hold on life that HarperCollins find it well worth while always to keep a large selection of them in print.

Nor is this surprising, for the books have an excellent selling record. As far as numbers go, the first year figures are the most remarkable: in the six months between May and October 1967, 198,539 copies of Chalet paperbacks were sold — 169,938 at home and 28,601 in the export market. But right up to the present day annual sales continue to top the 100,000 mark; and, despite the relatively modest price of paperbacks, the author's annual percentage has always been a very respectable sum.

Elinor must have welcomed those royalties. For, contrary to what her fans may have imagined, she never made a great deal of money from her writing; and there are hints in correspondence that, up to the advent of 'Armada', Elinor often worried about financial matters. But perhaps she enjoyed the success even more. Certainly she would have rejoiced that the Chalet School was being introduced through 'Armada' to a completely new readership both at home and abroad. And, to begin with at any rate, she was delighted with this latest presentation of her stories. 'I am so glad for everyone's sake [she wrote to her 'Armada' editor] that the books are selling well. I think the "Armada" set-up is most attractive and I love the jacket illustrations. Will you please tell your artist this, and also how pleased I am about the way he/she is sticking to the descriptions of the various characters in the books.'

Perhaps it is fortunate that Elinor did not live to see some of the later jackets which portray her Chalet girls and even the grown-up Joey in miniskirts, or she might have been less happy. She was, in fact, quite critical on occasion of the way in which some of the books had been abridged, and in particular of well-meaning attempts to update them:

> As you will see I have had to make various alterations in the cuts [she wrote when returning the proposed revision of *Mary-Lou of the Chalet School*]. One or two made nonsense of the M.S. and quite a number used phrases and words that just are not me . . . One thing I do want to impress on whoever does the alterations. The Maynards never called their parents Mummy or Daddy. They were brought up from the first to say Papa and Mamma and, indeed, there are not only two or three pages explaining all this in *The Chalet School in Exile* [one of the first 'Armada' batch], but a brief explanation is given in the majority of the books into which . . . [the Maynard children] come.

After that it was arranged with Elinor that all alterations would be left to her; and for some years after her death this task was taken over by Mrs Matthewman. Some abridgement of the books was probably essential, for the originals had often run to 70,000 words and more. But many Chalet fans, in all age groups, have expressed regrets about the cutting; and this may partly explain why the ready availability of the paperback edition has not lessened demand in the second-hand market for Chalet School hardbacks, which are always unabridged. Nowadays the most ordinary 'reading copies' will fetch far higher prices than they did when new; and collectors are ready to pay sums in three figures for any of the early books in the original illustrated edition with dust wrapper, as well as for certain particularly scarce titles.

This boom in second-hand Brent-Dyers is just one facet of the whole extraordinary Chalet School legend — a phenomenon that one of Elinor's readers has named 'Chaletomania', which will form the subject of the coming chapter. But one other piece of evidence about Elinor's popular success may be given here. It was mentioned in a letter that Sydney Matthewman wrote to Collins on 21 February 1969: 'I suppose you know that Elinor has now reached the summit of literary fame: she is (as we used to say) "given away with a pound of tea". In other words, if you send up eight coupons from Lyons' Harvest Pies you can have a copy of *Rivals of the Chalet School*.'

And, according to Sydney, Elinor 'was tickled to death when . . . [she] discovered this'. Yet another Historic Day for the Chalet School?

CHAPTER XXI

'A ROMANTIC WORLD IN ITSELF'

In the late 1920s Elinor's fan mail included a letter which began: 'We hope you won't mind two schoolgirls writing to tell you how much we appreciate your jolly Chalet Stories. They are all so ripping that we don't know which book to say we like best . . . such a novel and delightful change from the ordinary school-story.'

That fan letter was to be quoted on the dust wrappers of all Chalet books published in the thirties and early forties. And the 'two schoolgirls', even though unnamed, thus became the best known of Elinor's early fans.

Most likely the two were also quite typical of their generation — undoubtedly so, to judge from their choice of adjectives. Schoolgirls did naturally form the largest group among Elinor's readers in the early days; and this continued to be the case during the pre-war period and right through to the 1960s. Even today, with the 21st century approaching, the selling record of Chalet School paperbacks (see previous chapter) indicates that Elinor still has plenty of youthful admirers.

Of course, critics and experts in children's literature sometimes refuse to accept that book sales provide any evidence of children's tastes. Books, as they eagerly point out, are bought not by children but by parents, who often choose their own childhood favourites. And this is undeniable. But the experts are perhaps forgetting the average child's talent for resistance. The most nostalgic parents will hardly go on and on buying books that their children persistently refuse to read. And it is impossible to believe that the thousands upon thousands of Chalet paperbacks sold during the past twenty-eight years have all been bought by misty-eyed, middle-aged Mums, to be rammed down the throats of unwilling daughters.

It is true that Elinor's older readers do include many 'mothers who enjoyed the books in their own girlhood and have now passed them on to their daughters' (*Chalet Club News Letter* 1); and that the majority of adult Chalet fans did first meet the Chalet School during their childhood. Nor is this surprising. The remarkable thing is that the adult group should contain so many people who had never so much as heard of the Chalet School until they were grown up. From this category, five may be singled out:

> A Canadian school-teacher, who for some years lived and worked in Hertfordshire, in a local infant school; in 1975 she picked up a copy of *The Princess of the Chalet School* at a jumble sale for 5p, and enjoyed it so much that for the next year or two she gave much of her spare time to finding and reading the other fifty-eight stories.

> An eighty-one-year-old New Zealand lady who became fascinated by the series when visiting her grandchildren.

> A Scottish lady, Miss Georgina Moncrieff, who was already nearing sixty when the first Chalet story appeared; her greatest love was Dante (on whom she published a book at the age of eighty-four), but she remained an enthusiastic Chalet reader to the end of her life, caring nothing for the

> raised eyebrows of her friends and relatives.
>
> A middle-aged Englishman, who used regularly to borrow the copies that belonged to his schoolgirl daughter — and not to send them up, either: he was quite put out when she later passed her collection to a younger reader, and he then devoted much effort to finding copies for himself.
>
> Another Englishman, the late Hilary Maurice Bray (oddly enough a descendant of the original Margaret Roper); he first encountered the Chalet series, as he himself recounts, when, 'searching for *The Secret Garden* in a library under B for Burnett, I saw a book next to it with girls in skiing clothes on the cover . . . took it out . . . [and] since then . . . have been reading them, like painting the Forth Bridge, beginning again at the beginning when I have got to the end'. Later, although never blindly uncritical, he was to become one of Elinor's most fervent admirers: 'I think . . . the Chalet series is a unique achievement. I know nothing about school stories but suspect that E. B.-D. raises them to a new dimension.'

Hilary Bray must be among Elinor's most unexpected fans. But then Chalet enthusiasts are to be found in an astonishing number of places, age groups, and walks of life. Fan letters used to reach Elinor from 'England, Scotland, Ireland and Wales. Letters from Canada, Australia, New Zealand, the Barbadoes, India, France, Belgium, Switzerland, South Africa, Kenya and [as Elinor herself puts it] other places'; Singapore, Malaysia and Hong Kong were some of those she did not mention.

Nor did the stream of letters end with Elinor's

death. Throughout the twenty-five years since then people have gone on writing; in the first place to Elinor's two main publishers, W.& R. Chambers and HarperCollins 'Armada'; later, to the author of this book. And yet another tribute to the Chalet School's enduring vitality is provided by the existence today, in the mid-1990s, of two successors to the original Chalet School fan club.

The older of the two, the Friends of the Chalet School, originally began in Australia, where it was founded in 1989 by Ann Mackie-Hunter, a committed fan of the Chalet School, who was then living in New South Wales. At first the group consisted only of a few dozen Australian enthusiasts; but the society's reputation spread so quickly that by 1994, the year of Elinor Brent-Dyer's centenary (more of this in the coming chapter), it had grown to over a thousand members, representing among them ten or more different countries. The other society, the New Chalet Club, which began only in June 1995, has grown at an even more remarkable rate. After barely two months it already had a worldwide membership of more than four hundred, and every week the list continues to grow.

Both societies issue quarterly magazines, and hold occasional meetings and other events. And although, not surprisingly, the majority of members live in the United Kingdom, Chalet fans have joined, just as in Elinor's day, from Ireland, France and Switzerland, as well as from all around the English-speaking world, including more recently the USA.

Australia has always been particularly well represented in Chalet School circles — possibly because there was at one time an Australian edition of the books, published by Dymocks. And back in the mid-1970s, when *Behind the Chalet School* was first being written, a particularly interesting letter arrived from a young Australian school-teacher, Rosemary Gunn, aged then about twenty-six. Born and brought up in modern Australia, she had no personal links with Britain, or Europe, or with the English boarding-school tradition; but she became so caught up with the Chalet books and their author that she decided to base a thesis on the subject. This involved her, among other things, in persuading several of her friends to read through the series; and she furnished a most entertaining account of some forthright comments these friends had made, including the following:

'The first exploded at one point: "Why, oh why are they always eating?"; and the second: "If another of them marries a doctor I shall scream!" But she didn't — just reached for the next book.'

And later in her letter she confirmed that many schoolgirls in present-day Australia were reading and enjoying the Chalet series.

No doubt about it — the Chalet School appeals to an audience that is far wider than many of Elinor's critics would acknowledge, or perhaps even realise. This point was emphasised by a fan in Scotland, who had always enjoyed the books as a girl, and became specially interested 'when, as a school librarian I found that . . . [the stories'] popularity was as great as ever among girls of all grades of attainment and social class'.

Possibly 'as great as ever' could be a slight overstatement. But certainly there are inumerable Chalet enthusiasts today — albeit sometimes in secret — among the pupils at both independent schools and large comprehensives. Not so long ago, a twelve-year-old schoolgirl from Aberdeen proclaimed: 'Apart from some of the expressions they use, like "top-hole", I always think of the

Chalet School as happening today'. And quite recently another twelve-year-old described the series as 'Apsalootly [sic] wicked' — a 1990s term of youthful approval for which some older readers may require a teenage interpreter.

Leaving the world of school, there are Chalet fans to be found today working in the BBC, and in the British Library. More than one young editor in go-ahead London publishing houses has confessed to being 'an avid fan of the Chalet School'. One older reader in Hereford presented several of the books to her daily help 'because her [the latter's] mother always enjoys them so much'. One of Elinor's lifelong fans, Judith Humphrey, was so full of admiration that, in the midst of looking after home, husband and two pre-school children (not to mention compiling French textbooks for schools and singing in a choir), she somehow found time to embark on a detailed 60,000-word survey, now the nucleus of a PhD thesis, which aims to establish Elinor's pre-eminent place in the school-story genre. And a university librarian wrote of a friend, 'the Head of a Science Department in a College of Technology, [who] . . . has even based a holiday in Switzerland and Austria on . . . descriptions of places in Chalet books'. Nor would this be unusual nowadays, for in the 1990s there have been several occasions when fans have joined organised group visits to Chalet School sites in both Austria and Switzerland.

Admittedly, many readers of the series could be decribed as middle-class, but the range of backgrounds is unexpectedly wide; and the memories of one fan, Mrs Sally Holloway, who grew up in a London working-class home, serve to underline the point that a child's imagination can be unfettered by social boundaries. She recalled that, although she could not afford to buy the Chalet books, she would borrow them regularly from the public library — having originally been attracted by the red covers; and she would often stand in their Clapham Junction backyard, apparently watching the trains rumble past: 'But I wasn't looking at the trains — I was watching the Tiernsee steamers arrive at the landing-stage beside the "Kron Prinz Karl".'

All in all, it would be quite impossible to put Chalet School readers, past and present, into any category — or even series of categories. They belong to no particular age-group. They come from various social backgrounds and from many different countries — although, for obvious reasons, the majority are British. Some have attended boarding-schools, others not. Some have travelled abroad and may have studied foreign languages; some have done neither. Many did first meet the Chalet stories during childhood, but a sizeable minority did not. A number go on reading the books with uncritical admiration; a few lose interest altogether; but many more, in all age groups, continue to enjoy the stories while remaining fully aware of their flaws.

The fans include children and teenagers and the whole age-range of adults up to at least the age of ninety (the oldest known to date was ninety-three); people married, unmarried, childless, with families large or small. They work in a variety of jobs, skilled, unskilled, intellectual or otherwise, paid or unpaid; attend schools or colleges (an interestingly high proportion of adult fans belong to the teaching profession). Many are housewives, with or without other jobs. Only a very few are ladies of leisure.

They include practising members of many different religious sects, and people without any religious affiliations — occasionally even an avowed atheist. They include people from widely different income brackets, and of opposing political views. They are certainly not all middle-aged women seeking to recapture their childhood. They are not even all females.

The one thing that unites all these people is their enjoyment of the Chalet books. And most of them, although the warmth of their enthusiasm may vary, also join in remaining unimpressed by any derogatory pronouncements of critics, or librarians, or other so-called experts in children's literature. But, apart from this basic agreement, the fans appear to hold very different opinions of the books, and especially about the reasons for their popularity.

For some, the sheer length of the series is part of its fascination. 'It's no good taking . . . [the Chalet Series] in small nibbles like cocktail biscuits . . .' writes Hilary Bray; 'It is a regimen, a diet'. Judith Humphrey thinks that 'the cumulative effect of the Chalet Series' would in itself entitle Elinor to a high place among children's writers, for it was by this means that 'she . . . created a living world with an imaginative reality [all its own]'. But a different angle is taken by another admirer, who considers that, since 'Elinor had already achieved this "romantic world" quite early on, . . . it is at least questionable whether she added to her achievement, or perhaps even diminished it, by going on and on [with the series]'. And that view seems to be shared by many readers, for it is clear that a majority in all age groups prefer the earlier stories — although perhaps few would go as far as one who wrote: 'I only ever liked the early Chalet books . . . Later on I think the long series got absolutely nutty.'

However there would probably be general agreement with the point made in a letter by the late Sheelagh Tatham, who was an acknowledged authority on the girls' school story: 'It was the fact that the Chalet books were a series that really ensured their continuing success, I think.' For there is no question that a series does tend to become self-propelling once it really gets going. At some point a kind of soap opera syndrome begins to operate, and people once hooked will find no rubbish too great to swallow. (Certain radio and TV serials come to mind.)

Neverthless, the cumulative factor alone cannot account for the success of the Chalet books. Apart from anything, it does not explain why the popularity of these stories has been greater and has endured for longer than that of other comparable series.

At quite an early stage Elinor's publishers already had their own ideas on this matter; and these were embodied in a blurb which appeared on the dust wrappers of pre-war Chalet books from about 1933 onwards:

> The 'Chalet School', situated among the Alpine pastures of the Tyrol, has . . . become to girl readers a romantic world in itself.
>
> The doings, ordinary and extraordinary, of Jo Bettany and her fellow Chaletians hold the reader's attention to the last page. At the same time, the descriptions of Tyrolese scenery and of the life and manners of the people make the stories as instructive as they are entertaining.
>
> There is a delightful freshness of incident and conversation, coupled with a skilful use of humour and pathos. Girl character is accurately drawn, and nowhere is the transition from rollicking girlhood to joyous womanhood more naturally portrayed.

Today the wording of that last half-sentence may be hard to take; but, allowing for the period language, the three short paragraphs manage to encapsulate in an expert fashion most of the ingredients in the Chalet School's magic recipe.

The exotic Tyrolean setting of the early books was unquestionably of prime importance. An informal straw poll among readers showed that this came high on their list of reasons for liking the stories. And Elinor's 'Briesau-am-Tiernsee' caught her readers' imaginations not only because of its beauty, but because it was fun. What girl would not prefer to forsake the ordinary bus or suburban train and travel to school by that 'quaint little mountain railway', and then onwards in 'the little white steamer' across the sapphire-blue lake, with breath-taking views on every side?

In this setting 'the doings ordinary and extraordinary of Jo Bettany and her fellow Chaletians' immediately became both more interesting and more convincing. The most ordinary school activities — walks, for instance — can seem glamorous in such a beautiful place; and the extraordinary adventures — two girls getting lost in the mist on a mountain precipice, or the Chalet being engulfed by floods during the spring thaw — can appear credible, given the school's alpine situation.

Then, right from the beginning, the Chalet School had the advantage of being 'different', with its mixture of nationalities and religions, its near-family atmosphere (in the early books) and its delicious-sounding meals. And the stories all contained — as indicated in the publisher's blurb, and expressed in the words of a grown-up fan: 'so many interesting historical and geographical facts, to say nothing of the local legends, which the reader could painlessly absorb.'

Another facet of the books was mentioned by a schoolgirl whose letter is quoted in *Chalet Club News Letter* 7: 'In reading the French conversation of the Chalet girls unknowingly I learnt quite a few words, phrases and idioms.' And although Elinor's own knowledge of French and German appears to have been, to say the least, limited (she sometimes makes glaring errors in both languages) there is no doubt that her stories really have encouraged many schoolgirls to try and emulate the prowess of trilingual Joey Bettany and her friends.

However, in spite of all this, it is plain that had there been no more to the books than a glamorous background and a lot of instruction more or less attractively packaged, the Chalet Series would long ago have been forgotten — like so many other school stories. Probably the stories' picturesque locations, in Austria, the Channel Islands, Herefordshire, Wales and Switzerland have helped; but today this aspect of things is probably less important than it was, for now holidays abroad have become almost the accepted thing for children, and this may rob the books of some of their former novelty.

That the Chalet School continues to survive after more than seventy years is mainly a tribute to the entertaining stories, the sense of comedy and fun, and above all to the characterisation shown in the early books. Here the pupils are neither the paragons of virtue nor the monsters of depravity so often found in school stories, but credible schoolgirls who may have a rather unusual number of adventures but still manage to behave and talk like human beings.

In fact, Elinor's principal achievement would seem to lie in having created, at the beginning of her series where it mattered most, a set of characters who (as discussed in the previous chapter and elsewhere) gradually assumed an almost independent existence in her eyes and those of her readers. It was this conviction that her characters were real people that carried Elinor through book after book; and it also helped to persuade all those thousands of readers into following the Chaletians' progress — and later that of their multitudinous children with unwearying devotion.

'I have read and re-read the series over the years [wrote a middle-aged fan whose daughter was beginning to follow in her footsteps] and . . . have always felt that with a very few words Miss Brent-Dyer was able to depict the character of any one of her numerous schoolgirls.' Another fan considered that Elinor's characterisation is of a very high order, and that in judging it 'the [school-story] context seemed irrelevant . . . [because] these characters are apt to explode out of the school gate'.

Yet another admirer paid tribute to the reality of the whole Chalet School world when she described how 'at Christmas time . . . and this has been in Japan, the USA, and once going up the Suez Canal' she is often 'far away, walking down the mountain path to Spärtz . . . having coffee and delicious rolls with Herr Anserl in the station refreshment room . . . setting out with Madge, Joey and the Robin to visit the Mensch family in Innsbruck'. And the author of this biography wrote to a friend about her experience in reconstructing the story, *Visitors for the Chalet School*, which is woven around the early Chalet School characters: 'People can say what they like — but I found it as easy to write about Elinor's Chalet School people as about my own family and the friends I know really well. That must mean something.'

What it does mean, or at least indicate, is that Elinor had managed in an extraordinary way to build what amounts to a personal relationship between her characters and her readers. And once this is borne in mind it becomes easier to understand why even the least satisfactory among her later Chalet books always found a faithful public.

It mattered nothing to the 'Chaletomanes' that the ideas in most of these books had already been used — and usually far more effectively — in earlier stories. And, seemingly, they were not bothered to find that genuine humour, which had been a delightful feature in the early days, was now in short supply, and that the jokes were often laboured. Decidedly nothing to match the fun of 'Shakespeariana' in the second book, or the snails episode in the third.

Nor were the faithful readers put off by Elinor's increasingly heavy-footed style of writing. And yet the interesting thing is that so many of them were obviously conscious of all these defects. For example, Judith Humphrey, who is herself an honours graduate in English and French, will allow that: 'Stylistically many of . . . [the later Chalet books] are awful, at best pedestrian and at worst incredibly clumsy'; also that 'by then [Elinor's] ability to sustain the structure had collapsed'. But she added — and is probably speaking for many: 'Despite this, there are good bits even in the worst books. I wouldn't really scrap any of them. Good "set pieces" with the parts in between [to be] got through as quickly as possible!'

Nevertheless, it would be fair to mention at this point that Elinor's style in her earlier books, which might still be open to criticism when compared with the standards prevailing among children's writers today, is noticeably superior to that of many others in her genre and period.

After all's said and done, it remains true that

Elinor, on top form, did produce some first-rate school stories. These undoubtedly rank among the best examples in their field. Whether they are judged to be the best of all will depend largely on taste. But it is worth noting that *Jo of the Chalet School*, published in 1926, is one of the few school stories of its period where an attempt is made to keep the story moving around ordinary school activities and characters (as in the books Antonia Forest and Mary Harris were to write twenty-odd years later); and where all the adventures, allowing for the Chalet School's alpine terrain, might easily have happened in real life.

Four further points should be taken into account in any assessment of the Chalet School's amazingly enduring popularity. One results from the tireless crusade that, throughout Chalet School history, was waged against the use of slang expressions. In the stories, the avowed object of this anti-slang rule was to prevent the girls who were not native English speakers from acquiring a vocabulary of undesirable slang expressions; and in real life, the fictional ban has meant that much of the dialogue in the Chalet School books now appears less dated than that in some other school stories.

Another important factor has been the role played by religion in the series. This has already been considered at length in Chapter XVI; so here it need only be emphasised once more that a majority of Elinor's readers have quite evidently welcomed and appreciated this religious aspect of the stories.

Then there is the theme of international fellowship, which is sometimes discussed and always implicit in the Chalet books. Here the reaction of Elinor's most fervent masculine admirer, Hilary Maurice Bray, to a particular side of the wartime books is of interest: 'for me, with the recollection of those years of genophobia and the deliberate "strategic" generation of hatred, E. B.-D. lighted a small but inextinguishable candle — in the Chalet School Peace League.'

Finally, there is the concept of the Chalet School itself as an abiding institution, with defined and well-established traditions, which through much repetition became comfortably familiar to the fans. And clearly Elinor's readers enjoyed the idea of being, as it were, part of the Chalet School's extended family. There can be no doubt that this quasi-reality of the school has been one of the two most powerful factors in binding together and even to a certain extent unifying the whole mammoth series. Only the continuity of the characters has been more important, 'Whatever happens to us, the Chalet School must go on,' Joey Maynard proclaims at the end of' *The Chalet School Goes to It*, published in 1941.

'The Chalet School . . . [books] are not just school stories; they are an entire way of life' (*Chalet Club News Letter* 18, July 1968) a schoolgirl fan wrote — an opinion that some might dismiss as an exaggeration, but one that nevertheless expresses a genuine tribute to the books.

And the last word in this review of the Chalet School legend may fittingly be given to Elinor herself. When asked in 1964 about the future of her series, she replied: 'I can't say, for I honestly don't know how long the series is likely to continue. As long as I do myself, I hope' (*Chalet Club News Letter* 12, December 1964).

At least that hope was to be more than realised, as will be demonstrated in the chapter which follows.

CHAPTER XXII

THE CHALET SCHOOL SEVENTY YEARS ON

Before coming to the final years of Elinor's life, some consideration of the events that took place during 1994 follows logically from the previous chapter.

It is always tempting to try and picture how people of a bygone era might have reacted had they suddenly been transported a hundred years forward in time. No doubt about it — Elinor's family and their friends and neighbours in South Shields would surely have been dumbfounded if, on the day of her birth, 6 April 1894, they could have foreseen what would happen on that same date a hundred years later. For, on 6 April 1994, a ceremonial gathering in South Shields, attended by the Mayor, with other officials of the South Tyneside Borough Council, and numerous Chalet School fans, not to mention local visitors and representatives of the media, marked the first in a series of events to commemorate Elinor Brent-Dyer's centenary.

At this first celebration, a memorial plaque to Elinor was unveiled; not at the actual place of her birth, which of course no longer exists, but, by an ironic twist of fate, on the house in Westoe Village where the Misses Stewart had their school, recording, as well as the dates of Elinor's birth and death, the fact that she had been a pupil there between 1906 and 1912. Would the ladies perhaps have been a little surprised?

South Shields certainly did Elinor proud that day. 'Now it's wor Elinor' — announced the headline in the *Shields Gazette*; and the Borough Council not only provided transport to and from Westoe Village for the many guests but, after the unveiling ceremony, laid on a splendid reception and sit-down lunch at the Town Hall — itself an impressive building, and one that must have been a familiar sight to Elinor as she walked around the town.

Next came the turn of Hereford, where the City Council was also most co-operative. Among other things, they sponsored the erection of a plaque at the gate of Elinor's former home in Bodenham Road (where she had run the Margaret Roper School); assisted with the arrangements for a Brent-Dyer exhibition at the Central Library; and laid on an evening reception in the Bishop's Palace.

More than 160 Chalet School enthusiasts attended an April weekend of celebrations in and around Hereford — some had come from as far afield as Australia. And the non-stop programme of official events included a celebration dinner at Belmont Abbey (where one of the speakers was a former pupil of the Margaret Roper School, Mrs Luella Hamilton); a visit by coach to the second-hand bookshops of Hay-on-Wye; a special Mass of Thanksgiving at St. Francis Xavier's Church in Hereford — the church Elinor herself attended; a fiendishly difficult quiz, covering just about every aspect, known and unknown of Elinor's books; and a hilarious group photograph session. Throughout the weekend the flow of chatter and laughter could hardly have been matched on a first day of term at the Chalet School itself.

Later in the year a comprehensive exhibition was staged at Edinburgh's Museum of Childhood; and this was opened by Mr Tony Chambers, a former director of Elinor's publishers, W.& R. Chambers, who, in relating some of his own memories of Elinor, provided a direct personal link with the Chalet School's author.

During the summer (thanks to the good offices of Martin Spence, who is prominent among the Chalet School's group of male admirers), a plaque commemorating Elinor's Tyrolean visit was erected outside the library in Pertisau-am-Achensee (as mentioned in Chapter XIII). This plaque particularly stresses the important role played by Pertisau as Elinor's inspiration in her Chalet School series.

The weekend of 16-18 September then saw a gathering in Guernsey, where the interest focused on both the Chalet School and the La Rochelle series. And, on Tuesday 20 September, the twenty-fifth anniversary of Elinor's death, a memorial and thanksgiving service was held in the Church of the Holy Family at Reigate, her parish church and scene of her funeral. This was followed by the blessing at Elinor's grave in Redstone Hill Cemetery at Redhill, Surrey of a specially commissioned headstone, paid for by subscriptions from Chalet fans all around the world.

The centenary year was rounded off in December: first with a conference in London, held at the University of Westminster. This not only dealt with many aspects of the girls' school story, but also provided an occasion for launching Bettany Press's newly published *The Chalet School Revisited* (a collection of nine essays on different facets of the Chalet School books), as well as giving an opportunity for Chalet fans to see Juliet Gosling's centenary video of the same title. And that evening a final celebration took the form of a Christmas party, Chalet-School-style, with the whole-hearted singing of Christmas carols being a notable feature. The programme even featured three of Elinor's own carols, including 'Oh, Busy World', from *Challenge for the Chalet School*, sung to the melody of 'Oh, Little Town of Bethlehem'.

Altogether a notably eventful centenary year. And its resounding success was undoubtedly due to the hard work of innumerable people in many different places, but above all to the enterprise and tireless energy of the Elinor M. Brent-Dyer Centenary Committee, Clarissa Cridland and Polly Goerres.

The former, who was at the time rights manager for an international publishers and is now working as a freelance agent, has made a special study of the illustrations and dustwrappers of the Chalet School series, on which she wrote an article for *The Chalet School Revisited*. Polly Goerres, who also contributed an essay to the book, had first made her mark in Chalet School circles when, in 1983, she chose to write the official dissertation for her degree at Sheffield University on: 'The Language, Traditions and Genre of the Chalet School'. And that, in the early 1980s, was both an unusual and an adventurous choice. At that time, critical attitudes towards the girls' school story were still predominantly hostile. And, although ideas have changed perceptibly in recent years, this softening in the climate of opinion did not begin to show itself until near the end of the 1980s.

Up till that point, even Armada, despite the excellent selling record of Chalet School paperbacks, had always tended to adopt an attitude to the stories that was more apologetic than enthusiastic. It was only in 1989 that a change of outlook led to their commissioning, first, in September of that year, *Elinor M. Brent-Dyer's Chalet School* — a large format paperback including numerous coloured illustrations; and, four years later, *The Chalet School Companion*, which was published in 1994 as part of Armada's programme for the centenary year. Their other centenary contributions included the first ever completely unabridged paperback of *The School at the Chalet*, which was produced in facsimile style, with a reproduction on the cover of the original Nina Brisley dustwrapper. And it must surely have given Armada cause for thought, if not surprise, that during the summer of 1994 this book became number five on the list of bestselling children's books!

Without question, the interest and media publicity attracted by Elinor Brent-Dyer's centenary have played a part in focusing the change of attitudes towards the girls' school story that has been noticeable during this decade. And the numerous fan clubs that have grown up in the 1990s — supporting other writers in the genre, besides Elinor Brent-Dyer — could be considered both a symptom and a cause of this change. For one thing, the various societies have encouraged many adult fans to reveal the enthusiasm which formerly they felt constrained to keep hidden. This is made abundantly clear in the hundreds of letters sent by Chalet enthusiasts since the first publication of *Behind the Chalet School* in 1981, where a common theme has been the delight of thc writers at finding they were not, after all, alone in their addiction. To quote just one 1990s correspondent, who wrote from Invercargill, New Zealand: 'I have been a fan of the CS books for years (I am now 23) . . . [but], living at the bottom of New Zealand, and not liking to admit to sceptical friends that I still read "children's books", I [had never realised] . . . how many other adults still enjoy the stories.' And there can be few gatherings of Chalet fans where someone doesn't utter the words: 'And to think I always imagined I was the only one.'

Nor is it only among enthusiasts that things have

changed. Today, Polly Goerres' dissertation, which at the time was a pioneer in academic cirles, has a number of successors. Among them, one by a young Australian, Patrick Osborne; and an MA thesis by Juliet Gosling — who produced the 60-minute video, *The Chalet School Revisited*, mentioned above, and who will complete her PhD on the reasons for the popularity of the girls' school story in 1996.

Juliet Gosling is also one of the moving spirits in Bettany Press, an enterprising small firm which she and Rosemary Auchmuty began in 1994 with, as its first objective, the publication of *The Chalet School Revisited*. Since then, they have gone on to publish *Visitors for the Chalet School* (1995), which is Helen McClelland's reconstruction of the story missing between *The Princess of the Chalet School* (no. 3 of the series) and *The Head Girl of the Chalet School* (no. 4). And the remarkable interest aroused by this 'new' Chalet School book in the national media must, in itself, be a tribute to the way ideas have changed.

Back in the early 1980s, when *Behind the Chalet School* first appeared, it took the BBC well over a year to show any interest, either in the book or in what may be called the Chalet School phenomenon. In the end, a highly successful programme, featuring an interview with Helen McClelland and extracts from the books read by Kate O'Mara, was broadcast in January 1983 on BBC Radio 4's *Woman's Hour,* with two repeats, including one on Christmas Day. This was due entirely to the efforts of one producer, Pamela Howe, herself a great fan of the Chalet School, who also arranged, on 23 March 1987, for Martin Spence and Gill Bilski to appear on *Woman's Hour* and talk about the Chalet School series and why the books still appeal today. But without Pamela Howe's personal intervention it is unlikely, bearing in mind contemporary attitudes, that there would have been any reaction from the BBC.

Whereas in the summer of 1995, when *Visitors for the Chalet School* appeared, it became the subject of six radio interviews within the space of barely ten days, as well as being given an excellent review in the *Independent on Sunday* — one, moreover, that took the story seriously, something that would have been quite unlikely during the 1970s and eighties. Just at it would then have been unthinkable for the BBC to allow a *Mastermind* contestant to choose for her special subject 'The Life and Chalet School Novels of Elinor M. Brent-Dyer', as did Barbara Inglis, a librarian from Perthshire, in 1992.

Today, with the Chalet School still marching ahead and now even established on the Internet, it is impossible not to wonder how Elinor herself would have regarded all these latest developments. No one of course can say for certain, but Mrs Chloe Rutherford, who is now Elinor's literary executor, is probably better qualified to speak than anyone else. Perhaps it should first be explained, in order to avoid confusion, that although Chloe shares the surname Rutherford with Elinor's mother and her family this is purely co-incidental, and Chloe is not in fact a relative. Nevertheless, from an early age, she knew Elinor well and was much attached to her. And in April 1994 Chloe wrote a moving tribute to Elinor, which was read at the conclusion of the Hereford centenary weekend, and again at the memorial service in Reigate.

For many of those who heard it, Chloe's account brought Elinor to life in a quite remarkable way. In it she describes how, as a youngster, she had found Elinor's outward appearance 'rather daunting', but had slowly come to realise that her 'face of unmistakable authority' was in fact 'the outward mask of the working headmistress'.

> Behind that facade there lurked a complex, singleminded, lovable, clumsy, stubborn, forward-thinking, spiritual, dottily humourous personality of enormous charm and innate wisdom. Someone who almost whooped for joy and enthusiasm at the chance of encouraging and opening a young mind. . . . no old-fashioned 'fuddy-duddy' — but a very kind and generous woman, a mine of information and a fount of good common sense.

As to how Elinor would have viewed the extraordinary ongoing success of her books, Chloe's pen-portrait ends on this note:

> I know Elinor was delighted with and enormously proud of her Chalet School creations — but always in a quiet and humble way. You'd never have known that she was a highly successful and prolific author. I know she would be truly astonished at the books' continued success with later generations. But how rewarded she would feel . . . How thrilled and deeply touched to know that somehow, within her stories of a girls' school, she had found a deeper alchemy, and had given her readers a much more valuable gift of certain insights, perhaps a momentary resonance within a phrase, that would stay with them long after the final chapters. That, I feel has been her greatest talent, and that is why the stories continue to exert a spell. Long may it continue, and long may . . . [the] enthusiasm for her work be passed on to the many young (and not so young) minds so eager to share it.

CHAPTER XXIII

THE END OF THE STORY

The last part of the story can be quickly told. For more than seven years after her mother's death in 1957 Elinor struggled to continue living in Lichfield House, the enormous Victorian villa which had housed her school. Eventually, towards the end of 1964, her friends Sydney and Phyllis Matthewman succeeded in persuading her to sell up and join with them in buying a house at Redhill in Surrey. Thus, by coincidence, Elinor's days were to end as they had begun, in a shared establishment. And this household, too, was subject to certain underlying tensions. Not that the house lacked space. 56 Woodlands Road had two large and two smaller rooms on each of two floors, so there was no problem over dividing it into two independent flats, and it was agreed that Phyllis and Sydney would occupy the ground floor, while Elinor would live in the upstairs rooms.

This, in theory, was an excellent arrangement. But in practice things didn't quite work out; because, according to Phyllis, Elinor took to spending so much of her time downstairs with them that the Matthewmans began to feel the lack of privacy. Or, at least, Phyllis clearly did. For it can be deduced that Elinor's affection for Phyllis was much greater than Phyllis's for Elinor. Nor can it have helped matters that Sydney and Elinor always got on so well together. At no point was any suggestion made — by Phyllis or anyone else — that their relationship was other than totally platonic — but

Elinor (left) in Mumbles, South Wales, with Phyllis Matthewman in the early 1950s.

Elinor in the early 1960s, taken in a friend's garden.

Chalet School 'Golden Jubilee' portrait, 1963.

Commemorative plaque at Pertisau, 1994.

the two greatly enjoyed each other's company and conversation and would spend hours discussing the many interests they had in common. As a result Phyllis seems often to have felt left out of things, and she began to resent the fact that — as she put it: 'The only time Sydney and I could ever be alone together was when we were in bed.'

Elinor, it can safely be assumed, was completely unaware of her friend's reactions. Nevertheless, in many ways this period cannot have been an altogether happy one for her. For one thing, her health was beginning to fail. And it seems that for the first time her hitherto inexhaustible vitality and enthusiam were also flagging. This certainly is the impression to be gained from Vivien Pass, Elinor's friend during more than forty years: 'It was sad to see her on her last visit to us [about 1967], she was so frail.' In particular Vivien was distressed that Elinor, 'after having had two heart attacks . . . had lost her zest for life'; and that to a certain extent 'pain and depression had changed her disposition'.

However, the following year must have been a better one, for in September 1968 Elinor wrote a cheerful letter (characteristically she failed to note that she had dated it 'September 1568'), describing to a friend a week's holiday she had spent in Hereford: 'I had a delightful time picking up the old threads as far as I could. A week isn't long enough to do much of that . . . but I did contrive to visit a fair number [of friends] or we met in the city.'

But clearly this was only a temporary respite. In the following January, 1969, Sydney Matthewman mentions in a letter to 'Armada' that 'A new Chalet book is on the stocks, but Elinor hasn't felt much like writing for some time'; and he adds the comment that 'the last one took so long that it won't be out till the autumn'. And the book in question,

Althea Joins the Chalet School, did, it seems, take almost two years to complete, for no Chalet book was published between 1967 and 1969.

A month after this, Elinor was sent into hospital for a checkup; this (as related in another of Sydney Matthewman's letters) revealed 'a slightly dicky heart, high blood pressure, and a few other little oddments'. But Elinor was soon to be home again and 'back on to the latest Chalet book', seeming to retain some enjoyment in her writing.

Her death, when it came on 20 September 1969, was quite sudden. On the previous evening, when Phyllis and Sydney paid their usual goodnight visit, Elinor, who was already in bed, had mentioned that she was experiencing a certain amount of pain; but she had seemed otherwise perfectly herself and ready to settle down for the night. Before they left, Sydney suggested that Elinor should say the prayers of the rosary, since he knew that this always gave her great comfort. In the morning, the Matthewmans returned to find Elinor apparently sleeping quietly, the bedclothes undisturbed around her and her rosary still clasped in her hands. She had died peacefully in her sleep.

Her funeral was held at the Catholic Church of the Holy Family in Reigate, where, twenty-five years later, many of Elinor's fans would gather for the service of thanksgiving mentioned in Chapter XXII. And afterwards, Sydney Matthewman wrote at some length to Mrs Joyce Thorp (then William Collins's 'Armada' editor):

> I'm so glad you were able to turn up for dear Elinor's Requiem. With Mr Chambers coming too, *and* the Borough Librarian and the head of the Juvenile library, we gave her a good send-off, and I'm sure she must have been pleased. I must say,

a Requiem Mass is a much more satisfying memorial service than the ordinary funeral service.

It's a great pity she died so young — 74's no great age these days [Elinor was in fact 75], and her mother lived to be 88 with a similar heart condition. The truth is that she hadn't a very strong hold on life — it makes me quite angry as I go through her papers and find *hundreds* of letters which prove how her books gave not only pleasure but *inspiration* to so many people. Chambers (and perhaps you also) will probably be deluged with letters — we've even had some ourselves, just sent to the address given in the papers. *The Times* gave her a first-class notice — must have pleased her greatly as it was always her favourite paper. I thought the *Telegraph* was a bit mingy. The *Surrey Mirror* of course gave her a nice piece of the front page, but I don't know if the *Hereford Times* did anything. Someone said there was a mention in the *Evening Standard*, but I didn't see it.

We are, of course, having an awful time with the clearing up — apart from anything else there's an enormous pile of MSS . . . The day before she died, Elinor was working on [the abridgement of] *The Head Girl* [of the Chalet School] for you. . . . I will send it on to you tomorrow . . .

The letter ends: 'I suppose we shall get used to it but I'm still in the condition of "Oh, I must tell Elinor that"!' Seven months later, in the spring of 1970, *Prefects of the Chalet School*,the final story in the series, was published. And it seems a fitting tribute to Elinor that her beloved Chalet School books really did continue for longer than she did herself.

POSTSCRIPT

Looking back over Elinor's life, what was the measure of her real achievement? And what kind of person was the real Elinor? The following is a collage of snippets gathered from previous chapters.

The Chalet School has become a romantic world in itself.
Miss Brent-Dyer certainly captured the imagination of vast numbers of girls to an incredible degree.
I know she wrote books, but my children did not care for them.
The Chalet Series is a unique achievement.
I think the long series got absolutely nutty.
The Chalet School books are an entire way of life.
The stories are apsalootly wicked.

Miss Brent-Dyer was a wonderful teacher.
Poor old BD, we ran rings round her.
She was extremely kind to me and surprisingly understanding.
As a child I didn't like Elinor at all.
I liked everything about her.

A very kind and generous person.
A very eccentric and different sort of person.
Extremely excitable and full of enthusiasms.
A larger than life, flamboyant sort of person.
A very forthright person.
She was very reserved until you got to know her.
Her imagination really was amazing.

She was always scribbling away all her life.
I can see her now — sitting on a rock and telling stories.
I always kept the salt-cellar handy.
We didn't expect an authoress to be 'normal'.

Far from pretty, but she had a very mobile countenance.
I remember her wearing a knitted suit she had made herself without a pattern.
She could look quite distinguished when she took the trouble.
Her underclothing was tied up with string.
The most peculiar things used to happen to her manuscripts; the Managing Director was *not* amused.
She could make a most amusing speech — anytime.

ELINOR WAS NOT THE KIND TO BE EASILY FORGOTTEN.

One last comment. It was made by a child in a little group that Elinor came across by chance one day, as she was walking home from the shops. This was towards the end of her life, and she was beginning to find the steep road a little trying. So, at the top of the hill, she sat down on a wall to get her breath back. The children came up and stared at her.

'Are *you* Elinor Brent-Dyer — who wrote all those Chalet School books?' asked the one in front. Elinor indicated that she was. A short silence followed. Then: '*Crumbs*!' said the child. And they all scampered off. Perhaps that remark sums up everything pretty well. And that Elinor herself should have told the story suggests that her sense of humour always remained alive.

APPENDIX I

BOOKS BY ELINOR M. BRENT-DYER

LA ROCHELLE SERIES

(published by W. & R. Chambers, Edinburgh)

1. *Gerry Goes to School* (1922)
2. *A Head Girl's Difficulties* (1923)
3. *The Maids of La Rochelle* (1924)
4. *Seven Scamps* (1927)
5. *Heather Leaves School* (1929)
6. *Janie of La Rochelle* (1932)
7. *Janie Steps In* (1953)

CHALET SCHOOL SERIES

(published by W. & R. Chambers, Edinburgh)

1. *The School at the Chalet* (1925)
2. *Jo of the Chalet School* (1926)
3. *The Princess of the Chalet School* (1927)
4. *The Head Girl of the Chalet School* (1928)
5. *The Rivals of the Chalet School* (1929)
6. *Eustacia Goes to the Chalet School* (1930)
7. *The Chalet School and Jo* (1931)
8. *The Chalet Girls in Camp* (1932)
9. *The Exploits of the Chalet Girls* (1933)
10. *The Chalet School and the Lintons* (1934)
11. *The New House at the Chalet School* (1935)
12. *Jo Returns to the Chalet School* (1936)
13. *The New Chalet School* (1938)

14. *The Chalet School in Exile* (1940)
15. *The Chalet School Goes to It* (1941)
16. *The Highland Twins at the Chalet School* (1942)
17. *Lavender Laughs in the Chalet School* (1943)
18. *Gay From China at the Chalet School* (1944)
19. *Jo to the Rescue* (1945)
    The Chalet Book for Girls (1947)
    The Second Chalet Book for Girls (1948)
    The Third Chalet Book for Girls (1949)
31. *Tom Tackles the Chalet School* (1955)
    (first published in *The Second Chalet Book for Girls* and *The Third Chalet Book for Girls*)
    The Chalet School and Rosalie (1951)
20. *Three Go to the Chalet School* (1949)
21. *The Chalet School and the Island* (1950)
22. *Peggy of the Chalet School* (1950)
23. *Carola Storms the Chalet School* (1951)
24. *The Wrong Chalet School* (1952)
25. *Shocks for the Chalet School* (1952)
26. *The Chalet School in the Oberland* (1952)
    The Chalet Girls' Cook Book (1953)
27. *Bride Leads the Chalet School* (1953)
28. *Changes for the Chalet School* (1953)
29. *Joey Goes to the Oberland* (1954)
30. *The Chalet School and Barbara* (1954)
32. *The Chalet School Does It Again* (1955)
33. *A Chalet Girl from Kenya* (1955)
34. *Mary-Lou of the Chalet School* (1956)
35. *A Genius at the Chalet School* (1956)
36. *A Problem for the Chalet School* (1956)
37. *The New Mistress at the Chalet School* (1957)
38. *Excitements at the Chalet School* (1957)
39. *The Coming of Age of the Chalet School* (1958)
40. *The Chalet School and Richenda* (1958)
41. *Trials for the Chalet School* (1959)
42. *Theodora and the Chalet School* (1959)
43. *Joey and Co. in Tirol* (1960)
44. *Ruey Richardson — Chaletian* (1960)
45. *A Leader in the Chalet School* (1961)
46. *The Chalet School Wins the Trick* (1961)
47. *A Future Chalet School Girl* (1962)

48. *The Feud in the Chalet School* (1962)
49. *The Chalet School Triplets* (1963)
50. *The Chalet School Reunion* (1963)
51. *Jane and the Chalet School* (1964)
52. *Redheads at the Chalet School* (1964)
53. *Adrienne and the Chalet School* (1965)
54. *Summer Term at the Chalet School* (1965)
55. *Challenge for the Chalet School* (1966)
56. *Two Sams at the Chalet School* (1967)
57. *Althea Joins the Chalet School* (1969)
58. *Prefects of the Chalet School* (1970)

ADVENTURE BOOKS

Fardingales (Latimer House, 1950)
The "Susannah" Adventure (W. & R. Chambers, 1953)
Chudleigh Hold (W. & R. Chambers, 1954)
The Condor Crags Adventure (W. & R. Chambers, 1954)
Top Secret (W. & R. Chambers, 1955)

SCHOOLGIRLS ABROAD

(A series of geography readers
published by W. & R. Chambers, 1951)

1. *Verena Visits New Zealand*
2. *Bess on her Own in Canada*
3. *A Quintette in Queensland*
4. *Sharlie's Kenya Diary*

LORNA BOOKS

Lorna at Wynyards (Lutterworth Press, 1947)
Stepsisters for Lorna (C. & J. Temple, 1948)

JANEWAYS BOOKS

A Thrilling Term at Janeways (Thomas Nelson, 1927)
Caroline the Second (Girls' Own Paper, 1937)

SKELTON HALL BOOKS

The School at Skelton Hall (Max Parrish, 1962)
Trouble at Skelton Hall (Max Parrish, 1963)

OTHERS

Judy the Guide (Thomas Nelson, 1928)
The New House Mistress (Thomas Nelson, 1928)
The School by the River (Burns, Oates & Washbourne, 1930)
The Feud in the Fifth Remove (Girls' Own Paper, 1931)
The Little Marie-José (Burns, Oates & Washbourne, 1932)
Carnation of the Upper Fourth (Girls' Own Paper, 1934)
Elizabeth the Gallant (Thornton Butterworth, 1935)
Monica Turns Up Trumps (Girls' Own Paper, 1936)
They Both Liked Dogs (Girls' Own Paper, 1938)
The Little Missus (W. & R. Chambers, 1942)
The Lost Staircase (W. & R. Chambers, 1946)
Kennelmaid Nan (Lutterworth Press, 1954)
Nesta Steps Out (Oliphants, 1954)
Beechy of the Harbour School (Oliphants, 1955)
Leader in Spite of Herself (Oliphants, 1956)

APPENDIX II

THE 'PROBLEM' STORIES

The Mystery at the Chalet School, *Tom Tackles the Chalet School* and *The Chalet School and Rosalie* provide between them an account of one complete Chalet School year. *The Mystery at the Chalet School* is set during the Christmas term which follows *Gay from China at the Chalet School* (no. 18, 1944) and the summer holiday described in *Jo to the Rescue* (no. 19, 1945); and the story thus immediately precedes *Tom Tackles the Chalet School* (no. 31, 1955), which takes place during the Easter term; the events of the summer term then being covered by *The Chalet School and Rosalie* (1951). The stories themselves make this sequence quite plain, but since the three titles all have different origins, while two of them were published out of chronological order, readers often find difficulty in seeing where these stories fit into the series.

To take the three in order: *The Mystery at the Chalet School* is a title that may well be unfamiliar to many Chalet fans, since until 1994, when it appeared in an Armada paperback edition along with *The Chalet School and Rosalie*, it had not been generally available. Originally *Mystery* was part of the first *Chalet Book for Girls* — a kind of annual, which included stories, articles, cookery hints and so on, some having direct Chalet links, others not — that was published in 1947 by W. & R. Chambers. This collection was followed by two more Chalet School annuals, published in 1948 and 1949 respectively, and *Tom Tackles the Chalet School* made its first appearance in these, one half in each volume.

Until this point Chalet School stories had followed one another in the correct chronological order, and they continued to do so until 1955. Problems only began that year, when *Tom Tackles the Chalet School* was republished in book form, being then designated no. 31 of the hardback series. This, although theoretically correct, was misleading because, during the six years since *Tom* originally appeared in the annuals, eleven more Chalet School stories had been published and readers, both at the time and since, were unable to understand how *Tom* could possibly be no. 31 when the events it related had clearly taken place long before those in *The Chalet School and Barbara* — the book published the previous year and officially no. 30! This confusion lasted for many years and was only finally resolved in 1987 when the Armada paperback version of *Tom Tackles the Chalet School* was published, containing an explanatory preface.

Chalet fans have also been puzzled in the past about *The Chalet School and Rosalie*, especially as it was described at one point by the publishers as 'Not part of the series'. Probably the statement meant only that the book was not part of the hardback series, since, for some reason now unknown, *The Chalet School and Rosalie* was published only in a limited paperback edition, which appeared in 1951. And here again there were problems over Chalet School chronology. By 1951 the stories had moved from 'Armishire' to St Briavel's Island, which meant that events in *The Chalet School and Rosalie* were considerably out of date. In any case, the story quickly went out of print, due to the small size of the original edition; and until 1987, when it was first included in the Armada series, *The Chalet School and Rosalie* had been virtually unobtainable for more than thirty years.

Another minor problem concerns the numbering of these three stories. Chronologically they all take place (as explained above) in the school year immediately following *Jo to the Rescue*, which is no. 19 of the hardback series (Armada no. 21) and several years before the hardback no. 20 (Armada no. 24) — *Three Go to the Chalet School*. Obviously the hardback series cannot now be officially renumbered; but the correct chronological and reading order could be conveyed as: No. 19b *The Mystery at the Chalet School*; No. 19c *Tom Tackles the Chalet School*; No. 19d *The Chalet School and Rosalie*.

INDEX

Illustrations are indexed in italic.